Tribunes of the People

Tribunes of the People
The Past and Future of the New York Magistrates' Courts

By Raymond Moley

New Haven · Yale University Press
London · Humphrey Milford · Oxford University Press
1932

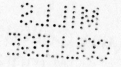

FOREWORD

THIS book is the outgrowth of a study of the magistrates' courts which I was asked to undertake in 1930 by Judge Samuel Seabury, and of a continuation of this study for the Commission on the Administration of Justice of New York State since the completion of Judge Seabury's *Report*. For facts and illustrations I am deeply indebted to these two official relationships.

I owe many personal obligations as well. The deep wisdom and enlightened sense of progress which Judge Seabury brought to the many discussions which we had on the subjects treated in this book were invaluable.

I owe a great debt to Magistrate Jonah J. Goldstein, not only because he has been an example of what a magistrate can do officially, but because of the many hours which he gave unselfishly to advising and assisting me with every aspect of this study. For generous aid in the collection of facts I am indebted to Jay Finn, Deputy Chief Clerk of the magistrates' courts of New York City. My friend Martin Conboy has read much of the manuscript and has offered valuable advice.

The contribution to this book made by my assistants, Celeste Jedel and Grace McCastline Waite, can be described only by saying that without their labors in collecting and arranging material and in verifying its accuracy the book would certainly not have been written. The care and skill which they displayed in this work cannot easily be described.[1]

R. M.

New York, October, 1932.

[1] Acknowledgments should also be made to the *New York Times*, Harper & Bros., and the Century Co. for their kind permission to reprint certain material used in this book.

Contents

TRIBUNES OF THE PEOPLE

CHAPTER I

PERSPECTIVE

STRIPPED of legal frills, the New York magistrates are
officials vested with the duty of passing upon the work
of the police. The great police bureaucracy, in its business
of maintaining order, makes arrests. Those who are arrested, charged with crimes or offenses, are brought before magistrates. The magistrates pass upon these charges,
in some cases finally, in others merely as an intermediary
authority. Legally and historically this function of the
magistrates stands out. They are, in a sense, charged with
the great responsibility of exercising what amounts to a
veto power over the enforcement of the criminal law.
With respect to this, their position is of vast importance.
The liberty of many people is at stake. To a great degree
the magistrates are to them the custodians of justice; they
are, in essence, tribunes of the people.

In this duty their courts come to be concerned with a
great variety of the problems of everyday life. To the
mind unfamiliar with the scope and variety of their duties,
magistrates seem to be concerned only with the petty offenders, *les misérables* of our streets. But a great range of
human beings passes through these courts. The cases they
hear involve an almost unbelievable variety of offenses,
ranging from homicide to a violation of a minor city ordinance, from felonious assault to peddling without a license, from Sabbath breaking to selling poisonous drugs.

From the standpoint of the number of cases which pass
before them, the magistrates are of tremendous importance. In 1930 alone, over a half million persons were arraigned. In their capacity of committing magistrates,
they examined approximately two hundred thousand misdemeanors and nineteen thousand felonies. Three hundred
thousand minor offenses were decided summarily, and the
magistrates sat as special sessions judges in one hundred
sixty thousand cases.[1]

There was a time when magistrates actively pursued
wrongdoers, some of them serving as detectives, arresting
officers, prosecutors, and judges all in one. But that was
in the days before great professional police departments
had grown up. It is an interesting fact that as police
departments developed, the legal powers of magistrates
shifted from the realm of prosecution to that of judgment.
As Maitland points out, the rise of professional police dif-
ferentiated their functions from those of magistrates and
when, in 1839, the control of police was taken from the
magistrates, "the judicial and executive duties comprised
in the conservation of the peace fell apart, and we were
left with learned magistrates and gallant commissioners."[2]

It is a far cry from the days when magistrates actively
pursued wrongdoers to the present time, when a magistrate sits in judgment between the pursuer and the one
pursued, protecting those who are innocent, fixing punishment in minor offenses, and holding for further action in
more serious crimes.

[1] *Annual Report, City Magistrates' Courts* (1930), Table 1.

[2] *Justice and Police* (London, 1885), p. 100. See also Moley, *Our
Criminal Courts,* pp. 14 to 20, for a discussion of this development of
magisterial powers.

Let us reduce to the terms of common sense what the magistrates' courts are supposed to do in our system of government. We have, as our chief defense against the criminal, a police department, a vast bureaucracy with approximately twenty thousand members. This powerful agency, organized on a semimilitary basis, is our first line of defense against crime. But experience has shown us that such a power, exercised as it is, has infinite possibilities for abuse. We do not have to criticize the administration of the police to say that in the face of such a power the city needs a means of protection. The magistrates' courts fulfil this need. They are the city's first line of defense against the unjust and improper use of police power.

They are, moreover, a sifting agency to determine which charges brought by the police are substantial and should be prosecuted further and which should be dismissed. Much of this work does not extend beyond the qualities of rough common sense. It requires in addition to common sense, however, some understanding of vast social interests, involving a feeling for human values and a determination that the law should be not only feared but respected. Administration in these courts may become a vastly important educational force in the community. The magistrates could, if they would, teach the heterogeneous population of New York a lesson in common sense, fair play, and respect for truly republican institutions.

Most magistrates, however, conceive of their function in a narrow sense. But sensitive and resourceful men have found ways of enlarging this simple rôle into a much more diversified and significant one. The variety of examples of social pathology that drifts through their courts suggests possibilities to such magistrates of linking through their judicial machinery many of the social agencies of the community. Many of the great efforts toward social welfare can well find common problems there. This is particularly true of certain specialized courts with whose officials private welfare bodies have an active connection. To a great extent the magistrate determines the extent and character of these connections. Here he may often perform most useful services. He becomes the means through which the good intentions and organized efforts of private citizens may be brought to bear upon social problems.

Any discussion of the magistrates' courts of the city of New York will utterly fail of its purpose if at the beginning there is not set forth some conception of how these courts actually work. It is, therefore, appropriate to introduce at the very outset a realistic picture of what they are doing from day to day and from year to year. Two descriptions have been inserted in the body of this chapter in order to enforce not only the general impression that they must leave with any person who sees below the surface but the added fact that the picture that we see is continuous and unchanging through the years. The first of them was written twenty-four years ago; the second, two years ago. These descriptions must not be viewed in the light of mere "color," although they are in truth colorful, not as mere "human interest," although they have that quality. Nor should they be interpreted as an attempt to show how badly the "job" is being done. In one instance, that of 1908, an excellent magistrate was sitting and conditions were as satisfactory as could be expected.

I. LIGHTS AND SHADES OF LIFE IN A CITY COURT[3]

> Here are Domestic Woes to Soothe, Black
> Eyes to Heal, Insults to Atone . . .
> and the "Majesty of the Law" to Sustain.

" 'HATS OFF!'

"Those words, combined with the native grandeur of
Lieut. Bill Ennis, stand for the majesty of the law at the
Jefferson Market Court. Beyond them there is little if any
majesty in the courtroom. Magistrate —— wears a solemn black robe, of course, and John Foley, who is cele-
brating this week the twentieth anniversary of his taking
charge of the bridge, may occasionally look askance at
irreverent traffic cops who chew gum while making complaints against cabbies, but the fact remains that the gum
is chewed. His Honor looks too bored to care, and besides
he knows that Lieut. Ennis, walking up and down before
the awed prisoners and witnesses and lawyers and spectators, will provide all the majesty necessary. So he yawns
and signs his name and asks people to hold up their right
hands and go through the formula ending with 'S'h'lp m'
G'd' and every now and then he thunders casually:

" 'Why were you obstructing the crosswalk?'

" 'I wasn't, your Honor,' declares the Italian of the moment, after the meaning of 'crosswalk' has been brought
home to him by an interpreter.

" 'How far were you from the crosswalk?'

" 'Tventa feet, your Honor.'

" 'Well, you should have been twenty-five feet from it.'

" 'Well, then, I was tventa-five feet from it,' declares
the obliging obstructionist.

[3] *New York Times,* Sunday, March 15, 1908.

" 'Fined one dollar.'

" 'Get out!' says John Foley, pushing the Italian away. The Magistrate suppresses another yawn, the reporters buzz around, and the majesty of the law goes hang.

"Next to the conspicuousness of the majesty of the law's absence the most striking thing borne in upon you at Jefferson Market is that you are nothing but an atom. However world-stirring your private affairs may seem to you personally if they ever figure before Magistrate —— you will find that they look like a minnow in the Atlantic.

"For instance, have you, a peaceable citizen, while walking along a presumably civilized thoroughfare, been approached by a total stranger and unceremoniously felled to the ground? You have? Well, that is quite an epoch in your life, isn't it? Yet what are you when you appear seething inwardly, before Magistrate ——? Just a 'black eye,' one of a dozen, doubtless, and it is more than probable that the other eleven surpass you in area, garishness of coloring, and picturesqueness of the circumstances attendant on their birth.

"And there are things far worse than black eyes, which dwindle to insignificance when looked at from the Jefferson Market point of view. In the seats, waiting for a chance to speak to the Judge, are a row of women. Some of them are weeping. Some sit in silent agony. It is easy to see that the presence of each in the courtroom is the climax of a home tragedy, none the less tragic because obscure.

"Yet John Foley, with a wave of the hand toward the grief-stricken group, says in a matter-of-fact tone: 'Nonsupport cases. Come here every day for summonses for their husbands. Hey, Josephine, you're next!' Is he a heartless brute? Assuredly not. If Jefferson Market acted differently toward individual cases there would be no such thing as private affairs; and, incidentally, there would be no such thing as getting through with court business in a Judge's lifetime.

"Magistrate —— takes his seat every morning at nine. Already the courtroom is fairly well filled. The witnesses in the various cases are there, leaning forward, expectant. And there are friends of the prisoners and professional bondsmen and lawyers and idlers.

"Exhibit A consists of an irate young man who runs a lodging house, and an ejected lodger, with a fearful and wonderful injury about the jaw, strikingly bandaged in order to interest his Honor. But his Honor seems far away.

"The bandaged one tells his grievance against the lodging house keeper. It is a tale of considerable length. When it is about one-tenth over, Magistrate —— quietly asks whether the speaker was intoxicated at the time of the disaster.

" 'No, yer Honor,' declares the ejected one, in a voice implying that he never looks upon the wine when it isn't sarsaparilla.

" 'He was,' declares the lodging house keeper.

" 'Aw, yer Honor,' put in the complainant, 'if you wuz to go into his lodging house wid one drink and fall asleep and talk in yer sleep that guy wud t'row yez out. An' besides, I've witnesses.'

" 'Where's the witnesses in this case?' shouts John Foley.

"Two extraordinary specimens of humanity rise and shuffle forward. One begins describing the innate orderliness and sobriety of the complainant. But he is interrupted by the lodging house keeper, who remarks:

" 'Didn't I throw you out of my house night before last?'

"No answer.

" 'Did this man throw you out?' asks the Judge, with a piercing look at the witness.

" 'No, yer Honor,' declares that outraged innocent. 'I got up an' I walked out like a gentleman.'

" 'Discharged!' says the Judge in a tired voice. And the lodging house keeper walks triumphantly away, without a look at his fractured ex-lodger.

"Exhibit B is a female black eye, with its inflicter, also feminine, who declares that she acted entirely in self-defense and that she was very roughly handled in doing so, your Honor.

" 'But there are no marks on you,' remarks the Judge.

" 'Of course there ain't; I never touched her,' cries black eye.

" 'Yes yer did!'

" 'No I didn't!'

" 'Ah, you —!'

" 'You gave this woman a black eye; you say she hit you. Where are the marks?' repeats Magistrate ——.

"The accused pauses.

" 'Well, I've a handful of my hair at home which she pulled out,' she volunteers finally. 'Shall I go and get it?'

" 'Out of a mattress? No,' remarks the Judge. And almost before the inexperienced understand just what has happened both women are out of the courtroom and another 'case' is talking volubly in front of the Judge's desk.

"It is Italian and absolutely unintelligible so an inter-

preter is summoned from the mysterious regions behind
the rail. As soon as the 'case' finds out that it may speak
its own tongue it bursts all barriers and starts off at a
mile a minute. The Judge allows the rush of Neapolitan
excitement for about fifteen seconds then cuts in with:

" 'But why did you hit him in the eye?'

"Being unable to explain this satisfactorily, the 'case' is
hustled out of the way by John Foley, and another, this
time German, talks volubly to the German interpreter.

" 'Ich war in einem drug store, ganz ruhig, and wollte
nur eine kleine Flasche kaufen, die mit so etwas—Wissen
Sie—'

" 'And then you hit him in the eye?' asks the Magistrate. The Teuton is unable to disown the soft impeach-
ment, so everybody loses interest in him, especially since
the information is passed around that a 'Black Hand
case' is about to come on.

"This consists of an excited lawyer, a 'threatening' letter, an Italian barber who evidently has no time to attend
to his own hair, and a very mild-faced 'Black Hand'
emissary.

"Unfortunately for the lawyer and the barber, they
have forgotten the most useful thing at Jefferson Market
—evidence—so they are pushed away by John Foley, in
order that an infuriated woman who claims to have been
called 'a liar in a public thoroughfare' may be heard.

" 'You talk too much,' the tired Judge tells her after a
while.

" 'No, I don't,' she answers coolly. But what she has
previously said is used against her denial; she becomes
more voluble than ever, and in five minutes it is extremely
difficult to know who is complaining against whom, and

who owned the dog anyhow, so the 'case' is allowed to go over.

"Next come two boys, not over 16, caught with a kit of burglars' tools, including a wicked looking revolver, which they were unable to explain away. 'Ha! something novel,' thinks the man on his first visit to Jefferson Market. Oh, no. This case is painfully commonplace.

" 'Reading dime novels. Wild West. Want to be bad men,'—is the official classification of this sort of thing. It happens with a frequency second only to 'black eyes' and non-supports, and is soon passed along to the next step in its development.

"But some real novelty is injected into the court proceedings by a delinquent whose defense consists of this: 'Don't lock me up. I was locked up last week.'

"Even the Magistrate gives a near laugh at that.

" 'He used vile language to me, the vilest I ever heard,' says a traffic cop, looking severely at the next 'case.'

" 'What did he say?' asks his Honor.

" 'He told me to go to - - - -.'

" 'One dollar,' murmurs the Judge.

" 'Next! Mayer! Wilhelm Mayer!' vociferates John Foley, casting his eagle eye over the benches.

"Wilhelm comes forward. He has been accused by a policeman of belonging to a select party of about fifty men whose occupation is loafing on a certain Second Avenue corner, but it transpires, to the great discomfiture of the policeman, that Wilhelm has stood on the corner only once in his life, namely, when he was arrested. 'I live in Brooklyn!' he declares heatedly, and the laugh is on the man with the brass buttons. Wilhelm throws a look of Teutonic scorn at the United States in general and Jeffer-

son Market Court in particular, and stalks majestically
away.

" 'Hats off! Take your hat off!' roar Lieut. Ennis and
John Foley and other zealous Jeffersonians. Wilhelm re-
moves his hat hurriedly, loses some of his majesty in so
doing, and is completely forgotten before he reaches the
door. The Judge is inquiring of a young husband, who is
standing beside his wife, but obstinately refusing to look
at her.

" 'Why don't you make up?'

" 'Too much mother-in-law,' grunts the husband sulkily.

"The couple is turned over to a kind-hearted policeman,
who starts to argue with them in a corner. Five minutes
later they walk away, still not speaking.

" 'Too much mother-in-law,' growls the young man as
he disappears.

"But nobody hears him because an infuriated female
wants to get out a warrant for 'petty lozenges.' What she
means is that a female friend, whom she has apparently
trusted implicitly for years, has so far forgotten herself
as to appropriate a pair of shoes. The owner of the shoes
flounces away with her warrant.

" 'Why are you drunk so early?' the Judge asks, in a
bored way, of the next 'case,' who can hardly stand, even
with the help of the rail.

" 'Can't you answer?' inquires John Foley.

"The case is unable to state whether it can or not, so it
is adjourned till four.

"And thus it goes on, day in, day out. 'Why are you obstructing the crosswalk?' alternates with 'Where's your
license?' and 'Then you hit him in the eye?' 'Violating
the speed limit' rubs elbows with 'non-support'; 'petty

larceny,' sitting on the bench, quietly awaiting its turn, talks amicably with 'forgery, wanted in Boston.' And among them all nothing interests his Honor like the signal to adjourn.

"At least that is the way things impressed a newcomer at Jefferson Market. When he first arrived he felt awed and hardly dared to sidle close to the rail and listen to what was going on. But as the hours went by and cases were heard and dismissed with astonishing rapidity and Lieut. Ennis and John Foley conversed without a trace of haughtiness and his Honor didn't seem displeased at all at his presence the newcomer grew quite bold and began to assume the blasé tone of Jefferson Market and act as if he, too, were a part of its machinery.

"And he said good-bye quite nonchalantly to the Lieutenant and the bridge magnate and swaggered airily up the aisle toward the door until brought back to a sense of his insignificance by a roar behind him of

" 'Hats off!' "

II. THE HOUSE THAT JUSTICE BUILT[4]

"THIS is the house that justice built. This is the castle of fair play. This is the place where wise men shall sit and contemplate our human jealousies, our petty quarrels, our wrong-doings. This, by the grace of God, is a magistrate's court.

"Set squarely down in a backwater street, it is not, for some disappointing reason, impressive. But the spangled

[4] This is a first-hand description of a busy magistrate's court in New York City. It was written by Milton MacKaye of the staff of the *New York Evening Post* and published in that paper on January 10, 1930, as one of a series entitled "The Magistrate Racket."

parade of a city's life passes here, gaudy and gay, drab and mean. The push of ambition, the drums of crime, the blare of pretension, and keen quiet of tragedy—all these are integral parts . . .

"This, then, is a magistrate's court set down on the backwater street. Approach its scummy portals, and an inevitable and inexplicable feeling of miscreancy overcomes one. There is something about its very environment that is repellent.

"The System has made this environment. All around the premises little windowed offices, crowded uncleanly offices. This one says, 'Attorney-at-Law'; the next one says, 'Bail, Bonds, Night or Day.' Rows of them, one after another, all alike.

"On one side of the street, on the opposite side of the street. 'Bail, Bonds,' 'Attorney-at-Law,' 'Bail, Bonds,' 'Notary Public.' These are business men of the court environs. They make their livings from woe. Trouble brings them trade. They sit and smoke in their windows and wait. Their good is a bad day.

"Well, into the court. The hallway is crowded. Rat-faced men in derbies, fat greasy men in derbies. A few scared, nervous men with mufflers about their throats, indecisive, perhaps waiting for someone, perhaps wondering where to go with their problem. A few young girls, most of them accompanied by two or three men companions. One beautiful girl, quite alone. A dozen old women, and a pimply scattering of side-burned adolescent boys.

"Up the stairs. Loitering along them some important-looking red-faced satraps. They talk with authority from the sides of their mouths, chew on cigars and punctuate their pontification by spitting in the direction of a passer-by's shoes. Occasionally they salute a policeman, or hail some newly arrived compatriot.

"Taking a deep breath is difficult. Tobacco smoke is everywhere and fresh air is an unknown quantity. There has been some effort at cleanliness, but the smell of the disinfectant only serves to accentuate distaste into nausea. No wonder a famous judge, broken in health, called these places pest holes. Combined with the odor of unwashed mankind, there is the peculiar taint of old buildings, effluvium from forty years of life and death.

"Upstairs all is confusion. The court, a little behind time, is about to open. People are crowding into the courtroom, corridors are filled. Policemen push their way here, there and everywhere; a few are listening to hopeful defendants who ask them to tone down their testimony, pal.

"Down the corridor some of the men met on the stairs are grouped around a closed door. There are the magistrate's chambers. The attendant brushes by them, then stops to shake hands.

" 'The Judge in, Joe?' asks one. 'Just dropped over to say hello.'

"He beckons down the hall to one of the side-burned boys. They confer together in low, secret tones. Then he nods and sticks out his lips reassuringly. Without a knock he walks into the Judge's chambers.

" 'Pat Blank,' boasts the boy to his companion, 'leader of my district. He knows his eggs.'

"Pat walks out a few minutes later, and another red-faced man walks in. There is the sound of loud laughter. Finally the door opens and magistrate and politicians appear. They are met by other men, all handshakers.

" 'Don't forget that chowder party! Well, see you at

the club tonight. Harry and Nate have a bone to pick with you.'

"In the courtroom, the attendant bangs his gavel. Hats are already off. There is silence a moment, but the gum still moves rhythmically in sixty pairs of jaws. The magistrate moves to the bench. He sits down, a short man framed against the American flag behind him. The gavel bounces again, and the wheels of justice begin to grind.

"After that first silence all is confusion again. Policemen, attendants, lawyers, bondsmen click in and out of the gates in the partition railing. The blue-coated bailiff on the bridge below the bench shouts out a number of names. A prisoner, brought in from the detention pen, and seated inside the railing, is pulled forward by a policeman.

"The magistrate is deep in conversation with a friend sitting beside him. The prisoner waits. The bailiff bawls out another indistinguishable name, then another. Two women, both between thirty and forty, pick up their coats and walk self-consciously inside the railing. They are motioned to stand by until the first case is disposed of.

" 'What's this case?' asks the Judge, and glances hastily over the complaint. 'Assault and battery. Where's the complaining witness?'

" 'Not here, Judge.'

"The magistrate looks up.

" 'What do you know about this, officer?'

"The officer doesn't know anything about it. He was called to the premises at 345 Umpty-Umph Street and made the arrest on the request of the complainant, who had a black eye. No, no more details. No, the defendant hadn't been drinking.

" 'Discharged. Next case.'

"And so justice grinds on. The confusion increases. The courtroom is jammed and hot.

"A robbery charge now. The black-haired, languid-eyed Assistant District Attorney stands beside the complainant. No, he hasn't investigated the case. He wants $1,500 bail.

"The defendant's lawyer, little faced and big eared, doesn't know the case either. But he wants $1,000 bail. The two young men are charged with stealing clothing from this woman's store. Of course they plead not guilty. The young man with the waxed mustache and blonde hair —he looks Scandinavian—was released from Sing Sing two months ago. No record of his scared silent companion. Consent to an adjournment. Yes; $1,000 bail.

"Tumbling along, one after another, the cases. This one dismissed, many adjourned, very many adjourned. Some other magistrate will hear them. Today is a rush day. The oath is given time after time: 'Do yousolswear tell truth-otruthnoth but truth?' It's hard to believe it's an oath. Perhaps it isn't; only an old legal custom.

"The bondsmen all around, sleek men, most of them. One silver-haired young man with a big mouth steps forward to handle a felonious assault defendant. The details are complete, but, presto, the prize is snatched away. The defendant's brother, late at the hearing, puts up cash. It's hard to beat a bondsman.

"The air grows hotter, becomes stifling. There is an impulse toward flight, a desire to see someone besides the magistrate (a really handsome man) who has a pleasing face, a face to be trusted. So many snide people here, so many snide lawyers and political hangers-on.

"This is a robbery case. The defendant, a boy of seven-

teen has his head bound in crimson bandages. That trou-
bles the magistrate until he hears the story, for it is
obviously the result of police manhandling. Then the
story: Robbery of a speakeasy. The bartender killed by
bandits. This boy's companions held on a homicide charge.
No bail. Take him away.

"A chorus girl appears against a company manager. A
beautiful, sulky, frightened girl next. She is a maid,
charged with stealing a mistress' dress.

"Now a moment when no case is ready. It is time for
the issuing of summons, the time for anyone who wishes
to speak to the Judge to step forward. The bailiff shouts.

"An old man stumbles forward. He has a face like Bat
Nelson's. It is pinched almost beyond human identifica-
tion, but there is still the shadow of Kilkenny there.
Streaks of dried blood fringe his eyes and the old man's
coat is filthy. He is sober, but he hasn't been for long.
Hopeless old man.

" 'I want to be committed for a while, your Honor. I'm
sick and I'm hungry and I want to lay up,' he says in
brogue.

" 'How old are you?'

" 'Sixty-five, and I can't keep a job.'

" 'When were you hurt there—?' pointing to the eyes.

" 'Two weeks ago.'

"The commitment to the Home for the Aged is made
out.

"Another suppliant approaches. He is small and shy
and young. His collar is dirty and his voice is so low-
pitched and bewildered that he is hard to understand. He
wants a warrant for his wife.

" 'She left me in Paterson and came here and I quit my

job and came after her. She's under age. She's with another man.'

" 'How old is she?'

" 'Fourteen.'

" 'How long were you married?'

" 'Three months. Her mother lives in Paterson and her father in Philadelphia. They're divorced. I went to Children's Society, but they couldn't do anything for me, because she's married.'

"There's no law to help the husband. What he needs is a social worker.

"This is a magistrate's court. The spangled parade of life passes here, gaudy and gay, drab and mean. The push of ambition, the drums of crime, the blare of pretension, the keen quiet of tragedy, all these are integral parts."

If, as we read these parallel descriptions, we realize that the passage of twenty years has scarcely altered the outlines of the picture, the business that is going on before our eyes seems a purposeless and futile process. The cost of conducting these courts has trebled[5] in twenty years. The public spent over two million dollars of its money in 1931—to what end?

The picture recurs from generation to generation. The peddlers who in 1908 were haled before the bar of justice, confused and hopeless, did not differ essentially from those who appeared in 1930. This is equally true of the prostitutes, panhandlers, bookmakers, gamblers—even the robbers and burglars. The number who appear, in relation to the population of the city of New York, is about the same. The excuses they give do not differ in any impor-

[5] In 1911, $705,550.00; in 1931, $2,161,073.50.

tant respect. The attitude of the magistrate changes less from year to year than from magistrate to magistrate. The dispositions of the offenders are the same. Little changes, except the faces of the persons who cross the stage.

To be sure, there have been some changes over these twenty-two years. Domestic wrangling and traffic violations have been taken into courts of their own. Policemen have been replaced by civilian court attendants. Complaint clerks have a room of their own. The "bridge," that wide and tangible gulf between the magistrate and the defendant, has been taken away. But the general atmosphere remains the same. There are more subtle barriers between the accused and justice than the mere removal of a physical obstruction can dispel. The intervening twenty-two years have been punctuated with reforms which many people believed were important. But all of the facts cry to heaven that nothing important has happened.

In spite of their excellence, these descriptions are a poor substitute for actual observations. The way to understand a magistrate's court properly is, first, to see it, and second, to see it with the spirit of one who reflects upon what he sees. To see a court is to be faced by a fundamental problem, if we reserve some detachment and some intent to understand meanings that are not on the surface. These occurrences are but symptoms of a pathological condition of society. Another peddler will obstruct the crosswalk; another prostitute will be summoned before the bench.

The task of the magistrate is hopeless unless he uses his position as would a doctor in a clinic, not only to treat each individual case but to study the cause of the disease.

A clinical doctor, or a clinical jurist, realizes that dealing with the fringe of the problem will do no good. Nor can we gain much by following a routine. The problem must be attacked at its source, in the mood if not the method of science.

Throughout most discussions of courts, people speak of how badly the "job" is being done; but, were they asked what the "job" really is, they would be at a loss to answer. This is because, in the last analysis, we do not know what we are trying to do in the magistrates' courts, or, in fact, in any criminal court. Some of us think of punishment, others of retribution, others of the safety of "society," others of enforcing the law, while still others, a bit more enlightened perhaps, but no less confused in their thinking, speak in more modern terms of such indefinables and imponderables as "social readjustment," "rehabilitation," "reformation," and the like. All of these are words. We do not know whether any of them has reality. The weight of evidence is that they do not. It is like a chorus of many voices, each carrying a different tune, dissonant, meaningless, and, apparently, without end.

CHAPTER II

TWENTY YEARS OF POLICE-COURT JUSTICE

I N 1907, public sentiment was aroused by unsatisfactory conditions in the lower courts of New York City. The Charity Organization Society asked Governor Hughes to appoint a commission to investigate these courts. No commission was appointed at that time, the general feeling being "that no change in the existing situation could be accomplished so long as the personnel of the magistrates and judges remained as it was, and that it was hopeless to expect to secure such legislation so long as political parties had the roots of their power in these courts."[1] In the light of present disclosures this statement is a significant one. In the following year, however, a commission, familiarly known as the "Page Commission," was appointed to inquire into inferior criminal courts in cities of the first class.

Conditions at the time of the Page inquiry were palpably vicious. An article, "The Farce of Police Court Justice," appeared in a magazine in February of 1907. Its subtitle, "Magistrates, Lawyers, Wardheelers, Professional Bondsmen, Clerks of the Court, and Probation Officers Join to Make a Mockery of 'The Supreme Court of the Poor,' " recalls similar conditions in our own day. It is worth quoting at length.[2]

[1] *The Forgotten Army*, Charity Organization Society, Committee on Criminal Courts, p. 13.

[2] Franklin Mathews, *Broadway Magazine*, Vol. XVII (February, 1907), No. 5. This article has been condensed in quoting.

"While testimony is being heard, papers which the clerks are preparing keep dropping on the magistrate's desk in reference to matters not related to the prisoner at the bar; and, of course, the magistrate's attention is thus distracted constantly. He frequently signs his name from four hundred to five hundred times a day and scarcely realizes what he is signing. The color of the various papers is his best clue.

"Things are hurried so fast that there is opportunity in plenty for corrupt policemen, for crooked lawyers and clerks to manipulate deals and so draw up papers that the magistrate's hands are tied in the disposition of cases, and even an honest one cannot begin to know all that is going on around him.

"Suddenly, a tip is passed about that there is 'something doing' in a case. A certain lawyer or a politician appears before the magistrate and an adjournment is asked for and is granted. The reason is well known to all parties concerned—and the divvy comes later. . . .

"Ten years ago there were from four to five lawyers in and around each of the police courts making a fair living.

"They were engaged on the spot by prisoners who needed, or thought they needed, their services. Now there are ten or a dozen at each court, some of them making from $10,000 to $15,000 a year. These lawyers are steered upon the prisoners by the police and other attendants who share the fees. The rule is to frighten every prisoner who can afford to pay.

"These lawyers distribute their cards in police stations and divide their pay with every one who gets them a case. They are vultures for the most part. It has reached such a stage that when an ordinary lawyer goes into these courts, as sometimes he has to do, he hires a police court lawyer to do his work, because the game is so complicated that he is afraid his client will not secure justice unless he has someone to plead the case who 'knows the ropes.' When certain magistrates sit, in the rotation scheme that is followed, the lawyer vultures disappear. . . .

"In the trail of the police court lawyer as a matter of necessity comes the professional bondsman. One of these with two lawyers and a magistrate composed the famous Essex Market Pickle Trust. A large batch of women would be gathered in by the police solely for the sake of plunder. These women hate detention for even an hour. By the payment of $5 each to the station house bondsman, who divided his fees with the police, they would be released at once to appear in court the next day. There the Pickle Trust got hold of them. The magistrate would hold up his hands in horror over the spectacle before him. He would declare that he would clean the streets and make them respectable. He would put the women under bonds for good behavior. The law gives him the right to detain them until he is satisfied with a bondsman. He would lock them up and then their satellites would scurry around for a bondsman. One after another would be produced, and all rejected. Finally the mysterious tip would be passed around that a certain man must be hired. His fee was ten per cent of the bond, $20 for a $200 bond, and so on. Most of the women would be put under $500 bonds. If there were twenty of them the Trust would have $1,000 to divide—pretty good picking for a morning's work. One of the magistrates was said to be a member of that trust, and although exposure has checked its work, it is still in existence in a covert form.

"The safest investment, and one of the most profitable in New York, is going on 'bonds for good behavior' in the police courts. More than 11,000 have been issued in the last eleven years. Not one has ever been forfeited. It is a 'sure thing.' A bondsman may sign one of these obligations and no matter if the next day the person under bond is brought into court again, no one will attempt to disturb the sleep of the first or any other similar bond in its repository in the criminal courts. They are an absolute farce. They make a mockery of justice. The system exists to enrich the professional bondsman.

"Another point. People wonder why the police arrest gamblers, and keep arresting them, and still the vice is not stamped out.

"No open or semi-concealed gambling can exist in New York or any other large city unless it is paid for. The men 'higher up' get this money, and the police know better than to interfere. Some of it filters to police captains or inspectors. When a district attorney or an anti-vice society makes a raid the gamblers have their lawyer and bondsman ready. The case drags along in the ordinary routine of criminal procedure. There is no need to pay for police court favors, for political influences take care of that. Political machine magistrates usually require the strongest possible proof to hold prisoners even on petty charges of gambling. They hold the men in the big cases, but politics sees to it that little comes of the matter.

"Why does such a state of affairs exist?

"Politics primarily is to blame. Since the time of Mayor Low probably not one magistrate has been appointed solely because of his peculiar fitness for the place.

"One magistrate was counsel for the Retail Liquor Dealers' Association. Later he was made a district leader.

"Another magistrate was a civil justice and a district leader when he was appointed.

"Another, it is alleged, was appointed because he was John Ahearn's man, and Ahearn's influence—he is the borough president of Manhattan and the Bronx—was needed in the Murphy-McClellan fight for the control of Tammany Hall.

"Again, it is alleged that a fourth was appointed because he was Jimmy Hagan's man. Hagan is a district leader and his influence was also needed in the Murphy-McClellan fight. This magistrate is the man whose numerous debts, as recorded in judgments in the county court, surprised the public. He was formerly associated with the notorious Bob Ammon (now in States Prison for conspiracy in connection with the famous Miller get-rich-quick scheme), and was once arrested with Ammon, but discharged by one of his present colleagues.

"Another of the police court bench is one of the most constant attendants at Charles F. Murphy's club and a graduate of Howe & Hummell's office, a firm of bad repute.

"Still another was appointed solely through politics. He was supposed to be strong with the German voters, and it was a shock to many of his friends to learn that just before he went on the bench he was compelled by the Federal Court to pay back into the assets of a firm in bankruptcy $1200 given to him by the firm for legal services to which the United States [District] court said he was not entitled. . . .

"One must consider certain things, the truth of which has not been questioned, that have become public recently concerning some of the fourteen magistrates who occupy the police bench in Manhattan and the Bronx. One of them has been accused before the district attorney of selling decisions, in one case the price being $1000 and in the other $400. Sinister voices have whispered that this magistrate paid $10,000 for his job. Another magistrate has borrowed money right and left from attorneys who practice before him and from clerks who work beside him and has given in payment checks—a score is a small estimate of their number—which have been returned marked 'no funds.' The attorneys have counted these unpaid checks an asset in practising before this magistrate.

"Another is accused of being the chief promoter of the above-mentioned Pickle Trust. . . ."

And so the stage was set when, in 1908, Governor Hughes appointed the Page Commission to study conditions in the inferior criminal courts.

The report of two years of work and study by the Commission was published in April, 1910, and several months later an Act Relating to the Inferior Criminal Courts of the City of New York was passed by the Legislature. The Page Commission worked quietly and with relatively little publicity. It was concerned with "the system, methods, and procedure of the Courts" rather than with "specific complaints against individual officials or employees."[3]

The magistrates' courts were, at that time, separated into two divisions,[4] "each having its own organization, consisting of a board of city magistrates, with a president

[3] *Final Report of the Commission To Inquire into Courts of Inferior Criminal Jurisdiction in the Cities of the First Class*, pp. 3, 4.
[4] First division—Manhattan and the Bronx.
Second division—Brooklyn, Queens, and Richmond.

selected by the magistrates annually from their own number."[5] The presiding magistrate thus had no "permanent tenure of . . . office nor a permanent responsibility and his control over the clerks [was] greatly limited. The assignments of the magistrates to the various courts [were] made by themselves, with no directing head."[6] In order to correct this "lack of adequate and authoritative supervision," to which the Commission attributed many of the "unwarrantable delays," and "lax methods," they recommended that a chief magistrate "charged with comprehensive administrative duties" should be designated by the mayor for each division. The chief magistrate "should prescribe the hour of the opening of the various parts of the court and for the attendance of the judges, clerks and other employees. He should establish and supervise a system for keeping the records of the court and should have authority to appoint the chief clerk and the chief probation officer."[7]

A board of magistrates in each division, composed of all the judges, should appoint all other clerks and employees of the court. The assignments of magistrates would be the duty of the board except in the case of the special courts, in which assignments would be made by the chief magistrate.

The Commission did not favor uniting the two divisions of the court into one. It believed that "the large number of separate courts [rendered] it necessary to retain the existing divisions in order to provide for efficient supervision." It was suggested that two joint meetings of the two

---

[5] *Final Report of the Commission To Inquire into Courts of Inferior Criminal Jurisdiction* . . ., p. 7.
[6] *Ibid.*, p. 22.   [7] *Ibid.*, p. 24.

boards be held annually, as a means of securing "uniform rules of practice and procedure, so far as practicable."[8]

The court attendants of that day were police officers. This meant that the magistrate had "only a qualified control over men who necessarily remain[ed] under the jurisdiction of the police commissioner"[9]—who could assign and withdraw attendants at his own pleasure. The courts' divided responsibility in handling a group of men who were, to all intents and purposes, governed by another department, was not conducive to a satisfactory performance of duty and caused friction between the police and the courts. Furthermore, the policemen received higher wages than the Commission believed it would be necessary to pay civilian attendants. It was estimated that their removal would save the city from $75,000 to $100,000 annually. The Commission recommended, therefore, the replacement of these police attendants by civilians.

The movement for special courts might be said to have started with the establishment of the night court in 1907. In referring to this court the Page Commission report says:

> The purpose of [this court] was to put a stop to the evil known as the station-house bond. It was claimed that certain of the police and certain bondsmen were in league, so that by constant arrests of prostitutes these women were compelled to get bail in order to be released until the following morning, and for that bail to pay heavily to the professional bondsmen.

The testimony before the Commission is somewhat conflicting as to the results of the night court.[10]

With regard to the problem of prostitution, of which we

[8] *Final Report of the Commission To Inquire into Courts of Inferior Criminal Jurisdiction* . . ., p. 30.

[9] *Ibid.*, p. 25.   [10] *Ibid.*, p. 47.

shall say more in a subsequent chapter, it is sufficient to
say here that other means to circumvent the lawmakers
were found by offenders. On the other hand, the night
court was an advantage from the standpoint of the hasty
disposition of minor offenses.[11] It freed many who might
otherwise have wasted hours in jail.

The Commission recommended holding two night
courts, one for women and one for men. The establishment of a separate court for women was hailed as a great
reform measure designed to exclude "doubtful male char-
acters" and allow a "concentration of effort" enabling
those "philanthropically inclined more effectively to give
their assistance to the prisoners as well as to the magistrates and probation officers."[12]

This was again urged in the establishment of a domestic
relations court where patient and careful attention could
be given to nonsupport cases. Magistrates would be especially assigned to the court by the chief magistrate. It was
also suggested that cases "to compel the support of aged
and infirm parents by their children," hitherto taken into
general sessions, be heard in the new court.[13]

The situation in the magistrates' courts, first division,
with regard to probation was most unsatisfactory. Policemen served as probation officers. They were not attached
to any particular court but rather to the person of a
particular magistrate. The officer followed his magistrate
from one court to another and was not assigned when the
magistrate was not sitting. He reported to the first dis-

[11] Felonies are not heard in night court.
[12] *Final Report of the Committee To Inquire into Courts of Inferior
Criminal Jurisdiction* . . ., p. 50.
[13] *Ibid.,* p. 46.

trict court each day "for the purpose of the police department records," but when the magistrate was not sitting the probation officer had little or no supervision. "The account which many of [them] gave of themselves was highly discreditable." Most of them "evidenced neither the capacity, industry, nor disposition necessary for this important work. The supervision by the magistrate was ineffective and inadequate."[14] As in the case of police-court attendants, friction was apt to arise between the police department and certain of the magistrates. There was, therefore, no permanence of assignment and a probation officer might be withdrawn at a time when his magistrate needed him most. The Commission recommended the removal of police probation officers and the appointment by the board of magistrates of civilian officers. These officers were to be attached to the court and not the particular magistrate and were to be supervised by a chief probation officer appointed by the chief magistrate.

The Commission was apparently perplexed by the complaints against attorneys. An alliance between the officers serving warrants and these lawyers had been hinted, but the Commission found it "exceedingly difficult to obtain competent proof upon the subject." In the summary of the recommendations no mention is made of this important problem, but in the body of the report we find it suggested that "as a necessary record the name and address of counsel appearing in any case should be endorsed on the papers." This, they felt, would place the chief city magistrates in a "peculiarly advantageous position to in-

---

[14] *Final Report of the Commission To Inquire into Courts of Inferior Criminal Jurisdiction* . . ., p. 66.

vestigate information or complaint as to the unprofessional conduct of attorneys. . . ." They concluded "that it is impossible to prescribe a remedy by statutory enactment but that the improvement in the situation must come from constant supervision and appropriate regulation, from time to time, as experience may suggest and that these results can be attained under the system of centralized responsibility which we have recommended."[15]

The assignment of deputy assistant district attorneys to the magistrates' courts was recommended by the Commission. Such assignments "under competent administration" would, they believed, "result in protecting many defendants against imposition by [unscrupulous] attorneys."[16] The assistant district attorney could examine complaints and otherwise expedite the process of justice; seeing that a square deal was given both to the defendants and to the people appearing against them.[17]

There were other less complicated reforms proposed by the Commission. Fines, hitherto paid to private agencies, were to be made payable only to the city. Summonses were to be legalized and a record of their issuance kept. In place of an arrest in certain minor offenses, a summons was to be issued. The magistrates were to be allowed to try violations of traffic regulations where pleas of guilty were made and it was a first offense. They were also to try cases involving cruelty to animals.

Provision for defendants confined at police stations or district prisons to communicate with friends or relatives

---

[15] *Ibid.*, p. 70.   [16] *Ibid.*, p. 71.

[17] A request by the district attorney for funds to carry out this plan was submitted to local authorities while the report was still in preparation.

free of charge supplanted the old method of using messengers, who were not city employees but who were privileged to serve in the prisons. It was rumored that these messengers were given to extortion; but the truth of these rumors was hard to establish.

The Commission's only contribution, so far as bail was concerned, was a provision for taking cash bail by the clerk. Formerly defendants could not give cash bail at the court but had to deposit it with the city chamberlain.

There were still other general provisions dealing with salaries, terms of office, provision for additional magistrates, and visits by magistrates to institutions to which defendants were committed. A system of record keeping and statistics was devised. As a gesture toward keeping magistrates out of politics, the Commission suggested that magistrates be forbidden to hold executive positions in political organizations.

Perhaps the most important contribution which the Page Commission made to the progress of the lower courts was the codification of the laws relating to the courts into one compact act known as the Inferior Criminal Courts Act, which grew out of the recommendations embodied in its report.

The recommendations of the Page Commission and its actual accomplishments were hailed by the social organizations with enthusiasm. The general atmosphere was one of hope that the abuses prevalent in the inferior criminal courts were about to be permanently eradicated. "The politician has been banished," they said, and

the public now recognizes that all men are treated alike there and that justice is to be had. These courts now are on a parity with the Supreme Court in the public mind, both as to dignity and importance.[18]

Looking back on the Page Commission from our vantage point, we are inclined, because of its failure to establish a court system of which the city could be proud, to minimize the constructive work that it actually accomplished. But its work was a very useful step in the evolution of our courts.

The changes which it made in the organization and practice of the magistrates' court system were important to the development of the court, but did not go deep enough. That the Commission was cognizant of the root of the evil is evidenced by the fact that they attempted to strike at the source of corruption by relieving the congestion around the judge's bench and forbidding magistrates to hold executive political jobs. Commendable as these changes were, they did not cut out the cancer of political patronage, which had penetrated into the very marrow of our inferior criminal court system. While a feeling of optimism did prevail, there were a few keen minds who were aware of the unconscious superficiality of the reforms recommended by the Page Commission. An editorial in the *New York Times* the day after the Page Commission report was made public illustrates this point. The writer approved the discontinuance of the bridge, the establishment of a domestic relations court, further development of the night court, and the appointment of civilian probation officers.

[18] Lawrence Veiller, *Three Years of Progress in New York's Police Court,* Charity Organization Society Committee on Criminal Courts (December 18, 1913).

But, after all, the faults of the lower courts are not due to defects of system and structure so much as to defects of judges on the bench. As the Report says, "many of the defects pointed out have not been due to lack of statutory provision, but to failure to observe them," and again: "We have pursued our investigations and arrived at our conclusions with an appreciation of the fact that laws alone cannot compel intelligent and conscientious administration. Over and above all in importance is the judge himself,—upon whom depends, in greatest measure, the careful and wise disposition of these thousands of cases dealing with people and subjects which touch the city's life at every point." Great things were expected when the police justices were legislated out of existence and city magistrates, who must be members of the bar, were substituted. Some gain resulted, but more of it was due to the general improvement of political standards than to the new law. Where the appointments were bad, the results were bad. "Battery Dan" Finn, City Magistrate, was no advance over "Paddy" Divver, Police Justice. Much of the discredit of the lower courts has been due to bad appointments. A good deal more of it—the ridiculous rulings of some magistrates, which have brought the enforcement of the criminal law into disrepute, for example—has been due to the irresponsibility of the magistrates. Once upon the bench, some of them become alarmed themselves. One of them may discharge all the "unfortunate" women arraigned before him. Another may make a specialty of turning loose all vagrants. Another cannot be convinced that the excise law is broken unless a chemist has analyzed the beverage sold. We do not see that the new law proposed will put any check on what Mayor Gaynor calls the "strutting" of the magistrates. A little while ago, some of them, or perhaps it was the justices of the minor civil courts, complained that the court clerks were irresponsible because their removal was possible only through action of the Appellate Division of the Supreme Court and this was too difficult. The argument probably applies to the strutters themselves.[19]

[19] Editorial, "Minor Courts Reform," *New York Times*, April 5, 1910.

After twenty-three years, we find the following statement by Judge Seabury:

The reason why we are no better off today under the Inferior Criminal Courts Act than we were prior to its enactment is that the Inferior Criminal Courts Act left unimpaired and free to flourish the basic vice in the magistrates' courts, *i.e.,* their administration as a part of the political spoils system. It left the magistrates to be appointed by a political agency, the mayor, upon the recommendation of the district leaders within his political party—and these men, as we know, have regarded the places to be filled as plums to be distributed as rewards for services rendered by faithful party workers. The courts are directed by these magistrates in co-operation with the court clerks, who are not civil service employees and who are appointed without the slightest regard to fitness or qualification, but solely through political agencies and because of political influences. The assistant clerks and attendants, though nominally taken from the civil service list, are still, in almost all instances, faithful party workers who, despite civil service provisions, have secured their places through political influence as a recompense for services performed for the party. The insidious auspices under which the magistrates, the clerks, the assistant clerks and the attendants are appointed are bad enough; the conditions under which they retain their appointments are infinitely worse, because they involve the subserviency in office to district leaders and other politicians. It is a by-word in the corridors of the magistrates' courts of the City of New York that the intervention of a friend in the district political club is much more potent in the disposition of cases than the merits of the cause or the services of the best lawyer and, unfortunately, the truth of the statement alone prevents it from being a slander upon the good name of the city.

Much, if not all, of the hideous caricature which parades as justice in these courts is avoidable; complaisancy, unconcern and corruption are alone responsible for it—and these causes, in turn, are the product of the system which permits what was intended to be a great instrument of justice to remain a part of a political system, the purpose of which is to retain and control the jobs and perquisites relating to government. As long as appointments to office in these courts are permitted to rest in the hands of a politically controlled agency, just so long must we expect the appointees to be recruited from the ranks of those whose only claim to appointment is their subservience to their political party, and as long as this remains the yardstick by which candidates for these places are to be measured and selected, there is no justification for expecting any substantial improvement in the administration of these courts.[20]

With due allowance for overly strong language here and there, laid on the background of the well-intentioned reforms of the Page Commission, this is a moving statement of the difficulty of substantial reform.

[20] See *Final Report of Samuel Seabury, Referee, to the Supreme Court, Appellate Division—First Judicial Department, In the Matter of the Investigation of the Magistrates' Courts in the First Judicial Department and the Magistrates Thereof, and of Attorneys-at-Law Practicing in Said Courts* (hereafter to be referred to as *Seabury Report*), pp. 14–15.

CHAPTER III

THE SEABURY INVESTIGATION

Viewing the courts of New York City in long perspective, the generalization is possible that the inferior courts were far better managed in the period between 1910 and approximately 1920 than during the last decade. It is not difficult to point out the reason for this.

William J. Gaynor became mayor of New York City in 1909. While differences of opinion may exist as to Gaynor's administrative capacities, no one is likely to question the fact that in his rough, direct way he understood the proper qualifications of a magistrate. Generally speaking, he appointed capable men. Following him came the reform administration of John Purroy Mitchel, who, likewise, sought the best timber for the magistrates' courts, regardless of party or political influence. These two administrations resulted in the filling of the magistrates' courts with a fairly capable and honest group of men, whose influence lasted for approximately ten years. When the terms of these men expired, they were generally replaced, during the administrations of Hylan and Walker, by a relatively inferior quality of men. In fact, some of the appointments of Hylan, and the earlier appointments of Walker, were infinitely below the standards set by Gaynor and Mitchel. The effect of this change in the quality of magistrates came to be evident in the early twenties and apparently grew worse as the personnel of the court came to be more completely changed.

Another factor upon which one is bound to dwell with

some hesitancy is the fact that although Chief Magistrate William McAdoo, who served from 1910 until his death in 1930, was in his early days a fairly capable public official within his political limitations, his control over the great court apparently suffered considerable diminution during his last years in office. It is not too much to say that, with a vigorous hand at the helm, the conditions revealed by Judge Seabury might not have developed. These conditions were not the result of any lack of good intentions on the part of Judge McAdoo. The difficulties of his problem simply exceeded the failing capacities of old age.

The decline in quality of the magistrates' courts in the past ten years was accompanied by a fairly general failure of confidence in the courts and in the judges of the city. It should be borne in mind that in 1924 the strongest leader that Tammany Hall ever had, Charles F. Murphy, died. It is stoutly asserted by those who knew and admired Mr. Murphy that he sought in every way to eliminate the influence of politics in the courts. He scanned judicial candidacies with a careful and discriminating eye. He followed the policy of noninterference himself and sought to enforce his ideas in this respect upon other politicians. It remains to his credit that few judicial scandals broke out in New York during the twenty years of his leadership. After his death no such discrimination existed. It is not strange, therefore, that unsatisfactory conditions in the judiciary began to appear. First there came suspicion, then humiliating accusations, and finally sensational exposure.

A judge of the Court of General Sessions, Francis X. Mancuso, resigned his position, because of disclosures in connection with a bank of which he was a director. Subsequently he was indicted and unsuccessfully prosecuted in connection with his business relationships.

A judge of the Brooklyn County Court, W. Bernard Vause, was charged with having received a fee estimated at $190,000 for negotiations in certain pier leases. While he was answering this charge he was indicted for using the mails to defraud in his activities promoting an insolvent finance corporation. He resigned from the bench, was convicted on the latter charge, and was sentenced to serve a term in the Atlanta Penitentiary.

A serious disturbance in the probation department in the Court of General Sessions, which, while it did not show criminal culpability, at least indicated a state of exotic administration, did nothing to increase public respect for the criminal courts. The sudden disappearance of Supreme Court Justice Joseph Force Crater added further unrest and mystery to the situation.

The colorful episodes centering about the political and judicial career of Magistrate Albert H. Vitale did not reassure the citizens of the city. They showed how the facile magic of politics bridged the gap between high office and the grimy company of the underworld. The genius of sardonic comedy never imagined a more weird gathering than that which attended the dinner in honor of Magistrate Vitale at the Tippecanoe Democratic Club. While judges, politicians, and the underworld made merry, six gunmen entered the hall, lined up the guests, and walked out with thousands of dollars of loot. Soon after, it was disclosed that Magistrate Vitale had effected the return of many of the stolen articles within a few hours after the burglary. A trial of the magistrate before the Appellate Division was then ordered. One of the accusations against

Magistrate Vitale showed that he had dismissed a charge of robbery against a man whom he ordered, immediately after, to make restitution of the apparently stolen property. Another charge was that during five years on the bench Magistrate Vitale had made deposits vastly exceeding his judicial salary, which he could not adequately explain. He was removed because his answer to the charges admitted that he had accepted a large loan from Arnold Rothstein, the notorious gambler. In view of this admission the Appellate Division deemed it unnecessary to take testimony as to the other charges.

Shortly after this scandal, George F. Ewald was charged with having bought his appointment for $10,000 from a Tammany district leader. He resigned before he was indicted on these charges. Subsequently, he was indicted for using the mails to defraud in connection with the sale of the Cotter-Butte mining stock. The Ewald case, with its strange coincidences, threw another shadow upon the courts.

During this entire period, the most insistent and continuous criticism was leveled at the magistrates' courts. As we have seen, the *Evening Post,* in January, 1930, printed a sensational and apparently uncontroverted series of articles by Milton MacKaye, entitled "The Magistrate Racket." A short time after this, another newspaper ran a similar series. These articles asserted that the appointment of magistrates was dictated by political considerations, and that their decisions were often dictated by corruption and political favoritism; that clerks made their courts pay dividends in bribery; that bail-bond laws were being flagrantly violated; that "neighborhood monopolies" of court attendants, bondsmen, policemen, steerers, and lawyers preyed upon litigants.

These articles were followed by demands for a thorough investigation of the magistrates' courts. A grand jury investigation was held. On March 14, 1930, it submitted a report which fairly generally indicated the conditions that prevailed.

The testimony before us is not legally sufficient to warrant the finding of any indictment. It leads us, however, to make the following statement:

FIRST. It has been brought to our attention that some magistrates have been indiscreet and lax to a degree which might lead to improper inferences in one or more of the following particulars:

By maintaining too close connection with political organizations and by being unduly active in politics.

By a lack of dignity in the conduct of their courts.

By a lack of consideration of persons having business in the court and permitting the same on the part of court employees.

By being dilatory in opening and premature in closing court.

By granting postponements in such number as to put an undue burden on complainants and witnesses, tending to thwart the administration of justice.

By seeing in chambers too many people who may be presumed to have business which should be heard in open court, giving rise to the suspicion that the magistrate is being subjected to improper influences.

By holding for the grand jury cases which, by the exercise of proper courage or intelligence, or both, could have been disposed of by the magistrate.

By the inadequate supervision of the issuance of bail bonds.

SECOND. The magistrates' courts in the county of New York are, almost without exception, inconveniently subdivided and arranged. The subdivision and arrangement facilitate and in some instances may perhaps lead to abuses. In and about these courts persons are suffered to loiter who have no legitimate business therein or thereabout. The presence of most of these encourages improper practices by court clerks, assistant clerks, and attendants, which includes the acceptance by some of gratuities for the performance of acts in violation of the law, such as drawing complaints in a lower degree than the facts warrant, unjustly advancing or delaying cases and allowing persons improperly to have access to defendants.

THIRD. The testimony suggests a pernicious business connection between professional bondsmen and attorneys leading to extortionate charges and in some instances to an illegal division by the attorney of his professional fee with the professional bondsman, through whose activity the attorney has secured the client. Bail agents in some instances are shown to have charged more than the legal fee for obtaining bail bonds.

Throughout the summer of 1930 criticism continued. Newspapers, leaders of the bar, and others called for an investigation, and in August, 1930, Gov. Franklin D. Roosevelt called upon the Appellate Division of the First Judicial Department, which comprises the borough of Manhattan and the Bronx, to institute an inquiry into the magistrates' courts.

On August 25 the Appellate Division entered an order designating Judge Samuel Seabury referee to conduct the investigation into the magistrates' courts and "the magistrates thereof" and to report to them on the basis of his investigation, so that "further action or proceedings may be taken as to this court shall seem just and proper."

Judge Samuel Seabury had extraordinary qualifications for his task. He had been judge in the City Court, then of the Supreme Court, and finally of the Court of Appeals. During the political upheavals of 1912 and 1913 he had presided in the second Becker trial and had learned at first hand of the corruption then prevalent in the city.[1]

At Judge Seabury's request, the Association of the Bar of the City of New York, the New York County Lawyers' Association, and the Bronx County Bar Association designated the counsel to aid him in the investigation. Isidor Kresel, their choice, was a lawyer of unusual ability. He was connected in the public mind with the activities of William Travers Jerome, under whom he had served as assistant district attorney; with an inquiry into race-track scandals in 1907; and, in 1929, with the prosecution of seventy-four lawyers for the solicitation of clients in accident cases. To his keen mind, his skill at cross-examination, and his tireless industry, much of the success of the investigation is due. Unfortunately, in February, 1931, Mr. Kresel withdrew from the inquiry.

The task which confronted the investigators was indeed a difficult one. Vast suspicions, vague charges by individuals and organizations, were their only leads. Proof was needed. Scores of suggestions and complaints of official wrongdoing were received, many of them anonymous. But diligent investigation of them yielded nothing.

This general search was finally changed to an intensive

[1] It should be remembered that, in the course of the two years during which he has carried on his activities, he has served in three separate and distinct capacities. At the beginning, he was appointed by the Appellate Division of the Supreme Court as a referee to investigate the magistrates' courts of Manhattan and the Bronx. Later, he was appointed by Gov. Franklin D. Roosevelt as a commissioner to investigate certain charges which had been made against District Attorney Thomas C. T. Crain. Subsequently, the Legislature created a joint committee to investigate the entire city government of New York and Judge Seabury was appointed counsel of this committee. The major part of the investigation of the magistrates' courts, however, preceded and, to a certain extent, paved the way for these other investigations.

examination of a single court, the Women's Court of Manhattan. The investigators proceeded to study hundreds of individual cases, collecting evidences of abuse. Seven weeks of labor were spent in this way. Hundreds of witnesses were examined in private, in order to obviate the necessity of introducing useless testimony into the record. At the same time, accountants were set to work analyzing the financial accounts of suspects.

The basic soundness of this method of procedure was demonstrated when, late in November, the second public hearing of the investigation was held. John C. Weston, who for seven years had served as assistant district attorney in the Women's Court and whose activities had been commended by reformers, repeated his confession made in private hearings that he had accepted $20,000 in bribes to "go light" in the prosecution of 900 defendants in the Women's Court. This money had come, he testified, from twenty-one lawyers and from various policemen who served as prosecuting witnesses in prostitution cases.

The dramatic testimony of Weston was followed, the next day, by revelations even more shocking. Chile Mapocha Acuna, who had acted as a stool pigeon or *agent provocateur*, described a strange and perverted type of police procedure. The power of the police to set in motion the machinery of justice by arraigning women in the magistrates' courts had provided an instrument to tap a golden stream of easy money. Acuna identified police officers whom he accused of perjury and extortion and enumerated case after case in which such irregularities had taken place.

Rumor began at last to be supplanted by an ugly reality. Once again the public began to see the *dramatis per-*

sonae of the magistrates' courts in a realistic fashion. The
multitude of witnesses who followed Acuna and Weston
revealed the details of an amazing racket, carried on under the guise of criminal prosecution. Their testimony
made it clear that after many so-called "raids," sup-
posedly made to enforce laws against prostitution, the victims of this racket, innocent and guilty, were obliged to
purchase freedom from the police by the payment of
money. In a number of instances immunity was bought
before an arrest was made. In other cases, when the prosecution was carried beyond the arresting stage, bribery of
the police would induce them to fail to make out a case
against the defendant.

The extraordinary enrichment of some members of the
police force attached to the so-called "vice squad" was
disclosed in the course of the investigation. Five of these
officers alone accumulated in a few years more than $500,-
000. The efforts of some of them to account for these ac-
cumulations were not without humorous touches. One of
them explained that $40,000 in forty one-thousand-dollar
bills had been given to him by his Uncle George while going to Coney Island.

The testimony disclosed, moreover, that when "fixing"
occurred, it was usually managed through the interposi-
tion of the bondsman. In fact, even in cases where no actual dishonesty was present, the bondsman played a vital
rôle. He appeared to the bewildered defendant as a ministering angel. He opened the doors of the station house.
He steered her to another ministering angel—a criminal
lawyer. He or the lawyer took the defendant's bank book
into custody. If she paid enough, usually five hundred dollars, strange changes of heart on the part of prosecuting

witnesses took place. The magic word "discharge" broke upon the defendant and reason returned in the cool light of the outside world. Five hundred dollars, divided among the bondsman, the lawyer, the arresting officers, and the deputy assistant district attorney, produced marvelous results.

John Weston's part in this ring was, after a criminal lawyer had made an "arrangement" with him, to fail to elicit at the trial the facts necessary for a conviction. He rode the horse to lose. Acuna's rôle, like that of a number of men he named, was to act as a kind of privateer in the war of the community upon prostitution—hired to help or induce people to break laws. Court *attachés*, too, often played a part in the vicious system.

The long story of corruption and bribery in the Women's Court was revealed in the course of many months. These disclosures involved thirty-five members of the police force, twenty-one lawyers, and thirty-eight bondsmen. Charges preferred against a number of the policemen resulted in the dismissal of some, the suspension and subsequent reinstatement of others, and the commitment of still others to Federal and state institutions. A number of bondsmen were convicted of making extortionate charges on bail bonds and were sentenced to serve prison terms. A report concerning sixteen attorneys implicated in the testimony was presented to the Appellate Division of the Supreme Court. Their trial was referred to a referee, who recommended the disbarment of one attorney, the censure of another, and the dismissal of the charges against the others.

In the meanwhile, evidence was being adduced which showed serious abuses in magistrates' courts other than the Women's Court. This, too, indicated that "fixing," extortion, and oppression were frequent. Lawyers, bondsmen, and court *attachés* were implicated. A typical example is cited by Judge Seabury in his report to the Appellate Division.

A storekeeper is solicited to put an illegal gambling machine into his premises—a machine which, on occasion, returns slugs after a coin is inserted in it, these slugs being redeemable by the storekeeper for cash or merchandise. This type of gambling has become so notorious that the New York Law Journal said, editorially, on March 5th, 1932:

"The distribution of 'slot machines' has become an underworld 'racket' of substantial proportions, if one may judge from newspaper accounts of the rivalry and resulting bloodshed among members of the gangster fraternity arising out of the struggle from many cities for the control of the 'racket.' "

The storekeeper is concerned about the consequences if he should be discovered and arrested. His attention is then called to certain instructions on the device, advising him to telephone a specified number in the event of an arrest and that such call will result in his being provided, gratis, with a bondsman to bail him out and a lawyer to defend him in the magistrates' courts. In due time he is arrested. He follows the instructions, and when he arrives in court he is met by a lawyer who does not know him and whom he does not know. This lawyer proceeds to defend him. Upon a long technical argument, based upon the distinction between the return of money and the return of slugs—all of which the defendant, and everyone else except, apparently, the court, knows is based on false premises— the attorney succeeds in procuring a dismissal of the charge and the defendant leaves the court room with his tongue in his cheek.[2]

Another aspect of the evidence related to the functions, the manner of their performance, and the unofficial activi-

[2] *Seabury Report*, pp. 20, 21.

ties of those who participated in the administration of the
courts—the magistrates, the court clerks, assistant court
clerks, court attendants, assistant district attorneys, and
probation officers.

The testimony of a number of magistrates frankly indicated the political nature of their appointments to office.
A minute examination of their judicial activities clearly
demonstrated that it was the practice of some of them to
pay back the district leader to whom they owed their office by receptivity to suggestions made by the leader in
reference to pending cases.

In the course of the investigation three magistrates resigned under fire. Evidence had been collected in private
hearings which pointed, in one instance, to unjudgelike
conduct off the bench, and, in another, to a failure to recognize irregularities in his court. Within twelve hours of
the time at which the record of these private hearings was
to have confronted them in public, Magistrates McQuade,
Goodman, and Simpson elected voluntarily to return to
private life.

Charges against three other magistrates were filed with
the Appellate Division. The trial of Magistrate Brodsky,
who had engaged in extensive real-estate and stock-
market transactions, resulted in an order exonerating him.
The trials of Magistrates Norris and Silbermann, however, culminated in orders for their removal.

With regard to the clerical staff of the courts, a generally low tone of administration was likewise indicated. In
the department of probation, too, while no dishonesty
was found, it was clear that careless, shoddy work was being done. An inferior staff had degenerated into routineers

without a sense of the complex needs of the persons submitted to its care and of its duties to these people.

It should be firmly fixed in mind that the investigation conducted by Judge Seabury, so far as public hearings were concerned, occupied itself in the main with only three courts—the Women's Court, the Essex Market Court, and the Harlem Court. The investigations into the two latter courts were brief. They were apparently made to demonstrate to the city that corruption and inefficiency were not limited to the Women's Court. The task of considering in minute detail all of the magistrates' courts in Manhattan and the Bronx would have been endless. The examination of the three courts served to indicate general tendencies. Judge Seabury's consideration of the magistrates themselves, however, extended to practically all of the sitting magistrates in Manhattan and the Bronx.

In March, 1931, Judge Seabury was appointed by Gov. Franklin D. Roosevelt to investigate charges against District Attorney Crain. His energies from that point on were in the main taken from the magistrates' inquiry. Public hearings on the magistrates were discontinued and the only subsequent act was the preparation of the final report, which was published on March 28, 1932.[3]

Meanwhile, a number of activities directed from within the official family were put under way, in order to remedy some of the abuses revealed by Judge Seabury's investigation.

In the spring of 1931, the Police Commissioner announced a change in the organization of those members of the police department who were engaged in the supression

[3] See footnote, p. 36.

of prostitution. He also forbade entrapment and the use of stool pigeons. Orders were given that the provisions of the Code of Criminal Procedure, as to forcible entries, must be strictly observed. Police officers who made arrests for prostitution were required to draw up typewritten reports concerning each arrest, and, if the charge were subsequently dismissed, superior officers were required to investigate the reasons for such dismissals.

Former Mayor Walker unquestionably exercised greater care in the appointment of new magistrates. During the year 1931, ten magistrates were appointed. All but one had received the full approval of both bar associations. The Mayor, whenever appointments were to be made, submitted the names of candidates to the Association of the Bar of the City of New York and secured from them indorsements of the candidates. All of his appointments in 1931 were made after such indorsement.[4]

Shortly before the Seabury investigation had begun, Chief Magistrate William McAdoo died and Magistrate Joseph E. Corrigan was appointed in his place. This appointment was greeted by general approval. Magistrate Corrigan had been in the service for more than twenty years and had earned a reputation for honesty and ability. His coöperation with the investigation was whole-hearted and effective. In April, 1931, however, he was appointed to another court and the Mayor appointed as his successor James E. McDonald, whose appointment was favorably commented upon by Judge Seabury and the bar generally.

4 Credit is due to Charles C. Burlingham, then President of the Association of the Bar of the City of New York, for his unremitting efforts to have the mayor submit to the two bar associations the names of prospective appointees to the magistrates' bench.

One of the first acts of Chief Magistrate McDonald was the appointment of a committee on the reorganization of the magistrates' courts, with Magistrate Jonah J. Goldstein as chairman. This committee has since worked industriously in the direction of a series of reforms in the magistrates' courts. The first report of this committee, submitted in December, 1931, contains a number of recommendations to which allusion will be made in subsequent chapters. It must be recognized that in the work of this committee many handicaps must be overcome. It is not easy for a group of magistrates, serving with others, who of necessity must bear some of the blame for the conditions which existed in the courts, to make recommendations without conflict in the ranks. Moreover, much of the political influence which has disturbed the magistrates' courts still bears heavily on all magistrates. Even an unusually strong chief magistrate finds it difficult to overcome this opposition.

A great deal of commendation is due to the chairman of this committee, Magistrate Goldstein. With quiet persistence he has forced a number of changes. It is fortunate that his activities as chairman of the committee are by no means concluded. In so far as there is hope for the improvement of the magistrates' courts from within, it is largely dependent upon his efforts and upon the disposition of the Chief Magistrate to promote actively the work of reorganization.

CHAPTER IV

ORGANIZATION, JURISDICTION, AND HOUSING

IT is probable that few people have any conception of the size and scope of the magistrates' court organization, or of the wide field of human activity with which they are concerned. In order to describe the organization of these courts it is necessary to point out that the city of New York is composed of five boroughs, each coterminous with a county.[1] These municipal divisions cover an area of 287[2] square miles and are inhabited by 6,930,446[3] people representing practically every race, nationality, and creed. To handle the legal problems of this heterogeneous population there has grown up a vast structure of courts. In general, criminal and civil courts are separate. On the criminal side, primary jurisdiction is vested in the magistrates' courts. Into these courts are brought persons arrested by the police and many others on summonses issued on the complaint of a police officer or private citizen. The hearing is conducted by a magistrate who acts as judge and jury in minor offenses. The Court of Special Sessions is the higher of the inferior criminal courts. It has original jurisdiction in only one type of case.[4] The bulk of its work

[1] They are New York County and the borough of Manhattan; Kings County and the borough of Brooklyn; and the boroughs and counties of Queens, Richmond, and the Bronx.

[2] *Statistical Sources for Demographic Studies of Greater New York, 1920,* New York City 1920 Census Committee, Inc.

[3] U.S. Census, 1930.

[4] Orders of affiliation (bastardy proceedings involving a determination of paternity).

consists in hearing cases which are sent to it by the magistrates' courts. The cases heard are of two kinds—misdemeanors (these make up the bulk of the cases handled) and appeals from decisions of the magistrates. There is no jury; but as the offenses triable in this court might lead, if there were a conviction, to three years in the penitentiary, the rights of the defendant are safeguarded by having the trial of the case conducted by three justices sitting together. However, only two of the three must concur on a verdict of guilty. Appeals from the decisions of this court are heard by the Appellate Division.

Beyond these two courts, the criminal jurisdiction is in the main subdivided by counties. There are five county courts for the trial of felonies. These courts are called county courts, except in Manhattan, where the name Court of General Sessions is used. These courts hear only cases brought to them by way of grand jury indictments. Indictment may be obtained in two ways, on information supplied either directly by the district attorney or through magistrates' court hearings.

The magistrates' courts might well be called the clearing houses of the criminal-court system. They are organized under the Inferior Criminal Courts Act of 1910. Their judges are empowered to conduct hearings in felonies and misdemeanors, and to exercise summary jurisdiction in offenses that are less than crimes. These offenses include violation of corporation ordinance (where not expressly declared by law to be a misdemeanor), disorderly conduct, disorderly person, vagrancy, and wayward minor.[5] The many details of this jurisdiction, which present

[5] For complete description of jurisdiction see Inferior Criminal Courts Act, annotated by Bruce Cobb, pp. 115–212. Page 126:
"All crimes, including every felony and misdemeanor, from murder to

a number of rather unique problems, will appear in the course of subsequent chapters. Its wide variety is indicated by the fact that while it possesses the jurisdiction ordinarily exercised by police courts, it has what, to the residents of other cities, will appear a curious power in relation to family support.

Scattered throughout Greater New York there are thirty-seven magistrates' courts. Of these a number are special courts—three traffic courts, two night courts,[6] three family courts, two women's courts, three municipal term courts, and three homicide courts. In addition, a commercial frauds court and a probation court are held by the magistrates to meet a need not met by the regularly constituted courts. These courts are presided over by 49 magistrates, and a chief magistrate who acts as administrative head of the organization. The magistrates are assisted by 37 clerks, 89 assistant clerks, and 118 court attendants.

The magistrates are appointed by the mayor[7] for a term

"the most trifling infraction of a minor statute (or even an ordinance if "made by law a misdemeanor in rank) whether *mala in se* or merely "*mala prohibita,* come before the magistrate for examination unless (a) "the grand jury first indicts thereon, or (b) it is one of the lesser mis-"demeanors tried by consent before a magistrate sitting as a justice of "Special Sessions under Article III A, Sections 43–46 of Inferior Criminal "Courts Act."

[6] One of these, the Brooklyn Night Court, is for the taking of bail only.

[7] Qualification of magistrates:

"No person shall be appointed to office of city magistrate unless he "shall have been admitted to practise as an attorney and counselor-at-"law of the supreme court of the state at least three years prior to the "date of such appointment, unless he was a city magistrate, or police jus-"tice, or was acting as a police justice on or before the first day of Janu-"ary, 1895."

Inferior Criminal Courts Act, art. iv, sec. 52.

of ten years, at a salary of $12,000 a year.[8] The chief magistrate is designated by the mayor and receives $3,000 additional compensation. He is assisted in his duty as administrative officer by the board of city magistrates. There is a peculiar division of labor between the chief and the board. The Page Commission, which evolved the plan for the centralizing of responsibility in a chief magistrate, did not want the other magistrates to be entirely relieved of their share of administrative responsibility, and so this board was given specific duties.

It must meet at least four times each year and may be convened at other times by the chief magistrate or at the request of ten or more magistrates. All complaints pertaining to the courts or to the magistrates, officers and employees must be received and investigated by the board and proper disposition made. It is responsible for altering and amending the rules regulating the practice and procedure of the courts.[9] It appoints all the clerks, assistant clerks,[10] court attendants, and other employees of the court,[11] with the exception of the chief clerk, deputy clerks,[12] and probation officer.[13] Assignments to special courts are made by the chief magistrate.[14]

In the borough of Manhattan, to which, in the main, the discussion in this book is limited, there are seven district courts, a women's court, a night court, a family court, two traffic courts, a homicide court, a municipal term court, a commercial frauds court, and occasionally a court held by the chief magistrate.

[8] Salary schedule: in 1920, salaries increased from $7,000 to $8,000; in 1926, to $10,000; and in 1928, to $12,000.

[9] Inferior Criminal Courts Act, art. iv, sec. 59.

[10] *Ibid.*, sec. 55.   [11] *Ibid.*, sec. 56.   [12] *Ibid.*, sec. 55a.

[13] *Ibid.*, art. vi, sec. 96.   [14] *Ibid.*, art. iv, sec. 51.

The housing of this tremendous organization has long been a source of criticism. At the time of the Page Commission, no article on the courts was complete without a description of their grimy interiors.

The Page Commission found that the court buildings were for the most part old and that detention pens were unsanitary and dingy. While sheet-iron partitions separated men from women, frequent overcrowding led to the mingling of the sexes in the corridor outside the pens. There was no segregation by offense or previous record, and the innocent were subjected to demoralizing influences.

The courtroom itself was a scene of confusion during the busy hours of the day.

"Behind a broad desk at the far end of the room sat a number of clerks noisily transacting the routine business of the court, amid a litter of books and papers and almost at the elbows of the judge, who could not readily be distinguished from the clerical staff, for he, like them, was attired in citizen's garb.

"Directly in front of the desk stood a small platform known as 'the bridge,' and upon this each policeman arraigning a prisoner at the bar took his stand, closely surrounded by reporters, lawyers, professional bondsmen, and privileged spectators of all sorts, who occupied every inch of space, clung to the steps of the platform and sprawled over the desk in their anxiety to see and hear. What took place behind this human screen no outsider could possibly ascertain. Frequently the complaining witness or sometimes even the prisoner himself was elbowed and jostled out of hearing distance, to remain in ignorance of the whole transaction except as it was reported by the policeman or others occupying posts of vantage. Again and again prisoners were 'tried' in this fashion without even catching a glimpse of the magistrate, and sometimes the first intimation they received of his decision was finding themselves being roughly hustled toward the lock-up or the street."[15]

Unsatisfactory as is the present physical condition of our magistrates' courts, a great improvement has been made in the past twenty years. To the uninitiated our court buildings are still scenes of dingy confusion; but contrasted with pre-Page-Commission days they are orderly tribunals. In the courtroom a table replaces the bridge and there is a witness stand to the left of the judge's bench. Complaint clerks interview their clients in the privacy of a complaint room. The removal of cases of nonsupport and the innumerable traffic cases from the district courts has greatly relieved congestion.

After the inception of the Seabury investigation, there was unusual activity in the old court buildings. Cracks were patched and broken benches mended. A score of "unemployed" workmen cleaned and painted courtrooms and detention pens. An inspection of the courts in Manhattan late in 1931 indicated no serious deficiency in actual housing of the courts.

Viewed in the light of recent progress in building and in the modern, attractive court structure which houses the County Court, the magistrates' courts are still somewhat repellent. Nor are the headquarters of the organization more impressive than the courts themselves. After the reorganization of the courts in 1910, the new chief magistrate found that no place had been provided for the chief

[15] Hill, the *Century Magazine*, LXXXIV, No. 1 (May, 1912), p. 88.

office of the board of city magistrates. He borrowed, sup-
posedly temporarily, the ancient and unoccupied building
at 300 Mulberry Street which, for years, had served as
police headquarters and there set up his office. This old
building is still the heaquarters of the most important judicial branch of our city government. In addition to the
office of the chief magistrate it houses homicide, traffic,
and commercial frauds courts and the headquarters of the
probation department.

The dreary condition of the courts is not wholly the
fault of the magistrates. Former Magistrate Corrigan said
in 1910: ". . . The magistrates never could get anything
from the Board of Estimate. Look at this gas light we
work by here. The Essex Market Court has been condemned by every grand jury for months, and at last it has
received a coat of paint. I suppose improvements will stop
there."[16] Fortunately, they did not. In 1916 a new Essex
Market Court was built.

While conditions in some of the courts are not entirely
satisfactory, they do not seem to warrant the expenditure
of any great amount of money at the present time in view
of the centralization plan which is about to be described.
Meanwhile, with the proper overhead organization of the
courts and an improvement in personnel all along the line,
it may be taken for granted that minor housekeeping defi-
ciencies will be eliminated.

Before 1910 the district courts were scattered units
with no central organization to bind them together. ". . .
The whole scheme of administration of justice in the low-
est criminal courts—pre-eminently the courts of the
people—was a haphazard, chaotic jumble, the ten sepa-

[16] *Tribune,* April 3, 1910.

rate courts doing their work independently, under heavy disadvantages, both physical and moral, and with no headship or headquarters or central place of authority or of record. They were as separate from each other as the courts of New York and Texas. . . ."[17] The inadvisability of such a plan is readily understandable. The Page Commission sought to unify the courts into two divisions based on geographical location. Manhattan and the Bronx formed one unit; Kings, Richmond, and Queens the other. Each of these was administered by a chief magistrate and board of magistrates.

In 1915 the Inferior Criminal Courts Act was amended so that the territorial subdivision of the courts was practically eliminated; but the actual functioning of the courts is still based upon a broad subdivision between the east and west sides of the East River, or as between Queens, Kings, and Richmond on the one hand and Manhattan and the Bronx on the other—and, to a lesser degree, upon the boroughs themselves.

When New York was a sprawling village, there was reason for scattering the police courts in various parts of the town. The growth of the city, the attendant expansion in the volume of business disposed of by the magistrates, and the recognized tendency for graft and corruption to thrive in the isolated domain of the district court have led to the development of a plan for a centralized court.

Over a long period of time the general principle of centralization has proceeded through the formation of specialized courts, of which there are now six in Manhattan. Specialization has given us the women's court, the family

---

[17] William Inglis, *Harper's Weekly*, February 3, 1912.

court, the traffic and homicide courts, and the municipal term.

Because of the social nature of the work done by the magistrates' courts, welfare organizations have had a particular interest in them. Under the guidance of these agencies and "socially minded" civic groups, there has been a tendency to separate certain problems, not strictly of a criminal nature, from the criminal-courts system and to establish separate tribunals for the hearing of these cases. More will be said of this when the consolidation of the inferior courts is discussed; but it is a tendency which has an important bearing on centralization.

Former Chief Magistrate Corrigan was one of the early crusaders in the movement for a centralized court. He found that "the only persons really benefited by the local courts are a few restaurant and lunchroom keepers in the neighborhood, and the police court lawyers, bondsmen, runners and hangers-on."[18] The "idea that the magistrates' court was a neighborhood court held by one of the neighbors" was not practicable, for "owing . . . to the inherent fallibility of human nature, the neighborhood judge sometimes became the neighborhood tyrant so that finally the Legislature provided that the magistrates must rotate.

"The second reason for scattered courts, and the only one that is now urged, is the importance of the courts being readily accessible to the poor complainant or witness; but when we look into the facts, this advantage is more fanciful than real."[19]

The centralization plan as suggested by Judge Corrigan would bring together into a centrally located building the

[18] Corrigan, the *Panel*, February, 1928.   [19] *Ibid*.

district and special courts of Manhattan. A central detention prison, bureau of criminal identification, bail bureau, and central probation department would be housed in the same building.

The plan received Judge Seabury's hearty approval. He pointed out that centralization would make possible a more immediate supervision of the work of the courts by the chief city magistrate and by the chief officers of the various administrative branches. A considerable increase in efficiency might be expected. Cases could be distributed so that fewer magistrates and fewer employees would be needed. This would be especially true of certain functions of the court, such as stenographic service, interpretation, probation, and prosecution, which "are used in a more or less casual way," and which "could be immediately available to all the courts operating in one building without the expense and delay now incident to bringing them from one court house to another." Further, the detention of prisoners in one place would make possible the elimination of a number of court attendants. "It is probable," Judge Seabury said, "that the economies thus effected would run into very large figures, probably enough to pay the interest on a capital outlay much larger than is necessary to build a new centralized court building." Moreover, part of the difficult bail problem could be solved by the centralized supervision of the fixing, taking, and custody of bail, and a closer watch could be kept over the members of the bar who practice in the courts. It is clear that public opinion could fall with a much more intensive light upon the workings of a centralized court than upon the operations of district courts. Finally, the cost of the erection of a centralized court could be defrayed largely by the proceeds of the sale of city-owned property now used as court buildings and detention prisons.[20]

There seems to be no reason to believe that the creation of a central court would eliminate all the evils that are now prevalent in the magistrates' courts. There are many factors that would not be cared for by such centralization. However, it is clear that physical centralization of the courts has tremendous advantages and would make a properly constituted court a much more effective working unit.

There are still some who object to the centralized court because of what may be called the parochial nature of much of the work in the district court. A vast number of cases involve the atmosphere of the neighborhood. A proper settlement of these difficulties can best be made on the basis of a consideration of the local situation. In this respect, an ideal district court could function more effectively. The fact is, however, that we have no ideal district courts. The advantage of local atmosphere is almost completely dissipated by the isolation in which these courts carry on their work. Moreover, it is essential that police be cognizant of the neighborhood problems involved, and with the police operating effectively in these various districts, it would seem to be unnecessary to maintain a second branch of government to attempt to study and solve neighborhood problems. While there is general agreement as to the advantages of a new centralized building, the financial condition of the city will probably delay its consummation for some time. Meanwhile, no inconsiderable efforts are being made by some of the magistrates to improve the condition of the courts by minor physical improvements.

[20] *Seabury Report,* pp. 188–191.

CHAPTER V

THE MAN TO SEE

To the uninitiated, the court clerk seems like the dreariest of routineers. Actually, he is preoccupied with neither voluminous docket books nor prosaic files. He is not the obscure functionary of tradition. He is a vital part of the court—the conduit between all those who have business with the court and the magistrate himself. In a sense, he is even more important than the magistrate. Magistrates come and go in the life of a district court. But the clerk stays on. He is permanent, fixed, intrenched. He is the man to see.

The clerical staff of the magistrates' courts, consisting of clerks, assistant clerks, court attendants, fingerprint experts, and interpreters, is under the general direction of a chief clerk. This official is theoretically the administrative officer of the entire staff, but, in fact, he is in charge of the clerical staff of the courts in Brooklyn, Queens, and Richmond. The deputy chief clerk supervises the staff in Manhattan and the Bronx. Each of these officials is, for all intents and purposes, the chief of staff on his own side of the East River. The question of precedence of one over the other is practically nominal. Because the present deputy chief clerk is housed with the chief magistrate, and also because he is a man with an instinctive sense of order and efficiency, he exercises more influence in the general direction of the work of the staff. A second deputy chief clerk is in charge of the appeal and information bureau.

The central office includes, in addition, a fingerprint and a statistical bureau.

The clerk in each court largely controls the administrative business of that court.[1] Theoretically, his duties are of a general supervisory nature. He supervises the work of the other members of the staff. He is responsible for the records and for the money which results from the business of the court. He is there to answer questions and presumably to advise people coming into the court.

No civil-service requirements are imposed by law in the appointment of the clerks. The fact is that these appointments are, by unwritten law, distributed among the district leaders. The testimony of a number of clerks given before Judge Seabury clearly indicated the political nature of their appointments. A typical example of their testimony is as follows:

"Q. Are you a member of a Democratic club? A. Yes.

Q. What is the name of the club? A. The John F. Curry Association.

Q. John F. Curry, and Curry, of course, is the leader of the club? A. Yes, the district I was born in and still live on the same avenue where I was born * * *.

Q. Now, when you were appointed corporation inspector, who sponsored your appointment? A. Mr. Curry.

Q. Mr. Curry did? A. Yes.

Q. And when you were appointed a clerk of the First District Court, he also sponsored your appointment? A. Mr. Curry, yes.

Q. Were you active in the club? A. For 25 years, but never held no political jobs.

[1] There are eighteen clerks in the magistrates' courts of Manhattan and the Bronx. They are appointed for a term of four years by a majority of the board of city magistrates. Their salaries range from $3,240 to $3,720; but actually all but two of them receive the maximum salary.

Q. Were you ever a captain? A. I was more than a captain. I was very active * * *."

Another instance is:

"Q. What political club are you affiliated with? A. Chickopee Democratic Club, 21st Assembly District. * * *

Q. Who is the leader of that club? A. At the present time Thomas F. Murray, the last year.

Q. Who was the leader prior to that? A. Edmund P. Hallihan * * *.

Q. Now when you were first appointed to the Department of Correction, who sponsored your appointment? A. Mr. Hallihan.

Q. And did he also sponsor your appointment as court clerk? A. Yes.

Q. Were you active in the Democratic Club to which you belonged? A. Yes.

Q. What was your position in that club? A. At that time?

Q. Yes. A. I had been acting secretary, or assistant to the secretary. That was not really an official title, but that is what I have done * * *."

A third typical instance is:

"Q. Now, with what political organization have you been affiliated? A. The Minqua Club, Democratic Club, 23rd Assembly District. * * *

Q. Who is the leader up there? A. John Mara, Deputy Commissioner of Plants and Structures. * * *

Q. Have you been active in the club? A. District Captain. * * *

Q. Now, did Mr. Mara sponsor your appointment to this position you now hold? A. I don't know. Mr. Mara, it was possibly through Mr. Mara I got the appointment, I don't know how far he sponsored it. * * *

Q. Who made the offer to you? A. Mr. Mara.

Q. Mr. Mara did, and that was shortly before you were appointed? A. Oh, weeks, and probably months, and he said would I consider such a position, and I told him I would take it under advisement."

The three foregoing illustrations are typical of the testimony of the court clerks generally. A substantial number of these clerks were captains of election districts for the local Democratic clubs; others held offices in the clubs, or were members of their county committee. Sixteen clerks in the magistrates' courts in the First Judicial Department admitted upon examination that they were active politically; their appointments were rewards for service within their political organization. The great majority of them had no previous experience or actual knowledge of court procedure or any form of preparation for the duties which they were called upon to perform upon their appointment, a number of them having previously held other city jobs of an entirely different character, to which they had likewise been appointed upon political considerations.[2]

It is, of course, incorrect to assume that political appointment inevitably means dishonesty and inefficiency. There are intelligent and honest clerks in the magistrates' courts. Nevertheless, in a number of instances, the fact that clerks were political appointees made possible a casual give-and-take of favors which seriously obstructed the administration of justice. The Seabury *Report* on this subject may be severe; but it is arresting.

The testimony of the clerks themselves shows this state of affairs to exist, although the degree to which the influence of political leaders extends is undoubtedly not fully admitted by their testimony. The following testimony of court clerks is relevant:

"Q. Have you ever been asked by a leader of the club to which you belong to do any favors for them in connection with your court duties? A. Occasionally.

Q. What type of favor would they ask you to do? A. Well, corporation ordinance cases, you know; having a stand on the corner where they sell from; sometimes these fellows have the

[2] *Seabury Report,* pp. 57–59.

stands too large and if they are too large the officer gives them a summons and sends them in. But not very often.

Q. Now, I do not quite understand what you are supposed to do there. How you help out the man that asked you to do something for him. You said when these stands are too large and violate a corporate ordinance, the summons is served on the owner of the stands and he comes into court. What could you do there, when he comes into court? A. Well, he would ask me if I would please help him out.

Q. Help the man that was served with the summons out? A. Yes. That was it. Sometimes I might go in to the judge in his chambers and ask if he would consider it, and sometimes he would say 'No' and sometimes 'Yes,' and I give it to him. * * *

Q. What do you tell the judge when you come into them with a case in which you want to help the defendant? A. Why, I just have a memorandum marked 'John Smith' or 'John Doe' and say, 'Corporation ordinance, officer so and so. Judge, this man is a poor man and says he is broke and has not any money and if you can see your way clear to help him out, O. K.'

Q. Does he? A. Sometimes.

Q. Does the judge know from whom the request for a favor has come? A. Sometimes. I won't say 'sometimes.' All the time.

Q. That is he knows that it is that particular leader who is asking the favor? A. Yes; yes. * * *

Q. How often do you say you have been asked to speak to the judge about a defendant in a pending case, such as that push-cart case? Do you get many of those requests from district leaders or other people? A. Occasionally we do. We get a few.

Q. How many would you say you would get during a year, roughly? A. Oh, we might get 50. * * *"

Several of the court clerks testified substantially in conformity with the foregoing testimony, and in each case they were very careful to state that district leaders did not attempt to intervene in felony or misdemeanor cases. Such care on the part of court clerks to draw the line for intervention of district leaders should obviously be taken with a large grain of salt, in view of the other testimony brought out in this Investigation.

Another witness whose appointment was sponsored by Mr. Briarly, a district leader, testified:

"Q. Since your appointment has Mr. Briarly or Judge Mahoney ever asked you to do any favors for them in connection with your court duties? A. Judge Mahoney never did.

Q. Did Mr. Briarly? A. Well, yes, in the way of a little violation. They would send it to me.

Q. A violation of a corporate ordinance? A. Yes, sir. We have had priests, men in all walks of life that would come asking for little favors on violations.

Q. And Mr. Briarly would occasionally call you up or see you about such things? A. No, I would not say he done it twice in his life, but he would like send somebody in with his card for some little violation.

Q. What would you do when you were supposed to take care of the little violation? A. I would tell the Magistrate; I would deliver the message to the Judge.

Q. Would the Judge know from whom that came? A. Apparently he took my word for it * * *.

Q. What would you tell him? A. I would only tell him that this was a friend was sent to me to ask him to intercede for this man * * *.

Q. Would he ever ask any favors in connection with a misdemeanor case? A. He never has asked me in a misdemeanor case, no. No. As a rule though * * * it would be more than I could do to reach a Judge on a misdemeanor or felony of any kind. I would not attempt it * * *.

Q. I suppose some district leaders demand more of that type of favor than others do? A. Yes. Some of them demand more. I must say that of Mr. Briarly. Of course, I have seen attorneys from our club come there on cases and I presume a thing like that Briarly would say, 'Give it to one of their lawyers,' and 'Go and see what you can do with this.'

Q. One of the attorneys from the club who represented a defendant in that court? A. Yes."

The evidence establishes that district leaders and other politicians exert great influence in these courts because of the hold they have upon the clerks.[3]

The evidence heard by Judge Seabury, of which that quoted above is typical, indicates that the function of the court clerk is essentially political. He spends his day talking to lawyers, defendants, political friends; advising the magistrate, in many instances; and serving in a general way as a connecting link between the world of politics and the lesser world of the court.

It is in no sense to condone the political activities of the clerk to say that the real vice of the situation lies not in the fact that the clerk is the channel through which small political favors flow, but in the utter wastefulness which his activities represent. In most instances the clerk performs almost no administrative work. He busies himself day after day with futile and trivial things. Chaucer's sly thrust is not inappropriate here:

> Nowher so besy a man as he ther n'as,
> And yet he seemed besier than he was.

In the course of Judge Seabury's investigation, an observer was sent to a number of magistrates' courts to make detailed observations of the activities of the clerks. One of his reports, a minute-to-minute account of a clerk's day in court, is included here. It describes a pottering about, a laxity and inefficiency, less spectacular but more deplorable than the trading of small political favors.

10: 00 A.M.   Court began. The clerk was in the clerk's room where he remained until 10: 10.
10: 10 A.M.   Walked out of room into fingerprint room and

---

[3] *Seabury Report,* pp. 59–62.

back to his own room again. He remained at
his desk signing papers until 10: 27.

10: 27 A.M.   Stood at the door of his room looking at the
court.

10: 30 A.M.   A man came up to him and the two men went
into the room where they stood talking for
three minutes.

10: 33 A.M.   The defendants, complainant and their lawyers
in a case just heard went into their room to
have some papers signed.

10: 42 A.M.   A peddler who had been fined $5.00 went into
the clerk's room with the complaining officer.
Gave the fine to the clerk, who handed it to an
assistant clerk sitting in the room.

10: 45 A.M.   The clerk was in conversation with the assistant
clerk.

10: 50 A.M.   The clerk left his room, went through the fingerprint room and returned to his own room a
minute later.

11: 02 A.M.   Got up from his desk and stood looking down at
the assistant clerk who was working.

11: 06 A.M.   Walked out into the courtroom and out downstairs with papers in his hand.

11: 10 A.M.   Returned to his room where he walked around
with his hands in his pockets. Then he picked
up some papers and began to look at them.

11: 15 A.M.   Began to stamp papers.

11: 20 A.M.   Two men walked in and handed him some papers
—he examined them.

11: 22 A.M.   Policeman and defendant walked in, handed him
fine and some papers which he handed to the
assistant clerk. He turned again to the two
men and continued talking till 11: 30.

11: 30 A.M.   Went to his desk, sat down and began talking to
the assistant clerk and then jumped up and
continued conversation with one of these two
men.

11:37 A.M. Walked into fingerprint room and back into his room.

11:40 A.M. Continued talking to two men until 11:43.

11:43 A.M. Went into fingerprint room and back. The two men left.

11:44 A.M. A man walked through the courtroom and into the clerk's room. He talked with clerk and then left.

11:45 A.M. He was seated again at his desk. Sat for 10 minutes.

11:55 A.M. He came to the enclosure and talked to a man who got up from a seat in the courtroom.

11:56 A.M. The man left. The clerk walked into the court-room to bridgeman[4] to whom he said a few words, picked up a book, walked into his room, stayed there a few minutes, came out with open book which he handed to the bridge-man who handed it to the magistrate. Stood at the rail next to the judge, listening to the case until 12:04.

12:04 P.M. Walked into his room and back again to the bridgeman. Talked to him and then went back into his room.

12:10 P.M. Came out of his room and sat by his door listen-ing to the case (theater case—re admitting children).

12:14 P.M. Came back into room, sitting at his desk examin-ing papers which at 12:18 he gave to the bridgeman. Stood listening to the case.

12:20 P.M. Went back into his room and out again to the bridgeman with papers.

12:21 P.M. He walked out of courtroom with papers.

12:30 P.M. Went back through courtroom, walked in and out of his room and stood at the rail listening to the case. Called into fingerprint room and

[4] The bridgeman is a court attendant who stands before the bench, handing papers up to the magistrate and calling the cases.

	talked to man in charge there; came out laughing and went into his room for a minute.
12:33 P.M.	Went back into fingerprint room and talked.
12:35 P.M.	He was back at judge's rail, listening to same case.
12:40 P.M.	Went into his room and sat down and began to smoke.
12:55 P.M.	Rocked back and forth in his swivel chair with his hands behind his head. He was still smoking.
12:58 P.M.	Walked into the fingerprint room.
12:59 P.M.	Walked back into his room, put on his hat and coat and walked out. Court was adjourned.
1:50 P.M.	Returned to his room and the assistant left. Sat down at desk. Court attendant entered room and stood talking to clerk.
1:52 P.M.	Got up, strolled into courtroom and back again to his room.
1:55 P.M.	Talking and laughing with bridgeman.
2:05 P.M.	Walked into fingerprint room and talked with man there.
2:10 P.M.	Returned to room, sat down at desk and talked with two attendants.
2:15 P.M.	Two men entered room. Clerk stood up and shook hands with them. Talked.
2:22 P.M.	Took some papers from one of men and went into fingerprint room with them.
2:25 P.M.	Back into his room talking with two men. Walked out of room and called for "Joe" (the bridgeman). Joe entered the room.
2:27 P.M.	Joe took papers and escorted the two men downstairs. Magistrate arrived. Bridgeman returned. At this moment the clerk was sitting in his room.
2:33 P.M.	Clerk got up and received a man for whom he signed some papers.
2:37 P.M.	Sat writing at desk. Several men walked in.

2:40 P.M. Walked out to talk to a man sitting in the court-room, outside the door of the clerk's room. Returned to his room.

2:41 P.M. Took papers from one of the men waiting in his room and stamped them.

2:47 P.M. Walked out of his room and walked back with another man who came toward the room.

2:50 P.M. Wrote out a paper for him. Clerk then came out into fingerprint room where he stood talking to several men who had walked in from the court-room.

2:57 P.M. Clerk returned to his room and talked to his assistant.

3:03 P.M. Man walked into room. Clerk let him examine some papers.

3:10 P.M. Two men entered, talked to clerk, who made out some papers for them.

3:13 P.M. Assistant clerk returned from lunch and went to work.

3:14 P.M. Judge left bench. No more cases.

3:17 P.M. Two men came into clerk's room. He talked to them, got some papers for them. They left.

3:18 P.M. Observer told to leave.

Sixty-six thousand dollars annually seems a good deal to pay for such services.

The assistant clerks of the court[5] perform, for the most part, the active clerical duties required of the court. Al-

---

[5] There are fifty assistant clerks in the magistrates' courts of Manhattan and the Bronx—an average of approximately three per court. Their salaries range from $2,700 to $3,480. Assistant clerks are civil-service appointees. An examination is given every four years, which is restricted to candidates who have been court attendants, probation officers, interpreters, fingerprint experts, or fourth-class clerks who have served at least three years in that grade. A large majority of assistant clerks, in fact, came from the ranks of court attendants.

though these men are appointed after civil-service examinations, the positions they occupy are to some extent rewards for political service.

Judge Seabury said in his *Report:*

Of the forty-eight assistant clerks who were examined, thirty-nine stated that they had been, or were, members of political district clubs. Not all of the remainder were specifically asked this question. It is significant, however, that such a large proportion of assistant clerks, whose appointments are said to depend only upon competitive civil service examinations, are active in political organizations. The explanation for this may lie in the fact that priority of appointment from competitive civil service lists may be made to depend upon political influences. * * *

A court clerk, after testifying that clerks are appointed from civil service lists, said:

"There is a remarkable tendency for people who have political connections to come out at the head of the civil service list at times.

Q. Yes. I have noticed that coincidence. A. It sometimes mystifies how that happens, but it happens too often.

Q. Some way or other it is evident that the political influence is potential in the selection of those clerks? A. Yes."

The significance of the foregoing testimony cannot be overestimated; it shows how political favorites may, and obviously do, avoid the effect of competitive civil service examinations.[6]

The chief work of the assistant clerks consists of the making out of complaints—a technical and important function. Judge Seabury's investigation revealed that in some instances the power of the assistant clerks to draw complaints was subject to serious abuse. The testimony of Joseph Wolfman, the "lawyer," who operated in a magis-

[6] *Seabury Report,* pp. 63, 64.

trates' court for three years, described a simple and effective means of corruption.

One of the complaint forms which an assistant clerk may fill out is Form 343, the so-called "O-14." Whenever in the judgment of the assistant clerk in charge of complaints the facts stated to him by a complainant are insufficient to justify a complaint, he notes the fact on a form, thereby expressing his doubt to the magistrate. When he receives such a form, it is for the magistrate to examine the complainant and to decide whether a complaint should be drawn and, if so, for what offense.

Wolfman's testimony was to the effect that he paid clerks for drawing O-14s instead of complaints in bookmaking cases, and he further testified that in this type of case magistrates, upon the receipt of an O-14, invariably dismissed the case. He testified:

"Q. What has been your experience in that court when the assistant clerk presents an O-14 to a magistrate? Does it often follow that the magistrate directs the taking of a complaint, or does it usually follow that that is the end of the case? A. It usually follows that that is the end of the case. In my experience I have not had a magistrate as yet order a full complaint when an O-14 was submitted for his consideration.

Q. In all the years that you were operating in that court— A. That is correct.

Q. There never was an instance when, if the assistant clerk submitted an O-14 to the magistrate, the magistrate directed the taking of a long complaint? A. There was never an instance when the magistrate directed it.

Q. So that the assistant clerk had it in his power to practically dispose of any of these bookmaking cases that he desired by simply submitting an O-14? A. Which he does."

Since the time when Wolfman practiced, a rule has been put into effect by former Chief Magistrate Corrigan, requiring that in every gambling case in which an O-14 is submitted to the magistrate, a copy must be sent to the office of the chief city magistrate.[7]

The investigation indicated, moreover, that some assistant clerks were practicing still another variation of corruption.

Wolfman, after testifying to the effect that detectives, other police officers, and bondsmen, turned over cases to him, or recommended him as attorney, in consideration of a fifty-fifty split in his fee, continued:

"Q. Now, you have spoken of the officers as one source of the cases that you got. Now, were there any other sources from which you got cases? A. There were.

Q. Now, what were the other sources? A. The assistant court clerk who draws the complaint.

Q. A little louder. The assistant court clerk? A. Draws the complaints, the complaints made by the arresting officer or the complainant.

*   *   *   *   *   *   *   *

Q. Now, just how were they in a position to give you cases? A. The assistant court clerk draws the complaint and he also draws the formal, that is the history of the defendant who is about to be arraigned, asking him his name, address and business and so forth. One of the questions that the assistant court clerk would ask the defendant is 'Are you represented by counsel?' Should the defendant say 'No,' the assistant court clerk usually drops his pen—

Q. Usually what? A. Drops his pen, walks out into the courtroom, calls me on the side and gives me the name of the defendant whose complaint he had just drawn. In the cases which I received from the assistant court clerks I do not file a notice of appearance, because of the fact that the defendant is not in the prison pen but is in the complaint room, and the only one who could object to my talking to a defendant is the clerk who gave

[7] *Seabury Report,* pp. 67, 68, 69, 70.

me the case. So I just walk into the complaint room, introduce myself as an attorney and talk to the defendant.

Q. And then you make your arrangements with the defendant? A. That is correct.

Q. And what did the assistant court clerk get out of that? A. He got half of whatever fee I received from the defendants.

Q. He got half of your fee? A. That is correct."[8]

The picture is not altogether surprising. These men are largely recruited from the court attendants, a group limited in number and intelligence. The objectives of civil service are not attained because of political interference. The staff is organized so that a man does not have a full load of work. Their idle hours are filled with political work, not only because there are so many idle hours but because politics is the stuff out of which the assistant clerks grow and in which their life is spent.

Court attendants[9] are scattered throughout the court, keeping order among the spectators and among those in the detention room, handing papers to the magistrate, informing those who are arraigned of their constitutional rights, sometimes making entries in the docket books, and carrying documents to and from the office of the chief clerk.

In this division of the clerical staff, too, the investigators found evidence of graft.

The court attendants vied with the clerks in acting as steerers of cases to attorneys, in consideration of a share of the

[8] *Ibid.*, pp. 70, 71.

[9] There are 101 court attendants in the magistrates' courts of Manhattan and the Bronx—an average, in Manhattan, of six per court, and, in the Bronx, of five per court. Their salaries range from $2,000 to $2,460. Court attendants are civil-service appointees.

fee. Wolfman, after referring to his relations with the clerks, described the other sources of his business as:

"The attendant in charge of the prison pen, the attendant in charge of the gate leading into the complaint room and the prison, the attendant in charge of the bridge, that is, that calls the cases; plainclothesmen, that is, officers other than detectives; bondsmen, and two steerers, that is, those two men who hung around the corridor steering cases to attorneys."

After giving the name of one of the attendants, his testimony continues:

"Q. Well, as court attendant did he assist you in your practice there? A. That is correct.

Q. And how? A. He gave me cases when he was at the prison pen and he was calling cases at the bridge and when he was the officer in charge of the gate leading into the complaint room and the prison pen."

Wolfman described how this sordid business was handled. This is his testimony:

"Q. Now, take the attendant in charge of the prison pen. How was he enabled to be of service to you? A. Well, the prisoners, before they are arraigned before the magistrate and before the complaint is drawn by the assistant court clerk, the attendant in charge of the prison pen books the prisoner and then locks him into that prison pen until his case is called. He starts a conversation with the defendants in that pen, asks them as to whether or not they are represented by an attorney. If the defendant says that he is not represented by an attorney, the attendant would then say 'Have you any money for an attorney?' The defendant, if he had, would say that he did and how much he had. He would then come out to the courtroom.

Q. Who would? A. The attendant in charge of the prison pen.

Q. Yes? A. He would call me on the side and say 'Wolfman, John Jones is in there and has got $60 or $50.' I would then file a notice of appearance as I would in the cases I received from the detectives. I would then present the notice of appearance to the attendant and, within hearing of the attendant, I would represent myself as an attorney and the defendant would want to know who recommended me, or how I came to know about his case. Of course, I would tell him, as I told other defendants, I had a case on the calendar and noticed his case among the many cases and that I would help him out. The defendant at times wanted to know as to what proof I had that I am a lawyer. I would call the attendant in charge of the prison pen over and he would say, 'Yes, Wolfman is a lawyer and he is all right.' "[10]

This testimony is merely one of a number of examples of "steering" by the court attendants. Apparently, according to Wolfman, all of the attendants in the court in which he was active sent him business, receiving in return half of his fee. The "split" was a fixed custom.

Here, however, as in the case of the court clerks, the really important findings of the investigation are likely to be forgotten in the face of an enumeration of petty wrongdoing. There can be no doubt that the manning of each court with five or six attendants represents wastefulness. One specific illustration of this is the fact that in every magistrates' court there has been established a system of rotation whereby one court attendant each week is used to carry papers to and from the office of the chief clerk. For such messenger service alone, then, at least $2,000 per court is required. This is typical of governmental lavishness. The needless multiplication of jobs is an old political game, safer and more profitable than graft or corruption. It is the real problem presented by the clerical staff, as it now operates.

The function of the fingerprint experts requires little

[10] *Seabury Report,* pp. 72, 73, 74.

comment.[11] They take prints of all persons convicted of certain crimes and offenses[12] in order that any previous criminal record of a convicted person may be submitted to the magistrate before sentence is fixed. One impression of the fingerprint is attached to the original records and filed in the court where it was made; a second is delivered to the police commissioner; a third is sent to the fingerprint bureau in the office of the chief clerk, where duplicates are made and sent out to the magistrates' courts.

Here, too, the problem involved is inefficiency and extravagance. In the words of Judge Seabury's report to the Appellate Division:

> This entire process is exceedingly wasteful. It involves duplication of effort and considerable unnecessary expense. There exists in the police department of this city an incomparable collection of fingerprints which should be utilized.[13]

It should be added that a report from the fingerprint expert in the magistrates' court that the defendant has no previous record is often dangerously misleading. Such a report indicates that only in the magistrates' courts is there no record. He may have served one or more sentences in state's prisons for serious crimes of which there is no record in the magistrates' bureau. A central finger-

[11] There are fourteen fingerprint experts in the magistrates' courts of Manhattan and the Bronx.

[12] Fingerprints are taken of all persons convicted of intoxication, vagrancy, prostitution, jostling, rowdyism on public conveyances, "mashing," and of degenerates, beggars, and confidence men. The presiding magistrate may, at his discretion, order fingerprints to be made of persons convicted of fortune telling, of disorderly conduct involving riotous conduct, and of some crimes involving serious and considerable injury to person or property.

[13] *Seabury Report*, p. 195.

print bureau for all courts of criminal jurisdiction in the city would be helpful.

When Judge Seabury's *Report* was sent to the Appellate Division the cost of the clerical staff of the magistrates' courts was $1,026,592.[14] There was no doubt that in days of economic depression and high taxes the expenditure of such an amount was indefensible.

Judge Seabury's recommendations with regard to the clerical staff contemplated what amounted to an almost complete reorganization. His object was twofold: to eliminate, so far as possible, political favoritism and corruption in the staff, and to cut away the deadwood in it.

His proposals first looked to the securing of competent and efficient clerks in each magistrate's court. These clerks, he said, should be appointed after civil-service examination.

Examinations should be rigid and should be limited by no such restrictions as are now imposed in the case of the assistant clerks. It should be possible for all persons with legal training or otherwise qualified by education, or with experience in responsible clerical positions in other courts, to take such examinations. It is inimical to the public interest to exclude from the examinations any person who has the proper qualifications.[15]

The clerks so appointed, moreover, should be given real work to do. The function of making out complaints should

[14] This figure was compiled from the city budget for 1931. It represents the sum of the salaries of the following employees only: 1 chief clerk, 2 deputy chief clerks, 38 court clerks, 89 assistant court clerks, 42 clerks, 40 interpreters, 181 court attendants, 1 supervisor of fingerprints, 1 assistant supervisor of fingerprints, and 22 fingerprint experts. This does not include wages of temporary employees.

[15] *Seabury Report,* p. 192.

be the clerk's alone, except, perhaps, in one or two courts which are so busy that he requires the help of an assistant clerk. Such assistance, however, is "not intended to relieve them of the important clerical duties of the court." Because of the technical importance of the work of complaint drawing,

. . . it should be done by a thoroughly competent person. The examination for clerk should be of such a character as to establish clearly the ability of the applicant to perform this important function.[16]

In order to improve the quality of the assistant clerks, the *Seabury Report* recommended that the restrictions which are now imposed upon the candidates[17] be removed. They shut out many who might be far better qualified to fill this position than former court attendants, interpreters, probation officers, and the rest.

Evidence that the effect of civil-service examinations was destroyed, because in some cases the priority of appointment from competitive civil-service lists was made to depend upon political influences, was the basis of another recommendation which supplemented those with regard to the appointment of clerks and assistant clerks. This proposal states that

. . . any person signing a waiver, or by any other means relinquishing his right to appointment to any position in the court in regular order on the civil service list, should automatically be dropped from the list, unless the waiver relate to a position paying less than the salary the person executing the waiver is then receiving or to a position offered in a city other than the city in which the person executing the waiver resides.[18]

[16] *Seabury Report,* p. 192.   [17] See footnote, p. 73.
[18] *Seabury Report,* p. 196.

The ease with which the complaint Form 343 (the so-called O-14) had been used for corrupt purposes by some assistant clerks in charge of complaints raised the question as to whether the clerk should have any discretion in the drawing of complaints. The *Report* states that

. . . the assistant clerk should have no discretion in the making of a complaint. If a policeman or anyone else wants to make a complaint, the duty of the clerk is to draw this complaint in proper form and then permit the magistrate to decide the case. It is his, not the clerk's, sworn responsibility to decide whether the facts justify a prosecution. To permit the complaint clerk to make a recommendation is not only unnecessary, but also invites political control.[19]

It was therefore recommended that the use of this form be discontinued. Objection to this recommendation has been made on the ground that the magistrates whose duty it was after receiving an O-14 to examine the complainant thoroughly and decide whether a complaint was justified were as responsible for the abuse of the O-14 as were the assistant clerks. Had their examinations been thorough rather than formal, had the O-14 served them merely as an expression of the doubt of the assistant clerk rather than as an invariable notice to dismiss the case, the abuses which have been described could not have grown up. In the opinion of those who make this objection, there is no need to abolish this form. They suggest, however, that its wording be changed to include a statement to be signed by the magistrate that he has inquired into the facts thoroughly and that, in his opinion, they do not warrant the issuance of a complaint. This would, it is claimed, be a continuous reminder of his responsibility.

[19] *Ibid.*, p. 193.

The requirement that clerks really be put to work would make possible a considerable cutting down of the number of assistant clerks. The *Seabury Report* stated that there were approximately twice as many assistant clerks as the work required, and recommended that the staff be cut in half.

It was likewise recommended that the staff of court attendants be cut in half.

While no hard and fast rule can be fixed as to the number of court attendants that are necessary, it is easy to see from any casual inspection of the courts that there are at present altogether too many. It is probable that fifty are adequate for Manhattan and the Bronx.[20]

It was suggested, however, that the messenger work which court attendants now perform be turned over to part-time workers or to a well-established messenger service.

The final recommendation with regard to the clerical staff was that the work of fingerprinting in the magistrates' courts should be taken over by the bureau of criminal identification in the police department. The bureau in the magistrates' courts involves merely a duplication of effort and expense. It was suggested that the police department make some arrangement to take over this work.[21]

Almost nothing has been done in the direction of carrying out these recommendations. It is true that the effect of the testimony with regard to conditions among the staff resulted in 84 transfers among the clerks, assistant clerks, attendants, and probation officers during the year 1930;

[20] *Seabury Report,* p. 194.   [21] *Ibid.,* p. 195.

208 transfers in the year 1931; and a considerable number in 1932.

But the staff has not been reorganized and reduced, even in partial conformity with the Seabury recommendations. Its cost, in 1932, was $1,027,652.[22] This is $1,060 more than in 1931.

[22] This figure is compiled from the city budget for 1932. It represents the sum of the salaries of the following employees only: 1 chief clerk, 2 deputy chief clerks, 37 court clerks, 89 assistant court clerks, 1 accountant, 43 clerks, 40 interpreters, 182 court attendants, 1 supervisor of fingerprints, 1 assistant supervisor of fingerprints, and 23 fingerprint experts.

CHAPTER VI

BAIL

CRIMINAL bail, particularly as it is related to the professional bondsman, is one of the unsolved problems of American city life. The history of the bail-bond business in New York City since 1900 is a record of scandals, well-intentioned attempts to regulate the evils by the making of new laws, and recurrent scandals. The spasmodic campaigns which have been conducted have not materially changed the personnel or the activities of those engaged in the furnishing of bail. The business has its roots deep in the political texture of the city.

Perhaps the most important fact about bail is that it creates bondsmen and provides them with the means of livelihood. Bondsmen become, almost of necessity, links joining together several factors involved in the administration of criminal justice. They are, in the first place, the link between the accused person and the court, responsible to the court for the appearance of the accused there. To the accused person, they are often the avenue through which contacts are made with lawyers. Moreover, because the business of a bondsman requires his almost constant attendance at court, he becomes a political personage, useful in countless ways to the clerks, the police, and the magistrates. If, as we should, we regard this sort of a generally useful man in these connections as an undesirable factor in criminal justice, his elimination becomes a major problem.

According to Harris, an outstanding authority on criminal procedure, admitting to bail consists, in theory, "in the delivery (or bailment) of a person to his sureties, on their giving security (he also entering into his own recognizance) for his appearance at the time and place of trial, there to surrender to take his trial. Meanwhile he is allowed to be at large, being supposed to remain in their friendly custody."[1] The original theory of a bail bond, in simple terms, was that it was given by a person of substance who knew the defendant and was willing to help him by signing his bond and thus becoming sponsor for his appearance in the regular course of trial.

Originally, bail was personal. The sureties were ordinarily householders, housekeepers, or freeholders and the bailed person was released into their personal custody. The security offered was real estate or household goods. Then an attempt was made to regulate the giving of bail by requiring that the surety furnish documentary evidence of the ownership and value of the property he pledged. This regulation was unquestionably a partial cause of the springing up of the professional bondsman as contrasted with a surety who was personally acquainted with the defendant, for usually the householder or real-estate owner did not have at hand the required deeds or mortgages. Moreover, as an added measure of caution, magistrates refused to accept bonds of real-estate owners on whose property there was more than one mortgage and the average property owner could not qualify under these restrictions. This was a further contributing factor to the increase of professional bondsmen.

These professional bondsmen flourished for years about

---

[1] Harris, *Criminal Law*, p. 301.

the courts and police stations in New York City. They established themselves in small offices in the neighborhood of the courts and either solicited business themselves or employed runners for this purpose.

Soon after the appearance of the professional bondsman, a number of surety companies began to do business throughout the state. It is only within comparatively recent years, according to the learned opinion of Attorney General Ottinger in 1927, included in the testimony (Vol. VI, pp. 2295–3007) that statutes have authorized, or the courts have allowed, bail other than personal. In fact, it was not until the drastic revision of Section 181 (now Section 109–a) of the Insurance Law by Chapter 182 of the Laws of 1913 that the authority of a corporation to engage in the business of giving bail was wholly free from doubt.[2]

For various reasons, there soon grew up in New York City a situation which is somewhat unique. While in most parts of the country an overwhelming majority of bonds are put up by private individuals or independent professional bondsmen, in New York City this is reversed. By far the greater proportion of bonds are corporate. Some idea of the relative numbers can be gained from an investigation of the number of individual and corporate bonds taken in the month of November, 1931. Fifteen per cent were individual bonds. Eighty-five per cent were corporate bonds.

It was generally felt by thoughtful persons who observed the development of this phenomenon that corporate suretyship constituted a great advance and that it was the means of placing the giving of bail on a sound, respectable basis. While this was theoretically true, the fact was

[2] *Seabury Report*, p. 103.

that these companies often employed agents whose reputations were shady and whose activities were demoralizing. They exercised little or no supervision over these men, or the "runners" whom they, in turn, employed. The fact that the companies themselves charged 2 or 3 per cent was no indication of the rates which defendants were forced to pay. There was, before 1922, no legal limitation on the charges which might be exacted for a bail bond. In many cases the agent of a surety company was obliged to put up collateral with the company and, if the prisoner jumped bail, the agent was called upon to make good the amount of the bond. Often the employees of agents received compensation neither from the agent nor the surety company. They were dependent upon payments from defendants. The tendency of these men was to squeeze as much as possible from the defendant. Sometimes as high as 15 per cent of the bail was required.

A series of crimes in 1920, committed by criminals out on bail, or by known criminals with long records of escaping the consequences of their acts through the process of bail, led to denunciations in the press of the bail system in the magistrates' courts. In 1921, hearings were held by a magistrate to investigate the abuses of the bail system. These hearings revealed that one company in 1920 had written bail bonds in cases of burglary or robbery amounting to $370,000. It was clearly indicated that some of the collateral accepted by agents from defendants was stolen property. This was not illegal at that time; but it was obviously an abuse. Several witnesses testified that the security had never been returned to them. The report of this investigation stated, in effect, that while no evidence was adduced which would warrant any indictment, the tone of the business was generally low. "Under proper regulating and control and wise amendatory legislation," it concluded, "there is no doubt . . . that this business can be conducted with justice to the community as well as those engaged therein."

Largely as the result of this investigation, a new section of the law[3] was passed in 1922. This applies to persons, firms, and corporations alike. All are forbidden to "engage in the business of giving bonds in criminal cases without being duly licensed by the Superintendent of Insurance of the State of New York, in accordance with the said insurance law." Every corporation engaging in such business in a city of the first class must procure such license for each of its officers or employees acting for it. Each corporation or person engaging in the business must file a $5,000 bond for the faithful performance of its or his duty. No person is to be so licensed until he has satisfied the superintendent of insurance that he is "a person of good character and reputation and has never been convicted of any crime or offense." The granting of such license is in each case discretionary with the superintendent of insurance, and such license is subject to revocation by him "whenever he deems it advisable for the public interest and in accordance with said insurance law." This act also provides that "the premium or compensation for giving a bail bond or depositing money or property as bail shall in no case be greater than three per centum of the amount of such bond or deposit."

Broadly speaking, the purpose of this section was to place two kinds of checks upon those engaged in the bail-

[3] Code of Criminal Procedure, sec. 554–b.

bond business. It attempted to provide for regulation by the State Department of Insurance and it gave the magistrate the definite power to ascertain whether the law was being complied with. It fixed a maximum rate and aimed at preventing the giving of security feloniously obtained by the defendant by providing that the magistrate may at his discretion refuse a bond or deposit if he is satisfied that any portion of it has been feloniously obtained.

The naïve belief that this measure would improve the bail-bond business to any considerable extent was soon exploded. As early as 1925, a number of disclosures were made which indicated that the law was being flagrantly violated. The Prison Committee of the Association of Grand Jurors of New York County reported that "the present unrestricted and haphazard practice of releasing arrested criminals on bail is probably the greatest single factor in nullifying effective work accomplished by the police department of New York City."

This striking charge was the signal for one of the most effective editorial and news campaigns in the history of New York City journalism. The *Evening World,* largely at the instance of Harry Pollard, its editor, published a series of articles asserting that "easy bail" constituted an "aid and urge toward committing more crimes." It declared that bail had become "a mere routine expense for the criminal in the uninterrupted plying of his trade. . . ." It set reporters to work on the records. They found cases in which a criminal with a long record was "released on low bail, rearrested for fresh crimes and again released on bail to pay his bondsmen." It called attention to two conspicuous cases which constituted "glaring bail bond abuse." Its comment on these, printed on December 1, 1925, is worth quoting:

. . . In each case the defendant had a criminal record, with several earlier charges against him still pending. In each case the District Attorney's Office, because of the defendant's record, made a special plea for high bail. It so happened that in both instances the same Judge of General Sessions and the same Justice of the Supreme Court were concerned. In the one case, General Sessions Judge —— fixed bail at $25,000, whereupon the defendant's lawyer took his client before Supreme Court Justice —— on a writ of habeas corpus and, despite the protest of the District Attorney's Office, got the bail reduced to $15,000. In the other case the District Attorney asked Judge —— to fix bail at $50,000, but before the bail figure became a matter of record in the General Sessions Court, Supreme Court Justice ——, again, against the District Attorney's protest, fixed the bail at $10,000. The defendant in the latter case held the proud distinction of having had various earlier cases pending against him postponed no less than thirty-seven times!

Obviously here is something wrong. The General Sessions Judge and the District Attorney have larger and more direct experience in dealing with criminals. They have studied defendants' records. They know the risks to the community of letting criminals go free again and again on easy bail. Yet a Supreme Court Justice in such cases reduced bail. Why? Is the Supreme Court Justice moved solely by that vague constitutional warning against "excessive" bail? Or is he influenced by other arguments that equally ignore the defendant's record and the public's need of protection?

Throughout the winter of 1925 and the spring of 1926 the barrage continued. Harried public officials answered public letters. Some deplored the inadequacy of the legal regulations; others urged the abolition of surety companies. Scarcely a day passed without vigorous prodding that something be done about "the bail travesty."

As a result, the Legislature in 1926 passed four bills designed to deny bail to professional criminals. They provided that no defendant charged with a felony or with any of six designated misdemeanors should be admitted to bail until he had been fingerprinted and his record had been submitted to the official authorized to accept bail. It was further provided that if the defendant's record indicated a prior conviction for a felony or two convictions for the specified misdemeanors, the bail could be accepted only by a judge of the trial courts. This made it impossible for a minor judge to accept bail in the case of a professional criminal. It also required that the judge know clearly the kind of person who was being released on bail.

In the same year it was provided[4] that an affidavit must be filed by the person or corporation giving bail, along with the bond or other deposit for bail, describing in detail the security, indemnity, or consideration promised or given to the surety, and by whom. Any wilful misstatement in such an affidavit was punishable as perjury.

But these measures, too, did not materially affect the bail-bond evil. Before the year was over, the public was informed by alert newspapers that abuses were still rife.

On February 24, 1927, the State Superintendent of Insurance placed agents in the police department bureau of criminal identification and instructed them to fingerprint every bail-bond agent who applied for a state license. The purpose of this was to rid the courts of the fringe of ex-convict bail-bond agents who were unlawfully writing bail bonds. At the same time, an investigation of affidavits filed with the State Department of Insurance by those to whom licenses had already been

[4] Code of Criminal Procedure, sec. 554–c.

granted was made. This indicated that a number of persons with criminal records had made false answers in these affidavits. As a result, in March, 1927, the licenses of a handful of men were revoked.

This same futile procedure was gone through in 1929, when two newspapers again printed series of articles asserting that violations of the Insurance Law and the Code of Criminal Procedure were rampant. Again, the Superintendent of Insurance ordered an investigation. In the course of the subsequent investigation, conducted by Judge Seabury, a representative of the Superintendent of Insurance testified, describing the unavailing measures which he took to check the abuses which had been disclosed. The account of his activities was not impressive. He said: "I followed up the daily papers particularly, took names from the papers . . . and confronted them with the facts that I had and what other facts I could get, and I revoked possibly thirty or forty licenses."[5]

The total result of this investigation was simply a continuation of the *status quo*.

Almost on the eve of the Seabury investigation, Justice Albert Conway, formerly a superintendent of insurance, pointed out to a number of surety companies that they themselves must take some action to clean up the deplorable situation that existed. The suggestion which he made to them was a modification of one which had been advocated for many years in this city. It had been urged that a central bail-bond bureau be established, in which a com-

---

[5] *Hearings before Samuel Seabury, Referee, In the Matter of the Investigation of the Magistrates' Courts in the First Judicial Department and the Magistrates Thereof and of Attorneys-At-Law Practicing in Said Courts*, VI, 3028.

plete record would be kept of all bonds and of all agents and independent bondsmen who did business in the magistrates' courts. A ledger would show at a glance the status of a given bondsman. At any time it might be determined whether he had exceeded the limit of his probable financial responsibility. This would bring order out of the bail-bond records in the city, which were buried in the individual files of various courts, police stations, detention prisons, and other county and city departments. Moreover, the bureau might investigate every bond, both as to the financial standing of the surety and the criminal record of the defendant, and make recommendations with regard to it to the judge.

In the face of the failure of the Legislature to establish such a bureau and of growing criticism of the failure of surety companies to agree upon any joint program for restricting the offenses to be bonded, for blacklisting unscrupulous agents, and for regulating the activities of their agents, Justice Conway declared that coöperative action by the surety companies was imperative.

After a number of meetings, eighteen surety companies agreed to establish a bail-bond bureau. Such a bureau was set up in August, 1930. It established a standard rate of premium charge of 2 per cent. No other charges were to be made, except a small service charge for bonds executed at night, on Sundays, and on legal holidays. No charge was to be made for reëxecution of bail when the defendant at the examination was held to answer for trial. When a deposit of collateral security was made, a numbered receipt was to be given to its owner and the collateral returned without any fee when the bureau was satisfied as to the termination of the liability of the bail.

This was certainly, in the words of the *Seabury Report,* "a well-intentioned effort on the part of surety companies to improve the quality of their business, to provide a means of assisting helpless defendants and to centralize responsibility."[6] But the fact is that a friendless and bewildered person caught for the first time in the tangle of judicial processes is unlikely to learn that the bureau is doing business until he has obtained bail from bondsmen who solicit business around the courts. Such bondsmen may be either independent or the agents of surety companies which did not join in the establishment of the bureau. Moreover, it is important to note that the three companies which did the greatest part of the bond business in 1930 were not among those which established the bureau. Finally, it is clear that the effort on the part of surety companies to reform their business was based on the assumption that it was necessary to maintain the institution of bail as it existed. This was the assumption that Judge Seabury's *Report* overthrew completely.

Judge Seabury's investigation gave the most lurid accusations of the previous twelve years complete confirmation. It put together finally a clear picture of the activities of the bondsman and demonstrated his significance as a corrupting factor in the administration of justice.

The investigation indicated that there were in 1930, in New York City, five classes of persons engaged in the bonding business. These are the individual or independent bondsman, the "chiseler," the corporation, the general agent, and the agent. The individual or independent bondsman directly solicits business about the courts, usu-

[6] *Seabury Report,* p. 105.

ally putting up either cash or real estate as security. The "chiseler" bears the same relationship to the individual bondsman as does the "runner" to a lawyer. He is usually hired by a bondsman; but in some instances he solicits business himself and peddles it to the bondsman who offers him the largest "cut." The corporate surety is, as we have already seen, organized under the State Insurance Law. It operates through agents, who receive 1 per cent of the premiums which are charged. The fifth group engaged in the bonding business, the general agents, stands midway between the corporate sureties and the agents who represent them. These general agencies do not hire, but supervise the work of the agents. Ordinarily they do not themselves originate business; their function is rather that of "pseudo-detective" agencies, in the words of the *Report*. Their compensation is often as much as 25 per cent of the territorial revenues of the companies they serve.[7]

Regardless of the class to which the bondsman belonged, however, he was characterized as a "general factotum . . . in the administration of business in the magistrates' courts."

With meticulous care he arranged every detail of the way out of the labyrinth of justice. He served as a sort of general agent for his client, frequently employing the lawyer, looking after witnesses, and, in many cases, himself providing the expert management necessary to "fix" the various persons indispensable in the business of bringing about the failure of prosecution. With his extraordinarily varied connections the bondsman constituted a sort of clearing house between the under-

[7] *Ibid.*, pp. 104–106.

world and the realm of lawfulness. The elimination of these people from the process of administering justice in the magistrates' courts would be an important and far-reaching forward step.

A few . . . cases will . . . illustrate the role played by the bondsman.

Miss —— ——, a nurse in a doctor's office, was framed by a stool pigeon. She was bailed out by . . . a bondsman to whom she gave her bank books as security for a bond of $500. At the time she had over $600 on deposit in the bank. [The bondsman] supplied a lawyer for a charge of $150 to cover all. [The bondsman] and another man then called on Dr. ——, the employer of Miss ——, in an attempt to get him to make up the difference between $1,000 and Miss ——'s $600 on the misrepresentation that the charge might have very serious consequences to [the nurse] and to [the doctor] himself. [The bondsman], in attempting to meet this doctor's objections, reduced his first demand from $400 to $300. Dr. —— paid no money to [the bondsman]. [The bondsman], however, took Miss ——'s entire savings of over $600.

Mrs. —— —— conducted a beauty parlor. She was arrested [on a charge of prostitution] and taken first to —— Street police station and thence by patrol-wagon to Jefferson Market Prison. There she was allowed to call her son by telephone and arrange through him for the production of her bank book and a bondsman. The bondsman . . . put up $500 cash bail. [He] arranged for the lawyer, . . . who had his office in the same building . . . and with whom he shared his telephone. While discussing terms in the lawyer's office, [the bondsman] informed her that it would cost her $50 for the $500 bond and secured her bank book, which he then turned over to the lawyer, who receipted for it. The next day (the day of the proceedings in the magistrates' court), [the bondsman] accompanied Mrs. —— to the Empire City Savings Bank, where she withdrew $150 and paid the same to [the bondsman], plus $10 more for his time and taxi fare. One hundred dollars of the $150 withdrawn was to pay the lawyer, who subsequently exacted $200 more before he returned her book.

—— —— and her cousin were arrested in June, 1929, by Officer ——, at about 9:30 in the evening. She was taken to the —— Street police station where some man came to her and said, "Why don't you call a bondsman?" They allowed her to use a telephone and recommended that she get in touch with —— ——, [a bondsman]. She did not know whether the suggestion emanated from a policeman or not, as he was not in uniform. She and her cousin stayed in the stationhouse waiting room until the arrival of . . ., an associate of [the bondsman]. Miss —— then went with this [associate] back to her apartment to get her bankbook. Her bail and that of her cousin had been fixed at $500 in each case. She explained to [him] that she had only $575 in her bank account, whereupon he said he would bail her out and then see what could be done about the cousin's case. [He] stated that the premium on this $500 bond would amount to $40, which was paid to him by Miss ——, for her own bond, upon the return to the apartment for the book, as stated. The cousin stayed in jail over night but was bailed out by [the bondsman] the next day on the security of Miss ——'s jewelry, which was delivered to [him] at his office near the court. This jewelry consisted of three diamond rings, worth probably $1,000. The premium on the cousin's bond was set at $35, which Miss —— paid to [him] in cash in his office. [He] then got the cousin released on bail and all three gathered in [his] office to discuss attorneys. [An attorney] was called in. [The bondsman] intimated that for $500 he would take care of the lawyer, his own bond charge and "the cops"—everybody who was to be taken care of. Miss —— agreed to pay this sum. After the discharge of her cousin and herself [the bondsman] accompanied her to the Union Square Savings Bank where she had a second account, and she withdrew therefrom $500 which she paid to [him] and recovered her first bank book on the Corn Exchange Bank and her three diamond rings. Her experience thus cost this witness $575—$500 for lawyer's fee, etc., and $75 for two bail bonds.[8]

These cases and many others indicate that it was the practice of bondsmen to extort premiums greatly in excess of the legal rate. In extenuation of their illegal activities, they claimed that they could not make a living if they adhered to the prescribed rate. Even if this claim had been valid, however, it could not have justified the gouging of unfortunate defendants by the charging of extortionate rates or the improper custody of the collateral deposited with them.

It is clear, moreover, that the bondsman's frequent representations to the prisoner that he must "fix" the case, were not always simply means to extort money. The bondsmen were, in many cases, "fixers" and corruptionists. They maintained friendly working relations with police officers, with court officials and sometimes with the deputy assistant district attorney.

The associations between certain bail bonding agents and lawyers which have been brought out by the investigation are censurable in the extreme. Frequently bondsmen shared lawyers' quarters and lawyers' fees. Given the strong motive which these brokers and underwriters admittedly have for increasing their earnings, it is not surprising that they found, through arrangement with unethical lawyers, a potent means to that end. It meant an increase in the business of the lawyer. It meant that the bondsman, in addition to offering temporary liberty, could talk also of speedy and complete freedom. He was in a better position to raise his prices. And he did not hesitate to take advantage of that fact.

The great importance of the bondsman as a factor in political life is well shown in the case of —— ——. This man, who is said to have written or acted as agent for 95% of all the bail bond business of the Bronx, carried on this interesting business

[8] *Seabury Report,* pp. 107–110.

while he was receiving a salary as a city employee. He was assistant supervisor of the department of public markets, attached to the open air division. He said on the stand that in carrying on his bonding business, he frequented every magistrates' court in New York City. He received applications from persons in every walk of life for bail bonds. He served as a general agent for the Greater City Surety and Indemnity Corporation and occasionally for the Capitol City Surety and Indemnity Company. He had several agents working under him. When he found time to attend to his duties with the open air division, for which he received his salary, is difficult to say. The political significance of a man of such varied attainments and connections is apparent.

Finally, it is perfectly clear that the easiest course for a professional bondsman is to become so completely associated with the underworld, which he serves, that his knowledge of the haunts of his clients, and of their previous records, will guide him in acting for them and protect him from mistakes which might result in loss. [One] bondsman, testified that he was Arnold Rothstein's principal bail bond representative during Rothstein's last few years, and that he had written bonds for "Legs" Diamond half a dozen times. In fact, in one instance, a picture appeared in the public press portraying [this bondsman and a magistrate] standing at the bedside of "Legs" Diamond. Many lesser lights of the underworld, of course, habitually call upon one particular bondsman. It is doubtless true that the bondsman's contact with the underworld often extends to an actual knowledge of criminal acts which a law-abiding person would immediately report to the authorities. Indubitably there are good, upright men in the business, but it is clear that its very nature causes men of far from admirable type to predominate. Largely, for this reason, many surety and indemnity companies will not go into the bail field at all. They feel that the contacts which the business itself necessitates are shady and degrading.[9]

The investigation into the bail-bond situation revealed,

[9] *Ibid.*, pp. 111–113.

then, that the machinery so hopefully designed during the previous ten years to control the abuses of the business had utterly failed. In part this was attributable to the inadequacy of the laws themselves, and in part to the failure of those who were responsible to utilize such powers as they had.

The process of licensing by the State Insurance Department was at best an ineffective gesture. The staff of the license bureau of this Department issues and is supposed to supervise approximately 146,000 licenses yearly, which include 50,000 life, 25,000 health and accident, and 50,000 insurance agents other than the foregoing, 20,000 insurance brokers, and 1,000 adjusters. The license bureau is composed of about thirty-seven employees. The inspection staff of the Department with state-wide responsibility is equally inadequate. In the words of the *Report:*

> The Department has only limited power and utterly inadequate inspectional facilities. Next, there is no real control over the rates of individual bondsmen or agents for companies. Nor can it reach the "chiselers" and runners who get, but do not execute, the bonds. In short, the chances of any effectual regulation of the situation by the Department of Insurance are very slight indeed.[10]

The action of the Department in 1927 and in 1929, described above, is perhaps the most conclusive argument on this point.

Nor did the provision that the magistrate may examine bondsmen under oath to ascertain whether the law has been complied with have any meaning in practice. It is important to note that this provision, had the magistrates

---

[10] *Seabury Report,* p. 113.

been sensitive to their duty and strictly examined the qualifications for sureties, might have been the means of reducing the bail-bond evil to the minimum. In most cases, however, the business of approving a bond consisted of a cursory glance and the hasty scrawling of a signature.

The magistrates have never made any real efforts in the direction of improving the bail situation. . . . Since the investigation, the magistrate has been required to affix his signature to the bond at six separate and distinct places, instead of at one. Mere multiplication of the signatures of magistrates, however, will not solve this knotty problem. The difficulties cannot be scaled on a ladder of signatures.

Recently the board of city magistrates has tried the experiment of providing that a large sign containing information about bail be displayed in each courthouse for the benefit of defendants. It indicates a number of warnings to the public regarding the giving of bail and displays prominently the legal rates that may be charged. If we assume that the defendant is able to read English, and has an adequate opportunity to examine the sign, and is in such a state of mind as to comprehend its meaning, and has not already been approached by a bondsman or "chiseler," or "fixer," or someone else, then we may assume that this is a helpful measure of precaution. But it is, to say the least, a trifling gesture.[11]

It is true, of course, that the magistrate had no real access to information which would guide him in the acceptance of bonds. Assistant clerks in each court (except the Family Court) fill out cards for each bond taken. But the information they reflect is inadequate.

The well-intentioned provisions in the Insurance Law and in the Inferior Criminal Courts Act which call for financial statements and detailed descriptions of the se-

[11] *Ibid.*, p. 114.

curity offered by bondsmen furnish the basis for no real check upon their activities.

Bondsmen stand bail in the station house, in the magistrates' courts, in the Court of Special Sessions, in the Court of General Sessions, in the federal courts, and yet there is no exchange of information between these as to who stood bail and what security was offered, which might form the basis for real regulation. The same property, for example, may be pledged in several of these different places at the same time, or the equity of the bondsman in real estate offered as collateral may be far below the total amount which he pledges. There is no routine check on such practices.

Judge Seabury pointed out, moreover, that in fixing bail the magistrates have gone a long way from the original idea of bail. Bail should be fixed according to the likelihood of the accused person to appear. This was by no means the case. The amount of bail fixed ranged from $100 upward with a median of approximately $500. A study of the bail-bond cards at the office of the chief magistrate, for the month of November, 1931, indicated that:

1. There is little distinction among the magistrates themselves as to the amount of bail accepted. There seems to be a more or less standard process of dealing with these cases among the magistrates.

2. There is much less difference among the various crimes as to the amount of bail required than might be suspected. Of course, for serious felonies the amount of bail runs higher, but on the average the misdemeanors, high and low, and other offenses, run between $500 and $1,000.

3. In only 7 of the 756 cases was less than $100 accepted. Only 11.5% were for less than $500.

On the basis of this study, together with the consideration of other aspects of the investigation, the conclusion is inevitable that in the fixing and acceptance of bail by magistrates there is no method of operation except a vastly careless rule of thumb. There is little differentiation among crimes, and certainly little differentiation among the persons who commit them. Take [the case of a furrier], for example. Judge —— fixed bail for [the furrier] at $1,000, thus requiring him to go out and pay a considerable sum as a premium to the bondsman. He later continued this bail in the same amount. A little investigation, which he apparently did not take the trouble to make, would have shown that [the defendant] had never before been in trouble with the police, owned his own . . . business, his own home, was a man with a family and many relatives in New York, who had never been out of New York for any length of time, knew practically no one outside of New York, and was in bad health and partially paralyzed. The idea that Judge —— considered a thousand dollars bail a necessary measure for preventing such a man from running away is too absurd to detain us long. The fixing of a thousand dollars bail in a case like that of [the furrier] has no relation to the purpose of bail, which is to insure the attendance of the defendant in court. [This] case is typical of what goes on in the magistrates' court every day. The actual result of the practice is to provide an income for an army of bondsmen, many of whom, according to our investigation, are little short of criminals themselves. The fact is that due to the careless, indifferent, and utterly irrational system of fixing and accepting bail, the court is keeping this army of parasites alive at the expense of the defendants who come into the courts.[12]

The testimony of the shrewd bondsman Stitch McCarthy is illuminating. He did not reach decisions as to whether he would provide bail on the basis of guesswork. He knew the kind of people with whom he was dealing and considered in a rough but nevertheless informed way what the chances were of safety in accepting bail. If, pre-

[12] *Seabury Report,* pp. 117, 118.

sumably, he had been called upon to provide bail for the furrier whose case has just been described, he would have considered the factors already presented, although the magistrate apparently did not consider them important. Over and over again McCarthy indicated that his whole business success has rested upon such informed determination. In the course of the investigation, he testified as follows:

Q. Now, Mr. McCarthy, how do you get your bail bond business? A. Well, I get it through my acquaintances.

Q. And how? A. Over the telephone, lawyers will call you up, friends will call you up. If any one of their employees get in trouble or any one of their friends, why they will call me up and on their recommendation I will bail out the man.

Q. They ask you to bail out persons whom they name; is that correct? A. Yes, Sir.

Q. What kind of risks do you obtain for the company? A. Well, I am personally responsible to the company. The company doesn't take any chances with me.

Q. Yes, I appreciate that. . . . Now do you receive collateral from the person to whom you furnish this bond in the magistrates' court? A. Well, sometimes I will bail a man out for $50,000 and $25,000 without even paying a nickel collateral, because sometimes the big bond is better than a small $200 bond.

Q. That is, the risk involved is better? A. Yes, Sir.

Q. Does that mean that you personally know the person who applies for the $50,000 bond? A. Yes, Sir. I know the person and I know the situation.

Q. So that you are able to gauge the risk that you run; is that correct? A. Yes, Sir.

Q. Now, in other cases, I suppose you do ask for collateral? A. Oh, sure.

Q. What do you do with the collateral after you get it? A. Deposit it with the company.

Q. And you get a receipt, I suppose, from the company? A. Yes, Sir.

Q. Do you suffer many forfeitures in your bail bond business? A. Oh, yes, plenty.

Q. During the last year, for example, did you have many forfeitures? A. Oh, $5000.

Q. A total of $5000 forfeitures? A. Two $2500's.

Q. Now, how many bonds did you write in the magistrates' courts during the year 1930, do you remember? A. Oh, I can't tell you that amount; maybe a couple of hundred.

Q. So that out of a couple of hundred bonds you had two forfeitures? A. Yes, Sir.

Q. Well, that is not a bad record at all, is it? A. Oh, no. It is very rare that you get a forfeiture.

Q. In other words, in issuing the bond you exact discretion as to whom you will bond? A. Positively.

Q. Do you furnish bonds in the magistrates' courts for persons who are charged with crimes like robbery? A. I do at times.

Q. To any large extent? A. Well, if I size up the situation in the case and I know there is nothing to it, I will bail him out for any amount, and if I haven't confidence enough in the person then they will have to give me collateral enough to cover more than the amount of the bond.

Q. Collateral in excess of the face value of the bond? A. Yes, Sir.

By the Referee   Q. What do you take into account in sizing up the situation, as you express it? A. Well, take a married man who has a wife and children and he is a foreigner, and if he is convicted, that is, liable to be convicted, will he run away from the country? Will he leave his wife and children? He will spend anything to get into this country and he ain't going to run out in case if he is found guilty, to do a year. Then, he takes a chance, being the first time he is ever arrested, and if he has a good character, that man may get a suspended sentence and be put on probation.[18]

---

[18] Testimony of Samuel Rothberg ("Stitch McCarthy"), *Hearings be-*

What we really do under the system as it now operates is to put it up to the bondsman to familiarize himself with the defendant, to find out in his own way what the court itself should know and what the court could know if it set about finding out.

Unlike the business of ordinary insurance, the giving of bail is regulated wholly by rule of thumb. It is difficult to see on what basis a rate of 2 per cent or 3 per cent is determined. If such a rate is based on any actuarial computation, no mention has been made of the fact. No allowance is made for the differences among risks. It is as though an insurance company were to charge all whom it insured for life, old or young, healthy or diseased, those engaged in hazardous occupations and those in non-hazardous occupations, at the rate of $50 per $1,000.

Judge Seabury's recommendations as to the bail situation are based upon a return to the original idea of bail. The purpose of bail is to secure the appearance of the accused when needed, at particular stages of the proceedings. The amount of bail fixed by the magistrate should be determined upon some decision as to the likelihood of the accused person to appear.

As the *Report* indicates, more persons are paroled annually, i.e., released on their own recognizance, unsecured, than bailed. In 1930, almost one hundred twenty thousand persons were paroled, and of this number only a few absconded.[14] Judge Seabury pointed out that there was no reason why more persons should not be released in this

fore Samuel Seabury, Referee, *In the Matter of the Investigation of the Magistrates' Courts, etc.*, VI, 3033, *et seq.*

[14] *Seabury Report*, p. 116.

way, after a quick investigation, probably by the probation department, as to their likelihood to abscond.

He recommended that in the case of dangerous criminals and those charged with very serious offenses, bail should be extremely high. The number of bondsmen who stood bail in these cases would necessarily be small. Only a few of the bondsmen now engaged in the business could subsist on these cases. Presumably, it would not be difficult to regulate and control this small number.

In all but these serious cases, the *Report* recommended that bail be radically reduced—the amount in such cases to range between five and ten dollars. Wherever possible, such low bail was to be cash given directly to the official of the court.

This is the system which is used in England, where bail presents no serious problems. Bail is low in minor offenses. The number of bondsmen is small. In New York City, too, the fixing of low bail could be made the means to rid the city of most bondsmen and corporate sureties by wiping out their profits.

Finally, Judge Seabury pointed out that if this idea were associated with the recommendations for a centralized court, its practical workings might be made extremely effective. A central bail-bond bureau in the centralized court could keep detailed records as to the status of all the bondsmen who did business in the court. A central probation office would make possible the immediate gathering of information as to defendants which the magistrates could use in fixing the amount of bail.[15]

The substance of these recommendations is that the

15 *Ibid.*, pp. 119–120, 201–202.

way to eliminate the evils of bail is to eliminate the bondsman, so far as this is possible. It is clear that the old idea
that a prisoner released on bail is in the custody of a
bondsman is a fiction. The bondsman takes his chance on
the return of his charge. He bases his judgment on what
he knows of this person and what he guesses as to the
probability of his return. The strength of Judge Seabury's
recommendation of very low bail or high, almost prohibi-
tive bail after an investigation is that the court can just as
well make this guess as can a bondsman, and that the in-
terposition of the bondsman is, therefore, entirely useless.

Moreover, if, even after careful selection, a prisoner released on low bail escapes, the net loss to the community
would probably not be great. When we consider the number of guilty people who are turned loose because of lack
of evidence and the number of persons who commit crimes
and are never apprehended, the small additional number
who might occasionally abscond is not important. Of far
greater importance is the compensating factor—the elimination of a vicious source of corruption and of the exploitation of the poor and unfortunate.

The committee on the reorganization of the magistrates' courts, headed by Judge Goldstein, has resolutely
undertaken to deal with the problem of bail. The first result of its study was the drafting of a bill designed to sim-
plify the prescribed procedure with regard to bail in the
magistrates' courts. Under the law, as it then existed,
there were three principal stages at which bail might be
taken.[16] Bail at one of these stages did not survive the

[16] These stages were (1) prior to arraignment; (2) pending examination or trial, if the case was a summary one; (3) upon being held to
answer before a higher court.

purpose for which it was given. In other words, a defendant often had to furnish new bail at each separate and distinct stage. The bill drawn and sponsored by the committee which became a law in 1932[17] provided that there be single consolidated bail bonds which would carry defendants through the entire proceeding. This act served not only to eliminate unnecessary steps in the progress of the defendant through the magistrates' courts, but to deprive bondsmen of some income.

Three of the magistrates individually have attempted to carry out Seabury's recommendation with respect to low bail; but it is impossible at this time to judge the results of their isolated efforts. The number of cases in which low bail has been fixed is too small to make any statistical determination valid. These magistrates have, moreover, been obliged to rely upon their own judgment and their own ingenuity in obtaining information as to the likelihood of defendants to abscond. It is obvious that their efforts have been severely handicapped.

There has been no organized attempt on the part of the magistrates to give a fair trial to the Seabury recommendation.[18] The importance of such a trial can scarcely be overestimated for, if the fixing of low bail is effective, it will practically eliminate the professional bondsman. It requires, however, for its operation, two specific things. The first is a sympathetic attitude on the part of magis-

[17] See Code of Criminal Procedure, sec. 557-b.
[18] It would be a simple matter, by the use of proper statistical methods, to make a determination after a trial of how the principle is working. It would simply be necessary to tabulate the cases in which bail was fixed, according to the amount fixed, to ascertain, after a period of time, the number of forfeitures in each classification and thus to determine whether an increase in forfeitures is caused by the reduction in the amount of bail.

trates who sincerely desire to eliminate the evils of bail; the second is that the magistrates be provided with adequate facilities for gathering information as to the person to whom they grant bail. The tremendous weight of routine thinking and unenlightened conservatism is nowhere found so much as in the attitude of the New York City magistrates on this subject.

CHAPTER VII

THE WOMEN'S COURT

IT is unnecessary to begin a discussion of the problem of prostitution by saying, as most writers do, that it is "age old." It is—and the harrowing details of its march down the ages can be found in easily accessible sources.[1]

The problem of its control is practical, immediate, and extremely complex. The legislator and administrator must take into consideration the religious, social, and health aspects in order that he may determine a governmental policy wisely. At various stages in the development of society, one or more of these considerations have set the standard.

The religious attitude was based on a recognition of prostitution as an evil in itself. Moses, the lawgiver, condemned it as a menace to health. The Greeks and Romans had no concern with the religio-health attitude. They did, however, recognize certain evils resulting from prostitution, especially with respect to the difficulty of establishing legitimacy. In order to protect the integrity of the family, prostitutes were established as a class apart. Houses were set up and maintained by the government, which recognized in them a valuable source of revenue. In the latter days of the Roman Republic, while strict laws concerning prostitution remained on the statute books, they were not enforced. The wealthy were left to do as

[1] William M. Sanger, M.D., *The History of Prostitution* (Harper and Brothers, 1858), 685 pp.; J. H. Greer, M.D., *The Social Evil* (published by author, 1909), 64 pp.

they pleased and the common people managed to evade the law. The early Christian leaders considered the world as abandoned to frivolity and license, and hence the new faith stressed personal chastity. The body, the "temple of the Holy Spirit," must be kept from lust, "a vessel unto holiness."

About the fifteenth century an epidemic of syphilis spread over Europe. Since the time of Moses, government regulation of prostitution had not been concerned with health measures. Physicians were, for the most part, unwilling to treat "secret" diseases, and where treatment was administered, it was only to the men, as "victims" of the prostitutes' wiles. The plague brought the people face to face with the problem of public health in relation to prostitution. Attempts were made to treat women as well as men. Licensed houses were for the most part closed for a considerable portion of the fifteenth and sixteenth centuries; but they reopened later and "lived by strength of traditional usage until replaced by modern reglementation."[2]

The early part of the modern era differed from the medieval mainly in its interest in the stamping out of disease through sanitary regulation and control. The medical profession believed that sex indulgence was a necessity, and that through segregation and registration they would be able to fight successfully the diseases attendant upon it. This attitude was challenged by the moral leaders of the day. Gradually—through investigation—it has been shown that regulated areas do not accomplish their purpose. Red-light districts were centers of vice, crime, and political corruption which were difficult to control. Fi-

[2] Seligman, *The Social Evil*, p. 20.

nally, an important part of the medical profession has come to recognize the fact that sex indulgence is not necessary to health.

The social-hygiene movement has dealt with the recognition of the relation between moral and physical health. At first there were two lines of endeavor in the new movement. One was represented by the American Vigilance Association, which attempted to repress prostitution, and the other by the American Federation for Sex Hygiene, which fought sex ignorance and disease. In 1914 these two organizations united to form the American Social Hygiene Association. The program of the new organization is fourfold: (1) law enforcement; (2) medical treatment; (3) sex education; (4) wholesome recreation.

The regulation, restriction, or prevention of prostitution by law opens the way to limitless discussion of the relations of government to individual morals. To ramble in this field of thought will not greatly help us to meet a specific problem; but an acquaintance with the legal aspects of the problem is necessary in order to gain a sense of direction.

The common law was developed at a time when governments and courts were seeking to avoid undue interference in moral questions because these were recognized as being the concern of the church. Gradually, however, the civil law was extended to cover moral conduct. Questions relating to health came to be more and more a subject for state control.

Annoyance was the criterion on which the English and American common law based their attitude toward prostitution. Prostitution under the common law was punished only when it became offensive to the passer-by. Statutory regulation is an outgrowth of a changing public opinion which looks on this form of vice as more than a passing irritation. Today in New York State it can be punished under a number of statutes.[3] Regulation, for purposes other than the punishment of offenses against public decency, is a product of the present century. Freedom from annoyance rather than the suppression of prostitution as such was the concern of our pre-twentieth-century legislators.

Fornication is not unlawful in New York State; but prostitution is. Fine distinctions arise in this field. The legal theory behind making prostitution an offense is that when money is the motivating force, a commercialized relationship is established and the law is justified in intervening. This, of course, works what many people consider gross injustice because many of those who secure financial assistance for what amounts to the same ultimate reason are largely, because of the magnitude of the gift they receive, exempt from the operation of the law. To discuss this question on grounds of moral right and wrong involves us in a misunderstanding of what the purpose of the statute against prostitution really is. It may be difficult to see a distinction in morals between the woman

[3] Cobb, *Inferior Criminal Courts Act*, p. 425. The court "shall hear and determine all cases and proceedings against women as follows: any violation of—

"Sec. 150—Tenement House Law.

"Subd. 344 of Section 887—Code of Criminal Procedure.

"Subd. 20 of Section 1458—Consolidation Act.

"Sec. 1466 of Consolidation Act, as amended, and commonly known as "Chapter 436 of the Laws of 1903, relating to wayward and incor-"rigible girls (now Wayward Minors Act) or intemperate women.

"Sec. 1146—Penal Law (keeping disorderly house)—and all offenses of "a prostitutional nature, at present or hereafter defined by law."

who accepts a few dollars and the one who accepts thousands of dollars as a species of retainer; but the law in this case is intended to meet a specific social problem which is accentuated by the offense involving a small amount and is not seriously affected by the more expensive type. The distinction may seem artificial; but from the standpoint of society it becomes necessary for two reasons. Prostitution as a commercial activity drags into its net not only those who go willingly, but many who are forced. Furthermore, personal freedom of action does not mean license to become a public nuisance.

New York City for the past twenty-five years has been pursuing a program of intense repression. The Seabury investigation revealed the startling results of this policy. It will be worth while to turn the reader's attention for a moment to the unique situation which developed.

Until 1910, cases involving prostitution were heard either in Night Court or in one of the district courts. Men and women were tried together under conditions that, according to competent observers at the time, definitely tended to encourage vice and disorder. There was divergence in disposition of cases due to the number of magistrates hearing them, and the small fines and suspended sentences which usually followed conviction did not serve to curb the activities of the prostitutes.

The Inferior Criminal Courts Act of 1910 provided for the establishment of a special Night Court for the exclusive consideration of cases involving women defendants. In 1913, four magistrates were assigned to the work of the new court by Chief Magistrate McAdoo. Judges were chosen who seemed especially suited to the work, and it was hoped that concentration of interest would develop a technique in the handling of the cases.

The Women's Night Court was discontinued in 1919 and the cases were transferred to the present Women's Day Court. Since that time there has been very little change in policy.[4]

One of the characteristics of American practice with regard to governmental matters is that after setting up a governmental institution and providing for it through public taxation, we establish private agencies at private expense to watch the public institution and to assist it in performing its functions. Even before the Women's Day Court was established, there had been in operation in New York an organization of public-spirited citizens, imbued with lofty idealism, who designated themselves the Committee of Fourteen. The citizen members of this Committee were busy people, and, as usually happens in such cases, the actual work of the Committee was delegated to a paid professional staff. This staff concerned itself with assisting the police in enforcing the law relating to prostitution, often accompanying them in the business of making arrests and carrying out raids.

In 1929 there were sixty-five organizations coöperating with the Committee of Fourteen in the suppression of vice. They dominated the Women's Court because they considered its business part of their special province. They wanted prostitution stamped out. They believed that law and the enforcement of law could accomplish this

---

[4] The Women's Court has summary jurisdiction in prostitution and wayward minor cases and conducts preliminary hearings in petty larceny (shoplifting) cases. See Appendix for a discussion of the illegal commitment of wayward minors.

delicate task. They gloried in a mounting scale of arrests. The degree to which reformers have wanted to regulate people's public and private morals has varied. They have emphasized the regulation of public morals but they have, in practice, attacked private morals.

Whatever other vices the big politicians in New York City may have, profiting from the proceeds of prostitution is not among them.[5] Voluminous as were the revelations of the investigation of the magistrates' courts, no district leaders were mentioned in connection with the "social evil."[6] Profits of prostitution, however, were gathered by the so-called "vice squad."[7]

The squad and its stool pigeons worked in conjunction with lawyers and bondsmen to reap tremendous profits. The ramifications of this sordid combine were revealed by the testimony of two remarkable witnesses, John C. Weston, former deputy assistant district attorney in the Women's Court, and Chile Mapocha Acuna, former stool pigeon.

Acuna came to the headquarters of the investigation in October, 1930, and voluntarily testified. Revenge was obviously part of his motive. He had been double-crossed

[5] Mr. Croker, one-time boss of Tammany Hall, is quoted by Lincoln Steffens as saying of prostitution graft: "Police graft is dirty graft. . . . "We have to stand for it. If we get big graft, and the cops and small "fry politicians know it, we can't decently kick at their petty stuff. . . . "I never have touched a cent of the dirty police graft myself." *Autobiography of Lincoln Steffens* (New York, 1931), p. 238.

[6] The district leader who figured in the trial of Magistrate Silbermann had nothing to do with the Women's Court. Magistrate Silbermann's activity, for which the Appellate Division removed him, it will be remembered, confined itself to the district court.

[7] The term "vice squad" was coined by a journalist in an early stage of the investigation and applied to the squad of plain-clothes officers handling vice cases.

and imprisoned for a year. When he was assured of protection, he told his amazing story. Although his testimony was given entirely from memory, it was carefully checked and found correct.

It was the duty of the vice squad to suppress prostitution, gambling, the liquor traffic, and the sale of narcotics. They operated in three units. The headquarters group or Nineteenth Division had for its territory the Greater City. Borough squads, under the leadership of a deputy chief inspector, covered the boroughs, and divisional groups operated within division limits. The members of the squads were patrolmen in plain clothes assigned to this special duty. They worked either on complaints received at the station houses and at headquarters or on information which they themselves gathered.

Arrests were of two types—direct and indirect. In the direct arrest, the officer was a party to the transaction. He paid the amount asked and arrested the girl as she prepared to fulfil the agreement. In the indirect arrest or "jump raid," a stool pigeon played the part of the "unknown man." At a prearranged time the officers broke into the girl's quarters, arrested her, and allowed her male companion to fade from the picture. This method of arrest developed many of the clever but infamous rackets which scandalized the public during the investigation.

The stool pigeons were essential to the system which the vice squad employed. The most notorious were Chico and Harry Levey, Pinto, Harry the Greek, the "Dove," Meyer Slutsky, and "Chile" Acuna.

The story of Acuna is characteristic of all of them. Several years after this Chilean immigrant came here he met two detectives. Because of his knowledge of Spanish he was able to pick up information concerning crimes unavailable to the detectives. He was well paid for this information and worked for them until 1929, when he joined forces with the vice squad because there was more money in it. He worked mainly in the Spanish district of Harlem under "Inspector Ryan" who was in reality Lieutenant —— of the —— Street station house. ["Inspector Ryan"] taught him the lessons of the vice squad stool-pigeon—he must give a false name or address, he must be prepared for a slight beating from the police during the raid, he must never go to court, and above all, he must deny any personal knowledge of the arresting officers. Acuna was then turned over to two members of the squad . . ., [one] of whom is now in Sing Sing as a result of prosecutions based on the testimony given in [the] investigation. Acuna worked with them until he was double-crossed and sent to prison. Stool-pigeons were a costly item in the police budget. ["Inspector Ryan"] testified that the average monthly bill submitted by each officer was $35. In the whole city the taxpayers paid approximately $100,000 per year for the use of these informers.[8]

The police and their informers formed only one half of the ring which surrounded the unfortunate women. Having "tracked down and captured" their victims, the officers commended them to the care of lawyers and bondsmen, who completed the task of mulcting.

The bondsman usually had an understanding with the arresting officer and was present to receive the prisoner or was summoned by telephone. He then recommended a lawyer, and the rest of the system went into action.

John C. Weston, former deputy assistant district attorney in the Women's Court, exposed these practices in his testimony before Judge Seabury. Most of the lawyers

[8] The quotations on this page and the pages immediately following are made from the *Seabury Report*, pp. 84–86.

with whom he dealt were tenants of Lawyers' Row, opposite the Jefferson Market Court House.

He testified that it was the usual thing for these lawyers to say to him:

"Any time one of my cases goes out I will see that you get $25."

Sometimes the bribe was larger. In one case he was given $150. Bondsmen were closely associated with many of these lawyers who operated through Weston to carry out the bargains made by the bondsmen with the defendants.

The system was a simple one. The officer—for a consideration—failed to appear or suffered loss of memory. Weston allowed the evidence to pass unchallenged and the magistrate then had no alternative but dismissal. If the ring was unable to extort the necessary funds, the police testified with great accuracy and the victim was usually convicted.

The picture of the ring is complete. The stool pigeon or the officer framed the woman, the officer arrested her, the bondsman bailed her out at an exorbitant charge and usually recommended a lawyer, the lawyer gouged her savings and either himself, or through the bondsman, "fixed" the arresting officer and the district attorney. The following cases illustrate graphically the fine flowering of the system in action.

Miss ——, a self-supporting woman, was in her apartment late one Saturday afternoon when Officer —— knocked at the door, forced an entrance, struck her and then arrested her for prostitution. She was taken to the —— Street station house. Here [the officer], suddenly turning helpful, advised her to get a bond of $500. When she said she did not know where to get the cash, he told her that this was unnecessary, that she could buy a bond. She was allowed one telephone call.

"Tell the person," [he] continued, "to go to Jefferson Market Station and ask for Bondsman ———. He will give you the bond. Tell the person going there to bring at least $50. That will be the cost."

At the same time she was informed that Bondsman ——— had a brother, an attorney, the best attorney in New York, and was advised to engage Attorney ——— to take care of her case.

In Miss ———'s case, however, although she followed this disinterested advice, paying the prescribed bondsman an extortionate rate and retaining the prescribed lawyer, her difficulties were by no means over. At her trial, [the officer], the only witness for the prosecution, gave perjured testimony. Miss ——— was subjected to a severe cross examination by both the magistrate and the prosecution. Despite her repeated denials of the charge, the testimony of the janitress of her house as to what had happened, and the testimony of her character witnesses, she was found guilty.

Six months later, the Appellate Division reversed her conviction and ordered a new trial. [She was subsequently discharged honorably.][9]

Mrs. ———, a Hungarian woman, was first arrested for prostitution by Officer ———. While she was held in the ——— Street police station, she was approached by [a] bondsman, who offered to bail her out. Her sister then turned over to [the bondsman] her bankbook, and Mrs. ——— returned home and paid him $40 cash for the $500 bond. The next morning [he] led her to the office which he shared with . . ., a lawyer. [This lawyer] asked her for $300 and when she protested, he said she could go to jail if she would not pay. Finally, however, he agreed to accept $150. She paid him $60 before the trial and $100 after. She was found guilty.

The second arrest of Mrs. ——— was made by the same officer, . . . as she stood in a subway station. She was taken to the same police station, approached by the same bondsman and taken to the same lawyer. This time [the lawyer] insisted that he must have $300 to divide up with everyone. The officer

[9] *Seabury Report,* pp. 91–92.

alone, he said, wanted $100. Finally, this price was agreed to. Mrs. —— was acquitted because the complaining officer presented insufficient evidence. Weston testified to the fact that after the dismissal of this case . . . the bondsman called him over and gave him $25.

A year later, Mrs. —— was arrested for the third time by two officers. She was taken to the same police station. While Mrs. —— was trying to get bail there, a woman in the next cell told her that her lawyer, [Mr. ——], and a bondsman were coming. When they arrived, Mrs. —— was called downstairs, where she met [this lawyer and a] bondsman, who bailed her out and then took her home, where she paid him a fee of $30 for the $500 bond and gave him security. She visited [the lawyer's] office several times following this, asking each time how much he was going to charge her. He replied that he did not know yet; he would have to talk to the officers and find out about it. Finally, he told her that if she wanted an acquittal she would have to pay him $400, $100 for each of the officers, some for the judge and some for the district attorney. If she did not pay this amount she would be convicted. Immediately after the trial, [the lawyer's] office boy accompanied her to the bank where she gave him the $400.

Approximately a year later Mrs. —— was "framed" by a stool pigeon. She was taken to the station where she was bailed out by [a bondsman from the office of the lawyer who had handled her case the year before]. She paid [the bondsman] $35 for a $500 bond. [The lawyer] asked her for $700, which she was unable to pay. He then declared that as she couldn't afford it, he would take only $100. Mrs. —— was found guilty and sent to the workhouse for 30 days.

Two months later the unfortunate woman was arrested once again by [the same officer who had originally arrested her]. At the —— Street police station she was bailed out by [the bondsman who had previously stood bail for her when she was arrested by this officer. He] took her bankbook as security. She then communicated with [a lawyer] to whom she promised the $300 which he demanded to get her free. She was acquitted on the grounds of insufficient evidence. She paid [the lawyer] $300.

In the first and fourth prosecutions, where Mrs. —— did not pay the extortionate rate demanded, she was found guilty; in the second, third, and fifth, where she paid at least $300, she was acquitted.[10]

The actual physical violence employed by members of the so-called vice squad in some cases illustrates only one of a number of methods of procedure. In a smoothly functioning system of extortion, physical abuse on the part of the arresting officer tends to be occasional and incidental, a demonstration of individual brutality rather than an essential element of extortion. Moreover, it is a manifestation of a definite mental abnormality so obvious that the exclusion of such men from the squad should have been easy. On the whole, the objective of the members of the vice squad who abused their office was not to find and maltreat a woman, but to find a woman with money and extort it from her. The woman with money was not the average prostitute, but the respectable married woman whose husband was gainfully employed, or the respectable working woman.

Undoubtedly, the "framing" of women [of this character] illustrates an inhumanity more exquisite than the use of physical violence; it means a cold blooded search for victims with money enough to make the sordid business financially profitable to everyone involved; it means, further, a thorough understanding of the potency of fear. The difficulty found in inducing women to tell their stories showed clearly how strong was the fear of publicity upon which the ring traded.[11]

It is apparent that following many of the alleged raids,

[10] *Seabury Report*, pp. 92–94.   [11] *Ibid.*, p. 96.

victims bought their liberty. No one will ever know how many threats of arrest have resulted in the fleecing of innocent women. Enough information has been brought to light to prove conclusively that this "framing racket" was a smoothly working machine.

An important source of data on the subject of this racket was found in the bank accounts of the vice-squad men. The explanations offered by the police for the startlingly large deposits shown in Judge Seabury's analysis were often even more startling than the deposits themselves.

Officer ———, who has since been convicted by the United States Government for filing false income tax returns, had been, until the time of his public examination, on the force for eighteen years. An examination of his and his wife's accounts indicated that he had banked in the past five years about $31,000 in cash, and his wife, the modest sum of $57,744.67, of which $30,016.20 was in cash. They had a joint safety deposit box which, they testified, was used merely for the keeping of insurance papers and jewelry. When asked to explain his accounts he said that he had won $10,000 at gambling. This money in cash was kept by [his] mother at home in a trunk for about ten years and, at her death, [his] father assumed the burden of caring for the trunk. Two years later [his] father died and [the officer] himself continued to care for [the money] in its repository. He kept it in this way until he married, when he gave it to his wife. The money had by this time, however, increased to $20,000, for [his] father had left him $10,000 in cash. A brother of [the officer], it appears, was left nothing, ·although [the officer] explained that he could have had all he wanted, but unfortunately he died, thereby relieving himself of the need for worldly goods. The $20,000 now in [the officer's] possession continued to grow. $3,000 of this was won at the races. The remaining $8,000 he refused to account for on the ground that it would tend to incriminate or degrade him. Unfortunately, Mrs. ——'s account was never explained, since, shortly before the day scheduled for her appearance before [Judge Seabury], she left for an unknown destination in Pennsylvania. In these circumstances [Judge Seabury] was forced to use the colorless story of an accountant to explain her bank accounts. She was, indeed, from the analysis given, a very saving woman.[12]

. . . Another member of the vice squad gave an extraordinary account of his financial transactions. He had been, when examined, on the police force for over 21 years. His wife had died in 1918 and he lived with a daughter and a crippled sister. [This officer] had no bank accounts at the time he testified. He had had accounts in the Franklin Savings Bank and in the Greenwich Savings Bank of $7,010.91 and $7,440.94 respectively. Both were opened on January 7, 1925, and both closed on May 18, 1928. But this money, [he] explained, did not belong to him. It seems that one day in 1925, —— ——, who served as a secretary in the Chief Inspector's office . . ., asked [the officer] to do him a favor. [The officer] was to deposit some money, under his own name, for ——. The only explanation of this curious request was that Mr. —— "expected some trouble." [The officer] obliged. Thereafter he met —— from time to time and got money from him, deposited it, and then returned the bank books to him. None of the money so deposited was withdrawn until —— requested him to close the accounts in 1928. At that time, [the officer] said, he returned all the money to ——. Unfortunately [the officer] chose to tell this strange story about a man who was dead. And inasmuch as no one but he and the dead man were supposed to have known of the transaction, [his] explanation of these accounts, fantastic as it seemed, remained unassailable. The fact that [he] had performed somewhat similar services for his sister, however, threw considerable doubt on the validity of his explanations. Apparently, in 1927, [he] opened an account in his own name in trust for . . . his sister. Two days after the opening of this

[12] *Seabury Report,* pp. 96–97.

account, [his] name disappeared from it, and the account was put in [his sister's maiden name]. He testified that he did not know what the sources of his sister's income were. He had an idea that it came from her husband—he was not certain whether her husband was living or dead.

Obviously, perjured testimony was given by still other members of the vice squad. Weekly visits to a safe deposit box were explained by [another officer] on the ground that he was putting in and taking out his wife's earrings and looking at his fire insurance papers. His story of his bank accounts was incoherent, rambling and contradictory. His testimony on this point fills fifty pages of the stenographic report of the hearings. It ends in utter confusion.[13]

[13] *Seabury Report*, pp. 98–100.

CHAPTER VIII

THE WOMEN'S COURT
(*Continued*)

T HE assignment of special magistrates to the Women's Court was hailed with enthusiasm by social agencies. Yet most of the magistrates who sat in the court day after day failed to realize the conditions that prevailed there.

The system already described, through which a large number of cases were there dismissed, had been in operation for a number of years. The magistrates sat in the court so frequently during this period that they became familiar with the members of the vice squad and should have become aware of the fact that perjury and bribery occurred almost daily.

In view of the fact that the magistrates hold preliminary hearings in all cases in which members of the police department are complainants, it is obvious that they must exercise unusual care in passing upon the work of the police, checking their evidence, approving or disapproving their decisions, and restraining their ardor when necessary in order to prevent the oppression of an unorganized public by a highly organized police bureaucracy.[1]

Yet the evidence presented before Judge Seabury in the investigation and the evidence which he presented to the Appellate Division show conclusively that at least two or three of the magistrates sat in the Women's Court for long periods of time during the *régime* in which these practices

[1] R. Moley, "New York's Indicted System of Criminal Justice," *New York Times,* March 15, 1931.

were relatively common without making any effective efforts to clear the courts of this kind of case.[2] It is unnecessary to enter here into a complete account of the extent to
which these magistrates failed in their duty to prevent
these evil practices. It is sufficient merely to indicate that
they missed important opportunities to prevent perjured
testimony from being presented.[3]

A striking illustration is the case of Mrs. ———, a licensed physiotherapist. This woman maintained an office
in her apartment. She had working with her a licensed
physician and an assistant (both women).

The arrest was made on direct evidence and [the officers]
filed a complaint, charging that the defendant received one
——— ——— (actually the Doctor's assistant) and deponent [one
of the officers] into a room for the purpose of prostitution.
During the trial an array of character witnesses, including a
traffic policeman, the defendant's husband, who was present
when the arrest was made, and a priest appeared in her behalf, but in spite of this and of the unsubstantiated story
of [the officer], Mrs. ——— was convicted and placed on six
months' probation. Her health was wrecked, she was dispos-
sessed as a result of her conviction, and she subsequently moved
to another state. An appeal was taken to Special Sessions and
the case was dismissed.

[2] One of the magistrates who was subsequently removed had suspected that perjurious testimony was being habitually offered and he
initiated the "Green Sheet." This sheet was a report filled out by the officer at the time of arrest in prostitution cases. It was sealed and sent to
the magistrate. The idea of the Green Sheet was to keep the officer from
changing his testimony. The magistrate who initiated the reports read
them for a time but finally ignored them after another magistrate said
they were not legal evidence. See *Seabury Report,* p. 126.

[3] For a detailed account of these cases see the newspapers of the time,
the *Seabury Report,* the brief filed by Judge Seabury before the Appellate Division, and *The Insolence of Office,* by W. B. and J. B. Nor-
throp (New York, 1932).

[The magistrate] said the only testimony as to what actually happened in the apartment was the testimony of the two women and the officer. In spite of the character witnesses he believed the officer, for the

"defendants are always presumed to endeavor to exculpate themselves."

When asked whether this theory was not a dangerous one, which left open a door to abuse by the officer, [the magistrate] said

"If the police officer wants to commit perjury, I do not think the court is to be held responsible for it."

In all his experience in the court it never occurred to him that a defendant was being framed. He said that if it had, he would have reported it immediately to the police commissioner. He finds the system of law at fault where there is an occurrence such as the one which took place in the [above] case.[4]

It was [this magistrate's] practice to dismiss a case if, after notice by the court to the assistant district attorney, the police officer failed to appear at the postponed hearing. During 1908, 1909 and the early part of 1930 [the magistrate] dismissed eighty such cases. The practice became so well known that all an officer needed to do to bring about a dismissal in a case in which [he] was presiding was to stay away on the date set for trial. It never occurred to [this magistrate] that corruption was rampant in the court or that ——, the assistant district attorney, was dishonest, and so this easy method of escape caused him no concern.[5]

Another case is that of a young Russian dancer.

This woman was a person of good character, who conducted a studio at which she gave private dancing lessons. The studio was in an apartment in which she lived with her mother. She was framed most shockingly by Officer —— of the vice squad.

[4] *Seabury Report*, p. 128.   [5] *Ibid.*, pp. 131–132.

Her arrest left her utterly bewildered and helpless. She fell into the hands of [a lawyer]. He mulcted her of all the money she had, telling her

"It is absolutely needed. If not, things will go wrong * * * You will see what will happen * * * It won't be good for you * * *."

The case came on for trial before Magistrate ——. He very properly dismissed it. [The officer] did not sustain the complaint; the case had to be thrown out. Magistrate —— believed that [the officer] had perjured himself, but he did nothing about it. Subsequently [the officer] was indicted for committing perjury in [this] case. He was found guilty and sentenced to a term of two to four years in States Prison.[6]

The third magistrate who sat frequently in the Women's Court

saw nothing to arouse . . . suspicion . . . because, . . . [of implicit belief] in the veracity of the police officers, inasmuch as they were "sworn officers of the law."[7]

During all this time, the Committee of Fourteen was assuring the public that they were watching. Yet so intent were they on securing arrests that they seemed not to have realized what was going on. They hired informers to cooperate with the police and in their 1927 report they told their contributors that "the undercover investigators may be said to be the 'eyes' of the Committee. Never before in its history, has the Committee had such good 'eyesight.' Never has it been so well equipped to know what is going on in the field of its activities."[8] The work it was doing came under three heads: "Court Studies," "Vice Investi-

---

[6] *Seabury Report*, p. 127.   [7] *Ibid.*, p. 132.
[8] *Annual Report*, p. 6.

gation," and "Promotion of New Legislation." The court studies were divided between the Women's Court and the district courts. Of the Women's Court, they said:

The thorough study of the records and practices of the Women's Court, which was begun 15 years ago, has proven of great value to the magistrates and court personnel, as well as to welfare organizations and social workers, interested in the court.

The busy magistrate or the overworked probation officer, rarely has the time to stop and take stock of what he has been doing, or to evaluate the methods employed. The work of the Committee in studying methods and in compiling statistics has therefore been welcomed. The fact that they are compiled by an unbiased private agency and not by an officer of the court who might be prejudiced, gives this activity of the Committee an added value.[9]

The Committee of Fourteen assured its contributors that estimable work was being done in the Women's Court. The magistrates who sat in court were hailed as "progressive, sympathetic and at the same time scientific." The trials, tainted, as we now know, in many cases with gross injustices, were described as having been conducted "in the words of Judge McAdoo, 'with that patient investigation which many of them require and with those protracted hearings which were often necessary in such important matters.' "

The New York court is specially notable for its well conducted trials, for the careful winnowing of the evidence, for the checks placed upon the possibilities of perjury by the police, by the high bail that is demanded of the defendant which insures her appearance for trial, care being taken not only to affix a

[9] *Ibid.*, p. 4.

large sum, but also to accept only such surety as will assure the collecting of the bond in case of forfeit.[10]

The probation department, which was very incompetent, was pronounced to be "excellent," and by way of a rounded summation of praise for the entire court, the secretary of the Committee of Fourteen concluded: "The trials were conducted very carefully and there were so many checks on the police that the writer believes that there is practically no possibility of an innocent woman being convicted of prostitution in this court."[11]

This last statement is amazing indeed, in the light of what we now know. That such a well-intentioned agency with the wholly good purpose of ridding the world of evil may develop such myopic vision with respect to what happens in its immediate vicinity, ought to be a lesson not only to itself but to all those who participate loosely and without a proper sense of responsibility in organizations whose protestations are of the best and whose practical operations leave much to be desired. It ought to be said,

[10] George Worthington and Ruth Topping, *Specialized Courts Dealing with Sex Delinquency* (New York), p. 401.

[11] However, in fairness to Worthington and Topping, it must be stated that they called attention to the fact that: ". . . many of the attorneys "who appear in the Women's Court seem to be of the shyster lawyer type "who are a disgrace to the profession. . . . Of the trials observed in "which defendants were represented by counsel, it was noted that two "attorneys apparently had a monopoly of the cases. It would seem that "here would be a fruitful field for investigation by the Grievance Com- "mittee of the Bar Association, to ascertain how it is that these two at- "torneys secure such a monopoly. It was noted that directly across the "street from the Jefferson Market Building in which the court is housed "were several law offices with the lawyers' names in large letters and that "in the same offices with the lawyers were the shingles of professional "bondsmen who appear in the Women's Court. This would seem to indi- "cate a very close connection between the bondsmen and the attorneys "who practice in this court" (p. 309).

in addition, that the extent to which private agencies participate in public law enforcement is dangerous and unwise and that prosecution should be vested in a public agency. This is a principle which experience teaches us is sound and wise. Private initiative with certain restrictions is commendable; but public law should be enforced by public officials.

It is one of the most unfortunate and demoralizing situations in the whole history of law enforcement that while the lawyers, bondsmen, police, and stool pigeons were filling their pockets with money extracted from defendants and in their feverish and illegal activity were constantly setting high records for arrests, the statistical results were filling the reports of the Committee of Fourteen with great satisfaction and self-glorification. Preceding the investigation of 1930 there was a marked increase in the number of arraignments in the Women's Court on prostitution charges, as is indicated by the following tabulation:

ARRAIGNMENTS ON PROSTITUTION CHARGES IN THE
WOMEN'S COURT[12]

1926	. . . . . .	1,742
1927	. . . . . .	2,457
1928	. . . . . .	2,884
1929	. . . . . .	3,924
1930	. . . . . .	2,807
1931 (11 months)	. .	513

Of course, it is a well known fact that since the beginning of the investigation the number of arraignments on this charge has declined. The month-by-month arraignments are indicated in the following tabulation:

[12] *Seabury Report*, p. 101.

WOMEN'S COURT ARRAIGNMENTS

(MANHATTAN AND BRONX)

1930–1931

Months	Wayward Minors	Shop-lifting	Prosti-tution		Total
1930					
January	39	108	284		431
February	61	83	268		412
March	39	108	324		471
April	39	156	282		477
May	50	104	343		497
June	46	81	379	(Note)	507
July	56	68	311		435
August	41	47	225		313
September . . .	33	99	208		340
October	36	142	112		290
November . . .	22	152	52		226
December . . .	20	215	19		254
Total	482	1,363	2,807	(Note)	4,653

Note: Includes 1 "Insanity."

Months	Wayward Minors	Shop-lifting	Prosti-tution	Total
1931				
January	13	94	19	126
February	13	96	24	133
March	15	156	16	187
April	8	146	52	206
May	11	102	35	148
June	5	84	39	128
July	3	30	52	85
August	20	34	58	112
September . . .	4	70	83	157
October	8	76	67	151
November . . .	2	94	68	164
Total	102	982	513	1,597

Two observations are necessary in explaining this decrease. The first is that apparently the figures for 1927, 1928, and 1929 were abnormally large, and as they mounted in such a marked way, it is a fair inference that the scandalous conditions obtaining during those years were in some way responsible for this increase. There was certainly no tremendous increase in the number of prostitutes in New York or in the amount of prostitution. The increase must be explained on the basis of some administrative process within the courts and the vice squad. Consequently, the sharp decline should not be due to any utter and abject failure to enforce a wholesome law. In large part, it is a return to a normal condition.

The other factor to be considered is that, after severe criticism, government officials are likely to interpret their public responsibilities in the opposite direction. They veer with public opinion and always exceed the normal and reasonable demands of that opinion. In any event, present conditions in the city should be interpreted by some agency other than that which failed so signally to protect the public interest when it was in almost complete control of the situation. The public ought to look to some source of information other than the estimates of the Committee of Fourteen for data on any increase in prostitution in New York at this time.

Many of the abuses practiced by the police occurred in the act of making the arrests of defendants. It is significant that in a very large percentage of these cases, the arrests were made in a manner contrary to law. The observance of the rule of law that, in misdemeanor cases, the police are not authorized to arrest without warrant, where the offense is not committed in their presence, would have obviated the making of many unlawful arrests of innocent women, and would have eliminated other serious abuses. It is likely that, to a great extent, the diminution in the number of arrests in prostitution cases is due to a closer observance of this law at this time.[13]

[13] *Seabury Report*, p. 102.

Since the investigation, there has been a change in the method of gathering evidence. Jump raids are no longer allowed. Evidence must be direct and the officer must convince the judge that he has not approached the girl but has been solicited without encouragement on his part. Stool pigeons are no longer used and, of course, the squad itself has been abandoned.

There have also been changes in the administration of the Women's Court. New judges now sit in the Women's Court; a new district attorney stands beside the court stenographer; the police commissioner has placed a police lieutenant in the Women's Court to scrutinize the testimony of the officers; a fresh group of men does the work of what was the vice squad. Most of the arrests are made under section 887, subdivision 4-e, of the Code of Criminal Procedure. Direct evidence by the arresting officer is necessary. The mere payment of money is not enough. The girl must expose her person for the purpose of prostitution. Under this arrangement the officer is asked in detail questions which may be necessary but are not of the sort that contributes anything to his self-esteem.

In the last analysis, the real argument against the policy of the city in the past ten or fifteen years is that the law renders enforcement without corruption virtually impossible. Young policemen are subjected to most degrading experiences and are expected to emerge with clean hands. Furthermore, it will always be a question of accepting the officer's word against the defendant's. Finally, the present practice certainly cannot be justified on the grounds of reclaiming the prostitute. Short workhouse sentences or even a reformatory term are not cures for the habitués of the street. Some of the younger defendants may be reached through probation, but the tragic inefficiency of the probation department in the Women's Court has not given us any measure of encouragement in the belief that probation in these cases can be successful. It is doubtful whether it would be successful even if the officers chosen were very considerably better than the group studied.

The present freedom of the city from houses of prostitution is not necessarily due to the strict enforcement of the law as it relates to the individual prostitute. It should be remembered that public prostitution is not in demand to the extent that it used to be. This is attributed by wise observers and students of the subject in part to a modification of public attitudes toward sex relations. Moreover, an important part of the medical profession is teaching that sex indulgence is not necessary to health, and the old idea as to this subject is largely disappearing. The attack by the medical profession through public health upon venereal disease is, of course, necessary and should be vigorously prosecuted. The attack on the whole question is one in which common sense, medical science, and sound legal judgment are so necessary that a very real danger is created. This danger is the easy acceptance of the statements of individuals and organizations with a single idea and a single purpose which oftentimes have degenerated into fanaticism.

"Many people believe even yet, that it is only necessary to 'pass a law' to eliminate any wickedness that exists. This has been the principle on which governments have regulated society for ages. The world has been legis-

lating against sin for thousands of years, but the sin remains just the same," wrote one student of the problem in
1909.[14]

Strict enforcement has been the rule in New York. This
policy was calculated to clean up the city. To a certain
extent it has—at least so far as flagrant abuse is concerned. What price has been paid for this outward appearance of morality? The Seabury investigation has shown
that the stimulation of arrests through the pressure of social agencies has resulted in a vicious maladministration
of the law which is much more disastrous than the evil
which it is intended to suppress. This policy has led to the
persecution and mulcting of both the innocent and the
guilty.

The American method of dealing with prostitutes

is bad not on account of any defect in the organization of our
police departments, numerous and serious as those defects are;
or on account of the political control of the police departments,
although this contributes to the evils of the situation; or on account of the stupidity of the police authorities, although they
are not seldom idiotic. It is bad because it employs a coarse,
blunt instrument to perform an operation requiring the highest
degree of keenness and skill. The removal of these ancient evils
from the body politic is a matter of social surgery; and a sur-
geon who made a practice of removing vermiform appendices
with a pair of pliers and a butcher knife would be a worse menace to his patients than the appendicitis. To protest against
such surgery is surely not to write oneself down as in favor of
appendicitis; but if it were, still the risk would be worthwhile.
For generations America has been the happy hunting ground of
every type of quack, medical, religious, social, and political.
. . . Of these the most dangerous by long odds, are the quack
reformers. These are the only ones who do not bring down swift

[14] Greer, *The Social Evil*, p. 61.

retribution upon themselves and their followers . . . [They] merely poison and pervert morality, which is a process so slow that its evil effects may not show up for generations. One of the most vicious follies which quack reformers have foisted upon America is the notion that the police are a proper instrumentality to be employed for the advancement of public morals. This idea is accepted almost without question, almost everywhere; yet it cannot survive even a superficial examination. What is a policeman? Essentially, he is a club and a revolver. Whatever may be effected by a club and a revolver he can accomplish, and no more. Clubs and revolvers can dissuade malefactors from overt acts against the peace and dignity of the state, but they cannot reform any man, still less any woman. Clubs and revolvers can maintain order, but the belief that they can promote morality is fantastic.[15]

When prostitution becomes so flagrant that the private citizen is willing to testify to its existence, it should be prosecuted. Public-health measures should be broadened to assure attention to venereal disease in both men and women. Procurers and owners of real estate used for houses of prostitution should be prosecuted to the limit of the law. Beyond this, no law can be honestly enforced.

Meanwhile, the agencies interested in the subject might do better to concentrate their energies upon a possible amelioration of the social and economic conditions which pave the way to prostitution as a profession.

[15] G. W. Johnson, "The Policeman's Bed of Roses," *Harper's,* May, 1931.

CHAPTER IX

PROBATION

PROBATION, properly administered, has a twofold function. First, it is a method of investigation. It provides for the consideration of the judge information concerning a defendant on the basis of which the judge may determine more wisely what his sentence should be. The second and more familiar aspect of probation concerns the supervision of the convicted person after sentence has been suspended and probation ordered.

In such courts as those of the magistrates, which deal so extensively with general social problems, probation, particularly the side which deals with investigation, becomes very important. Up to 1910 such probation work as was done in these courts was carried on by police officers assigned to the individual magistrates for that purpose.[1] There were, in addition to these police probation officers, several women officers paid by private welfare agencies. The Inferior Criminal Courts Act in 1910 made definite provision for professional probation officers attached to the court rather than to the individual magistrates, and subject to its direction and control.

In 1931 the probation department of the magistrates' courts consisted of 157 persons. Of these, 123 were probation officers and 34 clerical help and others. The cost of these courts to the taxpayers of Greater New York was $258,060.[2]

[1] See p. 29, *supra*. [2] *Seabury Report*, pp. 144, 145.

The probation department is organized under the supervision of a chief probation officer, with five deputy chief probation officers and two probation officers in charge of specific divisions.

The supervision of the family courts and of the Brooklyn district courts is assumed by the five deputy chief probation officers, leaving four court offices without the supervision of any person of a grade higher than probation officer in charge. The remaining office, at 300 Mulberry Street, to which are attached the officers assigned to the Manhattan district courts, is under the direct supervision of the chief probation officer, who has no administrative assistant in this office. The chief probation officer is, therefore, responsible for the functioning of eight distinct units with a staff of over 150 employees, located in five boroughs, of which one is under his personal supervision.

Unfortunately, a great deal of his time must be spent at his office at 300 Mulberry Street, as he has no deputy to assist him in his administrative duties, and so he is unable to exercise adequate control over the division offices. Deputies and officers in charge are therefore left to operate their own divisions as independent units without proper control.

While probation in the magistrates' courts theoretically is organized under one head, in the borough of Manhattan it is actually operating in three units—the district courts, the Family Court, and the Women's Court. The specialized courts have their own staffs and their own supervisors. In the Women's Court there exists a unique situation which has led to the virtual separation of this probation unit from the rest of the department. This will be discussed later. While the Family Court presents special difficulties, the chief probation officer exercises only slightly more than nominal control there.

There are certain failures which may be attributed to the entire probation system in the magistrates' courts, and there are others which arise from conditions peculiar to the several specialized courts.

Those failures pertaining to the system as a whole are: lack of coördination, due to the absence of an executive free to control his subordinates; failure in the past to hold staff conferences with a view to enlightening officers as to their duties under the law and their responsibilities as case workers;[3] failure to establish definite policies and to maintain a high level of efficiency by setting fixed standards; failure to use the resources of the community; and unequal distribution of the case load.

Each of the two functions of probation—investigation and supervision—requires a different technique and different personal qualities on the part of the officers. Investigation must be made quickly and thoroughly. It requires a person who can get at the facts, weeding out the important from the unimportant and giving a clear, concise, and accurate study of the defendant's life, home environment, work, recreation, employment, companions, etc. Supervision, on the other hand, is more intangible. It involves all the subtle technique, insight, understanding, and forethought and, above all, personality, which enable one to influence human behavior.

The investigation which takes place after guilt is established and before sentence is imposed, is of the utmost importance to the proper outcome of the case and to the suc-

[3] Since the investigation, staff conferences have been held.

cess or failure of probation, should that method of treatment be employed. In order to be of any real value, such investigations must be thorough. They must be written by a person who is able to report accurately what he sees and to understand and interpret the conditions which he finds. As a rule the investigations made by the probation officers of the magistrates' courts were wholly inadequate. The legal history of the case was frequently overlooked. The defendant's statement was often omitted. The recounting of the personal history of the defendant became a routine matter, and stock phrases were used in describing the home and character of the defendant. For example:

> The defendant is of good character and habits, with the exception that he stays out late at night, associates with undesirable companions, refuses to work, and will not obey the reasonable dictates of his parents.

In the writing of probation reports it is a fault common to many officers to fall into the habit of using certain stock expressions. This relieves them of the burden of describing precisely the situation with respect to the prisoner which ought to be conveyed to the judge. The tendency is greatly accentuated when probation officers are overworked or incompetent. But no matter how clearly the probation officer sees the probationer before him, he cannot convey the idea to the judge unless he expresses himself properly in English. Little attention has been given to this important question by those who have written and spoken on probation.

Hearsay evidence often took the place of careful searching of the more reliable sources, such as the Social Service Exchange and social agencies which might have furnished helpful case histories. Mental and physical examinations, so strongly urged by modern criminologists, were seldom made.

The probation staffs of the district courts and the Women's Court are not rigidly divided into investigation and supervision. Generally speaking, an officer does not investigate and supervise the same case; but he does perform both functions in the course of his daily work. The probation officers were no more efficient in their duties as supervisors than they were as investigators. In the first place, they failed to formulate a plan at the outset. Their contacts with defendants, as indicated by their case records, were haphazard. Clinical assistance was employed only in rare instances in spite of the fact that its use was frequently indicated by the very nature of the case. Nor were the recommendations of physicians, when made, followed up.

Few, if any, of the case records show real attempts to aid the probationers in obtaining employment. The law requires that the probation officer keep in touch with the probationer and familiarize himself with the employment, associates, conduct, habits, and recreation of his charge.

The probation officers state that they were never checked up on their supervision work, either as to quantity or quality, and that only exceptional cases would, on occasion, come to the attention of their Chief. It is, accordingly, not surprising to find that the members of the staff were not even informed of some of the duties expressly imposed upon them by law.[4]

The Seabury investigators found that there were alternating periods of light and heavy case loads and that the

[4] *Seabury Report,* p. 146.

character of the work was little better during the former periods than during the latter. This situation could have been improved had the probation officers formulated definite plans for rehabilitation of the individuals placed in their care. There was no record of any such plan. Nor was there any evidence that conferences were held between probation officers and their superiors for the purpose of discussing a plan of treatment. Very little use was made of medical advice concerning the mental and physical aspects of probationary supervision. Supervision was a routine matter rather than the operation of a definite plan of rehabilitation. The staff lacked the special training and intellectual background necessary to the proper execution of their duties. "This in turn is due, at least in part, to the inadequacy of the salaries paid to the members of the probation department. The work does not pay enough to attract the right type of person."[5]

Knowledge in the field of probation is advancing and an increasing volume of material on the subject is becoming available. Yet we are told that "the Chief Probation Officer . . . introduced into his department no measures for training or improving his staff. . . . [He] . . . failed to require the members of his staff to utilize or keep abreast of any of this information." No instructions or bulletins were issued "which would create in his workers a genuine interest in the new sociological methods and theories in relation to crime and the reclamation of criminals."[6]

In the district courts of Manhattan and the Bronx, which came directly under the supervision of the chief

[5] *Ibid.*, p. 163.
[6] *Ibid.*, p. 146. Since the investigation bulletins have been issued and courses of study have been arranged.

probation officer, as already stated, there was "no serious attempt to comply with the requirements of law" regarding contacts with the probationer.

It was found that officers had made 1,670 contacts with probationers, relatives, etc. Thirteen hundred and forty-nine of these were visits made to the officer and only 321 were field supervision contacts. The records of visits to or by the officers do not show that constructive advice was given or that much specific information concerning the activities of the probationer was received. Most of the entries were short statements to the effect that the situation had not changed.

The legal requirement of one home visit per month was not fulfilled. Judge Seabury's investigators studied 191 cases which should have involved 599 home visits. The records showed a total of 271 visits made, or less than half the legal number.

Analysis of these cases shows that in 52 of them the legal number of home visits were made; in 86 cases less than the legal number were made, and in 53 cases no home visits at all were made. Thus the law was complied with in only about twenty-five percent of the cases.[7]

Two typical examples of the work done by the district-court branch of the probation department will illustrate this.

John had reached the age of twenty-one without any apparent adjustment to society. Destitute, he entered a

[7] *Seabury Report*, p. 162. A great deal of time was wasted by officers: (1) in following up the routine of fingerprinting—this work could be cared for by a single clerk; (2) in giving the judge probation investigations which were not sufficiently comprehensive to obviate the need for the presence of the probation officer in court.

police station and asked to be "put away." He said he had no home or means of support. He was taken before the court and the magistrate held him pending investigation of his case. The investigation was not a searching one and only the immediate situation was brought to light. The boy had had eight years of schooling. His relatives found him unresponsive when they tried to help him. They said he was not anxious to work, slept during the day, and associated with boys of doubtful character at night. The probation officer who investigated the case expressed doubt as to his mental condition; but no clinical examinations, either medical or psychiatric, were made, although in this case the need for them was clearly indicated.

When the case came before the magistrate for final disposition, a married sister was in court. She asked the judge not to commit the boy and offered to assume responsibility for him. Accordingly, he was sentenced to six months on probation. Despite the fact that close supervision was obviously required, the record shows a deplorable laxity:

8–26–30   Probationer reported—unemployed—living with married sister.

9–7–30   Probationer reported—still unemployed—no material change.

9–21–30   Failed to report—wrote him a letter.

10–5–30   Another letter of warning sent.

10–14–30   Probationer reported—said mother died—has been in strict mourning for past four weeks—is unemployed with no prospects or signs of work.

11–16–30   Called at home of married sister because probationer failed to report—she was not at home.

12–22–30   Learned probationer had been arrested for possession of burglary tools—tried in the Court of Spe-

cial Sessions and found guilty—sentenced to
workhouse for period of four months.

And so the case was discharged by the magistrates' courts.

A classic in stupidity appears in a letter written by a
probation officer to an adolescent boy:

. . . There seems to be some doubt among several people,
including myself, as to your mental condition. It is not that we
think you are insane, but that you are probably not an average
boy mentally for your age, judging by the way you conduct
yourself. So to set all concerned right, arrangements have been
made to have you examined to determine your mental age. It
may be that you have only the mentality of a child about ten
years of age. . . .

Those failures on the part of most of the probation officers in the Family Court, arising from specific conditions
peculiar to that court, which have not been enumerated
already, are: more interest in their function as a collection
agency than in the adequate adjustment of the individual;
failure to consider the children as a real factor in the
problem; failure to coöperate with the Children's Court;
failure to be sure of the defendant's earnings before taking the case to the court; failure to make home visits, on
the ground that to do so would be productive of domestic
discord.

A conflict existed in this court between investigators
and supervisors, due to the origin of the two staffs, the ab-
sentee guidance of the Chief Probation Officer, and the division of work, which makes the investigators interested
in the complainant, while the supervisors are concerned
with the defendant.

Just as the Women's Court was the starting point in
the unfolding of the corrupt practices in the magistrates'

courts, so this highly specialized court, the *protégé* of social agencies and vigilance committees, was the first to have its probation records scrutinized. It was the only unit of the probation department to have a public hearing. That hearing disclosed a system of probation which was grossly inadequate and inefficient. The facts brought out in the investigation of this court led Judge Seabury to extend his inquiry to the district courts, which the Chief Probation Officer claimed came under his personal supervision and in which conditions would be found to be better.

The Chief Probation Officer testifies that the Women's Court presents a peculiar situation which, he says, is incapable of being handled there. The following is from his testimony:

"Q. Isn't it a fact . . . that so far as the Women's Court is concerned you have practically thrown up your hands and let it run as best it could? A. Well, it was very distressing and very depressing to try to cope with conditions over which you have little control. In a modern complex time you try to run a machine with old parts and not properly equipped. It is a rather difficult task, Judge."[8]

The task of running the probation bureau of the Women's Court had been left almost entirely in the hands of an elderly woman. The chief of the probation system testified that he held five or six conferences annually with the Officer-in-Charge, and made additional contact through consultation in special cases and on such weighty matters as vacations.

From a study of the case records and the testimony taken, it is clear that the Chief Probation Officer did not personally supervise the probation office in the Women's Court, and that the

[8] *Seabury Report,* p. 154.

Probation Officer-in-Charge did not, save in exceptional cases, supervise the work of her subordinate officers, except to apportion the work among them. The subordinate officers did not keep the supervision records of their cases written up, one of them being 2½ years behind; the legal requirements as to the frequency of home visits were not obeyed; the Officer-in-Charge made very few field investigation visits and supervisory field visits, but surrendered those functions to volunteer workers who had no legal court status. She shirked administration, presumably on the ground of her case duties, and then shirked her case duties by having them performed by others.[9]

Each officer worked practically independently. The judge was the only person who read the chronological case supervision. This he did when the case was ready to be discharged, and he had frequently as many as fifty cases to review in a single evening. When the cases were not written up, the judge was forced to rely upon the verbal report of the probation officer, the records being written up subsequent to the dismissal.

The quality of work performed ranged from mediocrity, at best, to utter abdication of the supervisory function, at worst, and this was due to incapacity and not to overwork. This is established by the fact that the quality of the work was no better when the case loads were light than when they were heavy. The contacts were, in many instances, with the parents in court on the day of hearing, when a calm, patient and exhaustive inquiry was manifestly impossible. A large proportion of the interviews were sketchy in the extreme. Contacts with other agencies were infrequent. A frequent practice indicative of the uselessness and the lack of contact of these probation officers consisted in sending "first contact" letters to parents at distant points informing them that their "daughter is in the hospital with an infectious disease" and was being held over in the Women's Court. Similar statements were broadcast via telegram

[9] *Seabury Report*, p. 148.

to police officers and others. The effect of these unguarded statements upon future relations between the probation officer and the probationer and upon efforts to reclaim the offender, particularly if she should be sent back to her home town, can be surmised.

Wayward minor cases, which were concentrated in the hands of the Officer-in-Charge, were generally not investigated by her, except for court interviews with defendants, and in some instances with their families. The real responsibility for the field investigation in these cases was entrusted to volunteer case workers, representing philanthropic agencies. The investigation reports were prepared by a worker from the Florence Crittenton Home and were afterwards signed by the probation Officer-in-Charge.[10]

These investigations are, therefore, not a measure of the efficiency of the probation department as they were gathered by persons not having official status in the court.

The Director of the Division of Probation of the New York State Department of Correction, after hearing the testimony of the Chief Probation Officer and the Officer in Chief in the Women's Court, said:

"* * * There has been some talk of the work which has been done by social agencies in connection with the Women's Court and I am rather impressed that there is some misunderstanding as to the meaning of cooperation with social agencies, when used by probation officers. I have gathered that today; that it means handing your job over to a social agency. If you are doing good probation work you go to a social agency to ask that agency to do one particular service which that agency is more able to do than any probation officer is. You merely go for specialized assistance or treatment to another agency and do not relinquish your hold or command of the case."

Supervision in the Women's Court was equivalent to almost no supervision at all. Save for letters written to the probation

[10] *Ibid.*, p. 148.

officer and for routine visits to the court office, there was absolutely no supervision of the habits and mode of living of the probationers. In hardly a single case did the probation officer take the pains to ascertain from regular visits to those among whom the probationer lived and worked whether or not she was telling the truth in her reports as to her conduct and manner of living.

The records of the Women's Court indicate that probationary supervision was neither socially rehabilitative nor supervisory; they indicate no attempt on the part of the court officers to do any socially constructive work affecting the health, employment or the recreation of these offenders. Moreover, the records indicate an almost unbelievable bareness of human warmth, sympathy and understanding in dealing with these girls; they convey cold formality, tactlessness and brusqueness at worst, and routine handling at best. So rare was a demonstration of friendly and cheerful helpfulness in the records of these cases, that these instances stood out as significant examples of what the other cases should have been, but were not.

In case after case, in which the probationary period ran for long periods, there was not a single visit to the home, and in not one case analyzed in this section of the report was the monthly visit to the home, required by law, made. In case after case the records fail to disclose any probationary supervision whatsoever.

The supervision of prostitution cases was lax in the extreme. Where the defendant lived within the city, the supervision—where there was any—was of such a nature that she might have plied her trade with impunity, with the probation officer being none the wiser. In the case of non-resident defendants on probation, the relationship between the probationer and the probation officer was entirely by letter. Frequently the probation officer allowed the probationer to send non-committal letters, which in no way described her actual conduct, and allowed months to elapse without seeking a corroboration or an elaboration of the facts from others in the home community. In one case, for instance, the "supervision" consisted of the re-

ceipt of a series of letters, running over a period of a year, of
which this is a typical one:

> "Dear Miss ———:
> I am well. Hoping you are the same.
> Oblige"[11]

It is always difficult and usually unwise to discuss the
qualities of a specific individual in connection with a question like this. The entire work of the Women's Court has,
however, for many years been so largely influenced and
dominated by a single individual that the system cannot
be described apart from her personality. The probation
officer in charge of the Women's Court has served since
the beginning of probation in the magistrates' courts. Her
activities there have won her wide attention in the social
work of the city. She has been loaded with honors and ac-
claim for this work.

A candid view of the facts that we now know concerning the Women's Court indicates that while her attitude
and policies have the merit of sincerity and a reasonable
degree of consistency, they have been enlightened by only
a slight appreciation of the multitude of factors relating to
the problem with which she was dealing. Her attitude
toward the persons who were brought into the court has
been characterized by a finality and fixedness of purpose
guided by her philosophy of what the problem required.
She showed little disposition to reconsider her policies in
the light of a frank study of the results of her cases. Subtle differences of personality, changing conditions of life,
shifting attitudes toward conduct, were largely lost in the
atmosphere of which she was a part.

[11] *Seabury Report*, pp. 149–151.

The Director of the Division of Probation, New York State Department of Correction, at Albany, testified that he had examined the statistics and records regarding the probation department of the Women's Court which are sent to his office in Albany and was familiar with the work of the department. When asked to make suggestions for the improvement of conditions in this department, he said:

"Well, I could not say specifically. You would have to begin with an entirely new concept of the job in that court; that anything you would say about the mechanics of it would be of little avail unless you had persons on the job who had a broader concept of the situation than exists today and knew how to do what they were trying to do."

He testified further that there should be more active direction over this bureau by the chief probation officer, but this, he said, would not excuse the seemingly total indifference which now exists.[12]

The Code of Criminal Procedure provides for the appointment, qualifications, and duties of probation officers.[13] To these regulations, which are of a general nature and which pertain to all the courts, the Inferior Criminal Courts Act adds regulations pertaining more specifically to the magistrates' courts.[14] It is apparent that while the

[12] *Seabury Report,* p. 155.

[13] Secs. 927, 928, 929, 931, 932, 936, 939.

[14] Art. vi, sec. 96. The chief city magistrate may appoint probation officers and "may from time to time appoint such additional probation "officers as the Board of Aldermen, upon the recommendation of the "Board of Estimate and Apportionment may authorize."

Art. vi, sec. 97. "Probation officers shall keep such records and conform "to such rules and regulations as may be established by a majority of "the . . . magistrates. . . . It shall be the duty of . . . each city mag- "istrate . . . to see that such rules and regulations are observed and "that such records are properly kept."

probation department is itself guilty of a deplorable laxity of administration, the magistrates are not altogether blameless. In the last analysis, the magistrates are responsible for probation, and if they permit, as they have in the past, political considerations to enter into the selection of probation officers, conditions will continue to be bad. The Chief Probation Officer, upon whom the brunt of criticism has fallen, is to a large extent the product of the system. It cannot be said that he himself is an active politician; but his hands have been so tied because of politics that evils that he might have corrected have been allowed to continue. Political probation is bad probation.

In 1930, 407,022[15] persons were convicted in the magistrates' courts for offenses which were subject to the final jurisdiction of the magistrates. Of these, 111,188[16] persons, or 27 per cent of all convictions, were given suspended sentences. Of those sentences which were suspended, 5,371[17] persons were placed on probation. Thus, of all suspended sentences in the magistrates' courts, only 5 per cent were placed on probation. The wide difference between the total number of persons placed on probation and those who got suspended sentences is not necessarily a proper subject of criticism. A true measure of the effectiveness with which probation is applied lies rather in a consideration of the wisdom of the selection of cases for this form of treatment. The disparity between the number of suspended sentences and the number of those placed on probation, however, led investigators to select a repre-

[15] *Annual Report, City Magistrates' Courts*, Table 10.
[16] *Ibid.*, Table 11.
[17] *Ibid.* (figure includes adjustments by agreement or reconciliation in family courts of Manhattan and Bronx).

sentative group of cases for study. A study of 196 sus-
pended-sentence cases, in which preliminary investigation
had been made, disclosed the fact that whereas all were
set free without further supervision, 123 of the defendants
were urgently in need of further treatment. Nevertheless,
these figures do not indicate that the needed treatment was
probation.

Probation is as definitely a form of treatment as is a
reformatory sentence. Compared with other methods of
handling delinquents, it is in its infancy and it is almost
impossible to appraise its value with regard to permanent
rehabilitation. It is stated that probation is 70 per cent
successful. That is true if we consider that 70 per cent of
the cases are closed with the notation "dismissed with
improvement"; but such a basis of measurement does not
give an accurate idea of what has actually taken place.
For example, one authority on probation said:

The other day I wrote a letter to a judge closing a probation
case with the statement that the probationer had shown a certain measure of improvement under supervision, and at the very
time I wrote the letter that man was before another judge for
the same kind of offense for which he had been placed on probation! It is true that I knew of his second offense at the time,
but it was inevitable that I should close his case "with improvement" because his actual term of probation had lapsed about
two days before the commission of the second offense. Now
that case, listed as improved or successful, does not indicate any
fact of value for scientific statistics.[18]

The probation officer is the central figure in the probation system. A wise selection of probation officers gives

[18] R. H. Ferris, *Treating the Family as a Unit;* Mr. Ferris is Director,
Domestic Relations Division, Recorder's Court, Detroit, Michigan.

attention not only to educational requirements but to certain elements in the personal equation which provide the means for understanding the complex problems of character that are presented. Because the general qualities of human sympathy are important in this work, it is likely that educational requirements will be minimized in the selection of probation officers. It goes without saying that such work should be done by officers who possess not only a reasonable amount of education but a good deal of common sense, patience, and sympathy with the human problems involved. The importance of those qualities that cannot be measured in terms of education leads generally to the appointment of merely well-intentioned, ignorant nobodies who say, because they seem to have nothing else to say, that they are interested in saving people. This enables the politicians to place in such positions an extraordinary range of misfits. Actually, the selection of persons on the basis of these subtle attributes of personality is exceedingly important. Probation, in order to be effective, must be under the control of extraordinary people. It may be taken for granted that the service is not commanding such people; in fact, it is a grave question as to whether, under present methods of selection, they can ever be secured. With a few illuminating exceptions, these observations are true of the entire adult probation field. The work which ought to call to its service inspired men and women is being performed for the most part by routineers and political menials. There is something grotesque in the expectation and pretensions of social work that the rehabilitation of human life can be performed by such a Falstaff's army of incompetents. The successful prosecution of probation work requires qualities of a very high order. To teach a person the ways of right living, to bring back self-respect, to temper the embitterment that has led to crime, to fire with new ambition, to win the confidence of the suspicious and warped mind—these are difficult. To do them will require the devotion and capacity of men and women possessed of both intelligence and spiritual integrity of a high order.

But regardless of the ability and efforts of the probation officer, little can be accomplished unless extreme discretion is used by the judge in the selection of subjects for probation. One of the main differences between a prison sentence and probation—assuming, of course, that both will attempt to rehabilitate the individual—is that the former seeks readjustment by segregation while the latter seeks readjustment through supervised freedom.

If probation departments are burdened with unfit subjects, they cannot be blamed for a high percentage of failures. The judge must, therefore, determine whether the defendant is the type of person who will respond to supervision. Will he coöperate with his officer; will he be willing to take the advice which is given him? Will he live up to the plan that is made for his rehabilitation? Does he sincerely desire to improve or is he looking for an easy way to get out of going to jail?

The mere fact that a man is a first offender is no indication that he will be a good probation risk, nor should the fact that he is a second or third offender bar him from the probationary method of treatment. The number of the offense relates to the number of convictions a man has had, not to the crimes he has committed. The astute criminal may have many more crimes than convictions in his record.

It is impossible to draw a line between good and bad material for probation. Generally speaking, those who are casual offenders, drawn into crime by a circumstance of the moment, economic pressure, or some other unusual temptation; or who, through bad companionship, have been the unwitting tools of a crime, may be considered good probationary risk; whereas drug addicts, alcoholics, degenerates, mental defectives, or habitual offenders are more apt to require institutional care. There is no hard and fast rule; rehabilitation is a matter of individual reaction to a given form of treatment. Probation should be used only "when a thorough preliminary study of the individual delinquent has shown that the seed of probation will fall upon fertile soil. . . . Probation is doomed if the court, the offender, and the public regard it as something connoting a form of leniency or acquittal."[19] The murderer may be more suitable material for probation than the degenerate or vagrant. Murders are often committed under the stress of the moment. Frequently the murderer is horrified at his act and could scarcely be forced to repeat it; whereas the degenerates and vagrants are habitual offenders. The offense committed must not be the determining factor. The decision should be based on all those intangible factors which compose the background of the individual's life.

A judge may pick a very bad specimen for probation. There is a case on record in General Sessions which illustrates this error. Tom has been before the courts since 1915, when he appeared in the Children's Court as a juvenile delinquent. His legal history follows:

[19] H. H. Lou, *Juvenile Courts in the United States* (North Carolina), p. 150.

Dec. 31, 1915	Juv. Del. (Playing Dice)	Child. Ct.	Discharged
July 26, 1916	Pet. Larc.	Magistr. Ct.	Discharged
Sept. 30, 1916	Disord. Cond. (Indecent Proposal)	Magistr. Ct.	N.Y.C. Children's Hospital
July 30, 1917	Disord. Cond. (Playing Dice)	Magistr. Ct.	Fined $1.00
Sept. 18, 1917	Disord. Cond. (Obtained $3.00 from a soldier on promise to secure woman for immoral purposes. Took money and disappeared.)	Magistr. Ct.	N.Y.C. Children's Hospital
May 17, 1918	Burglary	Grand Jury	Discharged to police and returned by them to N.Y.C.C.H.
June 23, 1918	Selling Liquor to Soldiers	Spec. Sess.	Acquitted
Sept. 18, 1918	Selling Liquor to Soldiers	Spec. Sess.	Acquitted
Nov. 14, 1918	Disord. Cond. (Playing Dice)	Magistr. Ct.	Fined $3.00
Nov. 25, 1918	Possession of Obscene Pictures	Spec. Sess.	Sentence suspended
Jan. 20, 1919	Selling Liquor to Soldiers	Spec. Sess.	Workhouse 30 days
Feb. 24, 1919	Selling Liquor to Soldiers	Spec. Sess.	City Reformatory—paroled July 18, 1919
Nov. 21, 1919	Pet. Larc.	Spec. Sess.	Reformatory—paroled Dec. 21, 1919
Feb. 10, 1920	Disord. Cond. (Masher)	Magistr. Ct.	10 days C. P.
Feb. 19, 1922	Disord. Cond. (Annoying)	Magistr. Ct.	Fined $2.00
Mar. 24, 1922	Rape	Genl. Sess.	Inst. for Def. Del.—paroled August 7, 1924
Dec. 6, 1924	Disord. Cond. (Pickpocket)	Magistr. Ct.	Workhouse 6 months
July 25, 1925	Viol. of Par.	Parole Bd.	Inst. for Def. Del.—paroled September 23, 1930

The defendant was then returned to the Court of General Sessions and placed on probation.

In the city of New York at the present time there are four distinct probation systems—General Sessions, Special Sessions, Magistrates' Courts, and Children's Court. In these four systems there is considerable duplication of work. A family which has rubbed elbows with the law is apt to find more than one of its members in trouble. Several courts become interested in it; separate investigations are made; there is considerable flurry and scurry and finally several probation officers descend on the family for the purpose of supervision. Such a procedure is not only wasteful; it may defeat its purpose.

Probation should not be regarded as the function of the individual courts, but as the social function of the entire administration of criminal justice. It could be administered more efficiently by a single large department with specialized branches and a health clinic, handling the entire probation service of the criminal courts of the city.

Judge Seabury recommended the creation of a central probation bureau having specialized branches and a medical clinic. This bureau would serve all the criminal courts of Greater New York and, in addition, the children's courts. The Appellate Division of the Supreme Court would designate the chief probation officer and his executive assistant from the civil-service list.[20]

The County Lawyers' Association approved the "objects sought" by Judge Seabury, namely, the improvement of the probation department; but they questioned the

[20] *Seabury Report*, pp. 213–214.

adequacy of the recommendation to accomplish these objects. They disapprove of placing the chief probation officer and his executive assistant in the hands of the Appellate Division and they also disapprove of including the Children's Court in the general scheme.

Meanwhile, nothing has been done. The probation department and its personnel remain the same. There have been far-reaching changes in the Women's Court. Two judges have been removed from the bench and others are no longer assigned to the Women's Court. The deputy assistant district attorney who resigned shortly before the *exposé* has been publicly disgraced. One lawyer practicing in the court has been disbarred and the others censured. The method of procedure in arrest and trial of both prostitutes and wayward minors has been changed. The probation department alone remains practically untouched. Two of the more inefficient probation officers have been sent not out of the system but into another court, while the probation officer in charge stays in command, her prestige somewhat impaired but her authority still in hand and her colors literally flying. The probation department, of course, was not corrupt, as the court itself and the lawyers practicing in it were corrupt, but it was negligent, inefficient, and ineffective.

While the plan suggested by Judge Seabury would greatly relieve the present situation, there is a more far-reaching change which I would venture to suggest. This change would involve the complete separation of investigation and supervision and their incorporation into a "social clinic." This "social clinic" would include departments whose work would give it a much broader scope than is covered at present under the head of probation.

The magistrates frequently need services which, strictly speaking, cannot be termed probation. Social work, clinical assistance, and vocational guidance are often in demand, even though the defendant will not be placed on probation. At present a magistrate may keep a probation officer hanging around the court for hours to help him out when such assistance might be handled more efficiently in some other way and the probation officer allowed the much-needed time for his prescribed tasks.

The "social clinic" would be divided into six departments: investigation, probation, health, vocational guidance, social work research bureau, and research library. The bureau of investigation would perform the investigation work now carried on by the probation department. The probation bureau would confine itself to the highly specialized work of supervision. The social work research bureau would take care of those cases which are in immediate need of assistance and are not probation material. This bureau would be supervised by a member of the staff of the social clinic; but the case workers would be representatives of social agencies and the cases referred to it would be cared for by the agencies. Social agencies do help in such cases at the present time; but there is no room for them in the court and their relation to the probation work, which is the responsibility of the court, is not well defined. By making them a part of the social clinic and assigning to them definite coöperative tasks, there would be no overlapping of work. The vocational guidance bureau would assist, in its specialized field, both the probation and the social research staffs. Effective social adjustment to a large extent rests on proper vocational adjustment. The health clinic, with its medical and psychiatric departments, would absorb the present Criminal Medical Clinic. The research library would keep workers in touch with progressive thought not only by the medium of books but by arranging lectures and by coöperating with universities and the New York School of Social Work to secure educational advantages for staff members.

The selection of the chief administrative officer and his executive staff is too vital to be left to political chance. It is therefore suggested that the newly created social clinic be placed in the hands of the Appellate Division and that they appoint a man of real business ability and social point of view to act as chief, and an executive assistant and department heads of corresponding capability. Other officers should be appointed from the civil list with the approval of the Appellate Division.

It is hoped that some of the beneficial results of the establishment of such a social clinic would be:

(a) An adequate intelligence service to which the magistrates may turn.

(b) Uniform, simple standards of probation work.

(c) Uniform salaries, which will eliminate the present unfortunate difference between the magistrates' courts and General Sessions. (This does not mean that those officers of inferior grade in the magistrates' courts should, *ipso facto,* be raised to the level of better-prepared and more capable officers of General Sessions.)

(d) Staff conferences and educational advantages, such as coöperation between the clinic and the schools and colleges.

The courts need an assistant—not to supplant them but to work with them, adding to their judicial function social and medical knowledge. If such a clinic were well conducted and could gain the respect of the judge, it might actually assist him in the sentencing of cases through conferences between its officers and the bench.

"An effective probation system will, in the final analysis, depend upon the extent to which human behavior can be scientifically analyzed and the results wisely applied."[21]

[21] N. F. Cantor, *Crime: Criminals and Criminal Justice* (New York, 1932).

CHAPTER X

DEFENSE AND PROSECUTION[1]

THE half million persons annually arraigned in the magistrates' courts of New York constitute not so much problems of law enforcement as of social welfare. They are, in large part, merely careless, defective, or unfortunate—beggars, vagrants, degenerates, crap shooters, peddlers without licenses, small shopkeepers who have violated some minor law, traffic violators, participants in neighborhood brawls, sneak thieves, "dopes," and small-time cheats.

Many of them are wholly unfamiliar with American institutions. Great numbers of others who are native to the country are amazingly parochial—familiar with only a few blocks in the city of which they are citizens. Most are bewildered, frightened, blindly seeking relief from their difficulties. Clerks, official forms, rules of procedure, laws, the police, and, above all, the robed magistrate are baffling and incomprehensible things. The ability to pass among these mysterious forces, customs, and agencies eludes their understanding.

It is not surprising that they blindly welcome the first sophisticated guide who presents himself. This guide is usually the criminal lawyer—a vastly important factor in the fumbling process of criminal justice. His knowledge of persons, conditions, laws, rules, customs, gives him a complete mastery over the persons among whom he works,

[1] Part of this chapter is drawn from an article of mine published in the *New York Times* on May 3, 1931.

whom he professes to serve, and whom he often seriously exploits.

In securing the assistance of a lawyer, the defendant faces the fact that the present practice of the criminal law runs counter to the traditional forms of legal service. Few of the commonly known relationships between client and lawyer are present. The contrast may be itemized as follows:

In the practice of law, as tradition and popular concepts have it, the client seeks the lawyer. In the criminal courts, the lawyer seeks the client.

For the most part, in civil practice, the client has money or the prospect of money. If this were not true, in practically every case, no legal issue would be involved at all. In the civil practice, at least half of the litigants seek the court. On the criminal side, the defendants are, of course, brought to court against their wishes. In most instances the defendant in a criminal action has little money. He is defending himself against what may be a tragic crisis in his life, and he must often depend upon the assistance of friends or draw upon his accumulated savings.

The lawyer of tradition is, for the most part, an individual agent or practitioner unrelated except in a very general way to any system or organization. The criminal lawyer is almost invariably part of a ring, a closely articulated organization in which bondsmen and others are integral parts.

Perhaps most important of all, the lawyer of tradition and of popular opinion is a person who is expert in knowledge of the law. He is supposed to be "full of wise saws and modern instances." The criminal lawyer offers little and, in fact, needs little of legal knowledge. His stock in

trade is a bag of tricks, a bold indifference to the approval
of the genteel, and a conscience callous to most considerations of fine ethical practice.

What, after all, do criminal lawyers do? Let us view a
typical day in a magistrate's court in New York. Twenty-
two cases were observed. Of these, defendants had lawyers in eight. The deputy assistant district attorneys participated in only two. In the remainder of the cases, the
magistrate did all of the questioning. In the eight cases in
which lawyers took part, four appeared only to ask for an
extension of time. This was granted in every case with no
discussion except that necessary to determine what day
would be satisfactory to the defendant. One lawyer moved
for dismissal immediately and, with no argument, this was
granted. In two cases, the lawyers cross-examined the officers and witnesses. But in neither case was the question
one involving the law or, in fact, any important matter of
evidence.

In only one instance was a point made by a lawyer in
which any technicality was involved, and that was when
he objected and insisted that the magistrate cause the following phrase to be struck out of the record: "So that
looked suspicious to me." In the last case of the eight, the
complaint was withdrawn before anyone could say anything in court, and the lawyer herded his clients out without apparently having done anything—in public, at least.

The foregoing is typical of the work in the magistrates'
courts—small items of varied interest, decisions made on
the basis of rough approximations of what the lawyers
call "barnyard equity." In this atmosphere, political influence, rough psychological skill, and other very common
attributes are all that seem to be needed.

An important example of this is the testimony given by Joseph Wolfman in the investigation before Judge Seabury. This man had been able to function as a criminal lawyer for three years without any legal training at all. He testified that on one occasion he had spent a week familiarizing himself with procedure in one of the magistrates' courts. This constituted his preparation. Yet for three years no one suspected that he was an impostor. To quote Judge Seabury's *Report:*

Indeed, on the occasion of the fifth anniversary of the appointment of one of the magistrates to office, it was Wolfman who, as spokesman for the Bar, addressed the Court as follows:

"Now if the Court please, on behalf of the members of the Bar, I want to congratulate you on your fifth anniversary as a Magistrate of the City of New York. I know that I voice the sentiments of every member of the Bar in saying that during the five years that you have been on the bench that your ability has been unquestioned, that you are a very able Magistrate, and that I hope before long you will hold a higher judicial office and that I will soon be able to come before you and say that you will still rise higher.

"I am pleased to see your mother, your sisters, your wife and children behind you this afternoon to see the honor being bestowed upon you and I hope the same persons who are here this afternoon will be able to see you when you are presented with higher judicial office."

To which the Magistrate responded:

"Mr. Wolfman, Court attendants, ladies and gentlemen * * *. I want to say I am very grateful and deeply thankful and if I am in the position to do you a good turn, I'll always be at your beck and call."[2]

Wolfman acted as a criminal lawyer and seemed to get

[2] *Seabury Report*, p. 123.

as good results as the best of them. He would come to the court at eight o'clock every morning and wait for police officers or bondsmen or court attendants to turn cases over to him. After a defendant had retained him, he would "approach" the arresting officer or try to "induce" the complainant to withdraw the complaint. This was ordinarily successful when they had been "taken care of," but when this failed he "approached" the assistant clerk, "who was very friendly with most of the judges," and "asked him to look to the magistrate and try to get the complaint reduced" or "have him throw the case out." He said also that on many occasions he "bribed clerks to prepare complaints on regular forms telling the court that the clerk had heard the facts in the case as submitted by the arresting officer and found them insufficient to constitute a complaint." Almost invariably the cases were dismissed. He said that in return for this service he would give the clerk half of his fee. So far as the pleading of cases was concerned, he apparently acted after the manner of the lawyers who practiced there. No one had occasion to suspect him because the activities he was required to perform did not involve any important legal knowledge.[3]

The compensation exacted by these criminal lawyers is in no sense as small as the quality of the service might dictate. In arriving at the value of these services, there is no standard of reaching a fair economic determination. All of the elements by which the buyer of a commodity is protected in economic life are absent in such a transaction as this. For the most part, as we have seen, the people who are arraigned in the magistrates' courts have had no previous experience on the basis of which to drive a bargain.

[3] *Seabury Report,* p. 124.

They are, moreover, too pressed for time, too helpless, to shop around and compare abilities, reputations, and fees. They cannot choose between competing offers.

In fact, the system has effectually suppressed competition, and, in most instances, the lawyer who appears on the scene is protected by privilege. He reaches the defendant through the entrée he has engineered by means of the traffic in favors or outright corruption. He is gratefully retained and he promises quick release. Finally, the services of the criminal lawyer appear to the defendant as a mysterious and intangible commodity which must be purchased without deliberation, without competition, without comparisons, and under the terrifying duress of impending punishment. The purchase is made upon faith almost wholly unsupported by knowledge.

Under such protection from legitimate competition and, frequently, with the aid of cajolery and intimidation, the lawyers exact grossly unwarranted fees.

The Investigation has provided many examples of such practice. In one instance, a lawyer answered the protests of a woman who had been framed by saying:

"Now don't worry, my child; I am not one of those who just plunder people."

After she had been assured by the lawyer, she paid him $150 on account, but the lawyer later returned and told her that he must have more money and she was induced to pay $100 more. Just before the trial he called her to his office and said:

"If you won't give me right now $100 you are going to see what is going to happen."

She yielded to his demands and promised to try to get half of the amount demanded, which she gave him after she had been tried and discharged. The lawyer was not satisfied and demanded that she should get him "the rest of the $100." Finally she raised this and received a receipt for payment in full, but this did not satisfy him completely and she continued to receive demands by letter and by telephone for more money. When the lawyer was questioned before [Judge Seabury], he declared that he did not remember how much had been paid him, but he thought, however, that "there was a little balance still due."[4]

While all the evidence heard by Judge Seabury shows that the bondsmen were the archactors in the various practices which prevailed in the magistrates' courts, there can be no doubt that the attorneys practicing in these courts ranked next to the bondsmen in the evil influences which they exerted. This is especially true with respect to the attorneys who clustered around the Women's Court and those who composed the West Tenth Street Bar, where the signs of lawyers showed them to be in close association with the bondsmen.

The *exposé* of their methods of obtaining clients threw light on the system of exploitation of which these lawyers were a part. In many cases, a bondsman brought the client to the lawyer with whom he worked. Such an association was necessary to the bondsman in order that the original bargain made by him with the defendant might be carried out. The attorney was often utilized by the bondsman to corrupt the police and, while Weston was deputy assistant district attorney in the Women's Court, to bribe him.

In other cases, the criminal lawyer was called to the police station by the arresting officer almost at the very moment that an arrested person was "booked." If he got the case, his informant was suitably rewarded. The very court attendants—the clerk who draws the complaints,

---

[4] *Seabury Report*, p. 122.

the attendant in charge of the prison pen, the attendant in charge of the gate leading into the complaint room and the prison, the court attendant who calls the cases—might direct clients to him in return for part of his profits. Regular steerers loitering around the courts brought him still others. Finally, the lawyer himself was active in the scramble for cases. He often came to the court daily, deposited his coat and hat immediately upon arrival, and participated in the activities exactly as though he were a paid *attaché*. He chatted with policemen, bondsmen, attendants, even the magistrate. He mingled freely with the unfortunates who were waiting in the court, and so got business first-hand. He had, with the others who monopolized most of the cases in that particular court, a permanent status there. He was a "regular." He was as definitely a part of the court machinery as the clerk, the prosecutor, and the judge.

In this respect, it might be added, conditions in New York did not differ essentially from those in Chicago. In a study of the criminal courts in that city, which I conducted for the Chicago Crime Commission in 1928, I found practicing in many of the municipal courts an interesting type of "concessionaire" criminal lawyer. It was apparently the custom for certain lawyers to obtain, through the favor of someone whose identity was never clearly defined, a sort of monopolistic privilege in given courts. They then made their headquarters in and about the courtroom. They received, in fact, free rent at the expense of the city because the greater part of them did not even maintain a law office of their own. Most of their nights were spent in political clubs, their days, in courtrooms.

Judge Seabury, in his report to the Appellate Division, pointed out[5] that there could be no substantial improvement in the magistrates' courts unless the character of the members of the bar who practice there could be improved, and that so long as the bar was composed in part of men willing to gain their livelihood by wringing what they could from the wages of prostitutes or the proceeds of rackets, reasonable men could hardly expect any improvement in this respect. The responsibility of providing an honest and competent bar, he said, was primarily that of the bench and secondarily that of the bar itself.

The basis of his proposal is that attorneys who practice in the magistrates' courts should be subject to certain regulations which would safeguard the persons who seek their services. He recommended that all attorneys who appeared in the magistrates' courts should be required to file written retainers with the chief magistrate and affidavits containing statements of the exact amount of compensation they are to receive directly or indirectly, of the names of any other persons whose aid they know the defendants have enlisted, together with the considerations paid or promised to such other persons. Such affidavits should be supplemented by any additional information which comes to the attention of the attorney between the time the affidavit is filed and the date of the hearing. These retainers should be subject to the approval of the chief magistrate and it should be his responsibility to eliminate any abuses which might be reasonably evident from the information contained in the retainers or affidavits. In addition, the attorneys should be required to keep accounts, which the chief magistrate might examine, of all

[5] *Seabury Report*, p. 217.

their income from all sources for at least five years. Finally, "the chief magistrate should have the power to investigate the conduct of any attorney with respect to any case in which he appeared in the magistrates' courts, and the power of subpoena of witnesses and documents in furtherance of such investigation." Any unethical act discovered in the course of such an investigation should be brought to the attention of the Appellate Division by the chief magistrate.[6]

Judge Seabury felt that if this recommendation were adopted and were vigorously carried out, it would effectively stop the extortion and other reprehensible practices which characterized the activities of many lawyers. Dishonest members of the bar would be driven out of the magistrates' courts. "While they would," he said, "under the system which I propose, possess the right of practicing in these courts, I think they would not find it profitable to do so—and the economic law would be self-executing."

Even if the exclusion of unscrupulous lawyers who resort to improper practices were effected, however, Judge Seabury pointed out the further need for the provision of lawyers of character and ability for defendants who had no lawyers.

It has been clear for many years now that the tendency toward "regularity" on the part of lawyers in the criminal courts suggests an essential need. The lawyers who serve the poor and unfortunate in these courts must be "regular" in the sense of being easily available to those who are in trouble. They cannot sit in law offices removed from the scene and wait for clients to come to them. Consequently, the more intelligent and constructive suggestions

[6] *Ibid.*, pp. 217, 218.

for improvement contemplate some immediate relationship to the courts.

The most commonly proposed remedy for the situation in New York City looks to the creation of the office of public defender to represent those who are accused of crime and who are unable to pay for legal services.

This system, financed by the state, is at the present time actually in operation in Connecticut, Minnesota, Nebraska, Tennessee, Virginia, and a number of California cities. Roughly speaking, it has two variations, the Los Angeles plan and the Connecticut plan, on which the other states have based their own public-defender projects.

The Connecticut plan provides that the superior court of each county appoint an attorney of at least five years' standing to represent any person charged with crime in the high court of the county. The accused, of course, pays the defender nothing; but if he has means he is required to pay a reasonable sum to the state. At the close of each term of the court, the defender submits a bill for reasonable compensation, which the court is authorized to allow.

The office in Los Angeles County is the outstandingly successful example of the other type of public defender. This was, as a matter of fact, the first official public defender created in this country. The holder of the office is appointed after a competitive civil-service examination by the Board of Supervisors of the county, which fixes his salary and makes rules and regulations covering such of his duties as are not defined in the city charter. The public defender represents all persons who are financially unable to employ counsel and who are charged with crimes that are tried in the Superior Court. It should be noted here that the Los Angeles public defender does not do police-court work; there has been created another public defender who is so employed.

On two occasions in the past five years I have visited this office. An original doubt as to the effectiveness of a salaried public defender has been dissipated by observation of the Los Angeles system. The office seems to be fulfilling its function admirably. At present, its chief, who has held office for many years, is apparently genuinely interested in performing his job without an eye to its political potentialities. Quietly, intelligently, and efficiently, he and his staff of eight young lawyers are defending the poor who are haled before this court. According to the reports of the public defender, about 50 per cent of the defendants appearing in the Superior Court are represented by his staff. The salaries of the assistants in the office are comparable with those of the staffs of the district attorney. Their ability is probably a bit greater.

A day's observation of their work was an interesting experience. I was particularly impressed with the possibilities of the idea after a visit to the jail with a representative of the office. In a large room reserved for conferences between defendants and their lawyers, it was strikingly apparent that the representatives of the public defender's office were the most competent looking and acting persons in sight. They were in pleasant contrast to the privately retained lawyers there, who clearly were providing a low and dubious form of assistance. My conclusion in this respect was amply sustained by what a number of defendants told me. Some of them had had experience with the criminal lawyers and also with public defenders. Their preference for the latter was marked.

A public defender's office does more than make it possible for unfortunate defendants to have enlisted in the solution of their complex problems the enthusiasm and intelligence of young, well-trained professional men. Seen from another angle, it provides for the young lawyer an interesting and instructive interneship at the beginning of his career. It may be that the greatest value of the system is just this linking up of young professional ability with the realities of criminal-law administration.

The possibility of providing counsel for the poor in the magistrates' courts by the establishment of a public defender never received any considerable support in New York City. The organized bar repeatedly opposed the creation of such an office on the grounds that to create it would merely provide additional jobs for the spoilsman and that the fine idealism of the institution would be smothered under the same dead weight of routine incompetence that distinguishes so many other public offices. Judge Seabury rejected the idea in his *Report* on this ground.[7]

The second possibility is to rely upon such agencies as the Legal Aid Society to represent indigent defendants. The Voluntary Defenders' Committee, organized in 1917, is the criminal branch of the New York Legal Aid Society. Its staff, which devotes its entire time to the defense of the poor in the Court of General Sessions, is paid by the Society. This organization has done useful and valuable work. It is unable, however, because of its limited funds and facilities, to include the magistrates' courts within its activities. For the same reason, it cannot take care of more than a third of the defendants in the Court of General Sessions who are without means to retain counsel.

[7] *Seabury Report,* p. 220.

The Bar Association of the City of New York and the New York County Lawyers' Association formulated a plan, therefore, which, in substance, was to constitute an extension of the work of the Legal Aid Society to the magistrates' courts. It was proposed that these two associations, jointly with the Legal Aid Society, appoint a permanent staff of attorneys and investigators under the direction and supervision of a single directing head, who was to be, in turn, responsible to a joint committee of the three organizations. This plan contemplated the compensation of the staff out of funds raised by the bar associations and the Legal Aid Society.

Judge Seabury, while he recognized the useful work which had been done by the Legal Aid Society and the praiseworthy effort which the proposal of the bar associations represented, felt that reliance upon such agencies would not meet the need in New York City. These organizations, he said, are dependent upon voluntary subscriptions, and the public obligation of manning the magistrates' courts with honest and competent lawyers is an official obligation which should not be dependent upon the ability of a charitable organization to raise funds. "The obligation to furnish these attorneys should be recognized as an official obligation."[8]

His alternative to both the proposal of an official public defender and that of voluntary legal aid was based on the power of the Appellate Division to provide attorneys for defendants without counsel. He recommended that the Appellate Division name a number of attorneys whose duty it would be to attend the magistrates' courts and serve as counsel at the direction of the presiding magis-

[8] *Ibid.*, pp. 220, 221.

trate. The attorneys who served in this capacity should be compensated for their attendance and the services they rendered, out of the public treasury, after the amount had been fixed by the chief magistrate and approved by the presiding justice of the Appellate Division. He suggested, further, that the bar associations and Legal Aid Society submit lists of names to the presiding justice from which he could select the lawyers who were to serve in this work.[9]

None of these proposals meets the essential need of the problem of defense. None of them has recognized that the work of a defender involves far more than legal knowledge. Counsel for the unfortunate must have a variety of qualities and techniques. He must be a lawyer, to be sure; but he must also be something of a physician, a psychologist, and a social-welfare worker. The person who is most useful in adjusting the complex human situations that are seen every day in the magistrates' courts must know not only law but the social institutions which are working in the field of public welfare. He must know what sort of treatment can be secured for the persons with whom he is coming in contact and where they can be most profitably sent. The ideal defendant's lawyer possesses all of these qualities. He is an expert in human nature, combining in one person much of the technique of the psychiatrist, much of that now applied by a good probation service, and many other qualities.

If we view the magistrates' courts not as a place in which to treat and dispose of symptoms but as a point at which we can try to determine with a degree of exactness

[9] *Seabury Report,* pp. 221, 222.

something about the conditions which produce these situations, it becomes clear that what is wanted, really, is a doctor of human relations, a new kind of lawyer. There is needed at each magistrates' court a lawyer to whom may come not only indigent defendants, but all of those who have business with the court. The man who serves such a purpose must develop for the criminal courts something akin to what has been developed in the medical profession in provisions for public clinics where science and public service develop side by side. If and when a central court for Manhattan is established, such aid could be set up in a kind of legal clinic in the building, serving at once all of the courts. Here able young lawyers might learn and apply a wider range of wisdom than they find in their law books; and the victims of a complex and exacting social order might find enlisted in their service genuinely interested and adequately endowed friends in court.

It is paradoxical to say that much of the problem of defense would be obviated if prosecution were conducted as it should be. It is none the less true. This fact the Page Commission had in mind when it sought to protect defendants against corrupt alliances between attorneys and police officers in 1910. Its report stated that it was impossible to prescribe a remedy for this situation by statutory enactment. Therefore the Commission proposed that deputy assistant district attorneys be assigned to certain of the magistrates' courts.

A competent administration of this work [it said] would . . . result in protecting many defendants against imposition by attorneys of the kind to which we have already referred, and if it becomes known that the district attorney is seeking, not for convictions, but for just results, the poor and ignorant will

soon find that there will be no need of employing counsel in
minor and petty cases.[10]

There have been representatives of the district attorney's office in the magistrates' courts, now, for over
twenty years. Let us see how the hope of the Page Commission has been fulfilled.

It is clear that the Page Commission's recommendation
was based on the theory that the prosecuting officer would
be a man possessing a legitimate zeal for public order, a
depth of understanding, and a scrupulous regard for fairness. It may have had in mind the rule of professional
ethics adopted by the American Bar Association in 1908,
which stated that "the primary duty of a lawyer engaged
in public prosecution is not to convict, but to see that justice is done." But such is the practice of prosecution in
the criminal courts of the United States that prosecutors
are intent not so much that justice shall be done as that
they may gain prestige through the piling up of convictions. Every state provides examples, on the part of prosecuting attorneys, of sharp practices, of disobedience to the
court, neglect of duty, threatening, extravagant and abu-
sive language, almost unbelievable ignorance of the law,
and demagogic appeals to the mob spirit.

As it happened, however, this almost universal charac-
terization of prosecuting officers does not apply to those
in the magistrates' courts. It is true that the deputy assistant district attorneys there have not been distinguished
by their activities to protect the rights of defendants; but
it is also true that they have not vigorously protected the
rights of the State. They do not defend or prosecute the

[10] *Final Report of the Commission To Inquire into Courts of Inferior
Criminal Jurisdiction* . . ., p. 71.

accused. They are neither shields of the innocent nor
scourges of the guilty. They do nothing.

These are Judge Seabury's findings as to their activities:

It is no secret that the District Attorney does not assign the
most able members of the staff to this work.[11] It is generally
looked upon as an assignment to be given to the novices in the
office. It is not taken seriously by them. They in general find it
irksome and maintain, at least to outward appearances, indifferent and casual attitudes toward the whole proceeding. In the
last analysis, these are semi-sinecures given to political leaders,
and by tradition they are indifferently looked after. The Weston story is a graphic illustration of this fact. Here was Weston
who had very doubtful qualifications for court work in any capacity. He had served as a jewelry salesman, an attendance officer for the Board of Education and later a process server in the
district attorney's office. While serving in this lowly capacity
he drifted into the Women's Court and began handling cases.
He became the representative of the district attorney's office
there. Throughout the eight years during which he served he
was certainly free from hampering supervision on the part of
the district attorney's office. Weston had made reports to the
district attorney's office the first year he served as assistant
district attorney, but he stopped "because they didn't bother
to read them." Thereafter, he devoted himself solely to his own
best interests and to those of his clients of Lawyers' Row. He
testified that occasionally he went to the office of the district
attorney, but that his chief purpose in paying these visits was
to get his salary checks. For a time, he attempted to attend certain general meetings at the district attorney's office, but his
court work lasted until late in the afternoon. He was in latter
years very irregular in attending these meetings. His entire existence seems to have been a kind of indefinite shadow in the

[11] There are nine deputy assistant district attorneys assigned to various
magistrates' courts in Manhattan. None are assigned to the Family Court
or the Night Court.

mind of the District Attorney, who saw him practically not at all and heard about him even less. During all this time, he helped to throw out 600 cases and stowed away a tidy fortune in bribes.

An examination of the material collected in the investigation, particularly the minutes of many cases tried in the magistrates' courts, indicates that the deputy assistant district attorney plays a very minor role in the magistrates' courts, except in the Homicide Court. In most cases he does not appear in the record at all. He stands in court, apparently merely as a casual and indifferent observer. In a few cases he asks a perfunctory question or two. The instances in which he takes an active part in presenting the case for the People are very unusual. In addition to an examination of the minutes of these cases, an observer for the investigation visited six courts in the Borough of Manhattan. He kept complete records of his observations, in which he noted exactly what took place in each case, and particularly the part that the deputy assistant district attorney took.[12]

One of these reports provides a picture of the activities of these assistants. It is the report of a day of observation of a district court in Manhattan.

Case 1

Should an adjournment be granted, the police officer testifying that the complaining witness had a lacerated head which kept him abed? The deputy assistant district attorney was not in court and entered during the argument, but took no part in it.

Finally the judge ordered the police officer to go out and get a doctor's affidavit. The officer returned in an hour with one, and the news that the witness would not be able to come for about a week.

The judge succeeded in persuading the lawyer for the defense

[12] *Seabury Report,* pp. 78, 79.

to agree to an adjournment for that period—rather than have a string of two day renewals.

Case 2

New lawyer on the case—asks for an adjournment on the ground that he is unfamiliar with the facts. Finally the judge said that there must be a preliminary examination on the summons, as complainant demanded it, but he would be lenient in regard to adjournments thereafter, and also gave him until the afternoon to prepare. *The deputy assistant district attorney was present, but said nothing.*

Case 3

Two negro women were arrested on a stabbing charge. The judge brought out the facts through a questioning of the police officer, the deputy assistant district attorney asking only a few questions in regard to the seriousness of the injury. No one appeared for the defendants and they were held in $5000 bail each.

Case 4

Case dismissed on failure of complaining witness to appear. A dispute arose as to the amount of money the police officer had taken from the defendant. *The deputy assistant district attorney said nothing,* and the court remarked that this was a police matter, and called the next case.

Case 5

The defendant, while intoxicated, ruined a telephone booth. The judge, upon bringing out through the police officer that it was non-malicious, suspended sentence, on defendant's promise to pay for the damage. *The deputy assistant district attorney said nothing.*

Case 6

Chinese libel laundry case. Defendant and attorney not present despite summons. A spectator informed the judge he knew the defendants and would call them up. Judge waxed eloquent and said he would send out warrants of arrest, if they did not come to court soon. Deputy assistant district attorney agreed generally. Some time later the spectator returned and said that he could not find them. The judge severely criticized the lawyer for the complainants, asking him what he intended to do. Finally the judge sent out an officer to get the defendants and said he would issue a warrant if they refused to come. *The deputy assistant district attorney said nothing.*

Case 7

Three disorderly drunkards committed on testimony of police officer. *The judge handled it entirely.*

Case 8

This is the only case in which I saw the deputy assistant district attorney really play any part. The deputy assistant district attorney put a taxi driver on the stand who in response to a few simple questions told the court that he owned a taxi worth some $2000, and that he missed it on coming out of a store at 2 o'clock in the morning. The deputy assistant district attorney next put on the stand a police officer who said that he saw the defendant alighting from the cab a mile or so away from where it had been missed by the complainant. The counsel for the defendant objected at several points and pointed out that there was no evidence that the defendant had ever driven the cab. Judge asked a few questions and finally set bail for the defendant to appear before the Grand Jury. The police officer gave what seemed to me to be "canned" answers—purely perfunctory and would probably have given them quite as readily had the deputy assistant district attorney not been present, and the judge had merely said "Now tell your story."

Case 9

On the testimony drawn from a police officer by the judge, an intoxicated female with no apparent means of support was sentenced to the workhouse. *The deputy assistant district attorney said nothing.*

Case 10

The judge disposed rather summarily of a complaint in regard to parking on a restricted street, and another dealing with improper garbage disposal. Facts were drawn from officers who made the arrest, by the judge. *The deputy assistant district attorney said nothing.*

Case 11

Complaint made of woman that she beat a young boy. The judge handled the whole case, questioning the boy, the woman, and their attorneys. On clear issue of fact the judge said that a complaint was proper and a hearing would be held later. *The deputy assistant district attorney said nothing.*

Case 12

The parties agreed to drop the case; apparently it was one involving a check issued with some chance of fraud having taken place, or perhaps involved compounding a felony. The judge asked some questions to find out the facts, but both parties stuck to their story that it was just an innocent mistake which they would settle. *The deputy assistant district attorney made a few observations in a low tone to the judge, and the case was finally dropped.*

The reports of this observer show, in the words of Judge Seabury's *Report,* "that so far as the administration of justice is concerned in these courts, the district attorney might just as well have been non-existent."[13] The deputy assistant district attorneys show interest only in potential cases to be bound over to the Court of Special Sessions or to the Grand Jury, and even on these cases their work is of doubtful value. The magistrate himself usually takes over the business of questioning, for the deputy assistant district attorneys are not ordinarily well prepared on the law or the facts. The magistrate invari-

---

[13] *Seabury Report,* p. 79.

ably makes the decision as to the disposition of the cases
without the benefit of their advice. For several years it has
apparently been the policy of the district attorney's office
of New York County that its representatives in the magistrates' courts must make no recommendations whatsoever to the magistrate even where he specifically requests
such a recommendation.

Judge Seabury's conclusions as to the activities of the
deputy assistant district attorneys in the magistrates'
courts were that the personnel was generally poor, that
their work was practically unsupervised by the district attorney's office, and that, in any case, the part they played
in the magistrates' courts, except in the Homicide Court,
was inconsequential. In his *Report,* however, he made no
striking recommendations concerning them. He merely en-
joined the district attorney to assign really competent assistants to the proposed Felony Court.[14]

A careful consideration of the conditions dictates, it
seems to me, a radical remedy which will not only provide
more effective prosecution in the magistrates' courts but
will materially assist in overcoming the evils of the third
degree. It cannot be expected that the district attorney
will ever provide, under the present political system, a
staff of adequate prosecutors in the magistrates' courts.
The staff of district attorneys provided by a ruling political power in New York City is very unsatisfactory. There
are hardly half a dozen out of the sixty-five assistants
who are competent trial lawyers. The extent of incompe-
tency in the staff is so great that its lower ranges are utterly useless. Nevertheless, these are the men who will invariably be assigned to the magistrates' courts because

[14] *Seabury Report,* p. 80.

this service is regarded as less desirable than other activities of the district attorney.

The remedy for this is to abolish the service entirely in the magistrates' courts, except in the Homicide Court and the Felony Court proposed by Judge Seabury. The district attorney's budget should be reduced accordingly. With the money thus saved, a legal bureau should be established in the police department. Such a legal bureau should be headed by a deputy police commissioner who is a lawyer. The staff should be subject to civil-service restrictions and to the general direction of the police commissioner. Every attempt should be made to keep the staff free from political intervention to an extent at least equal to the freedom enjoyed by police officers.

The function of this staff should be to assist the police officers in preparing their cases and in the interrogation of witnesses, to advise police officers on legal matters, and to arrange with them the order in which they present their cases.

This would be no innovation. It is practically in this way that prosecution has been conducted in England for many years. It should be understood that for the most part prosecution is the responsibility of the police in England, except in unusual cases of large public importance.

There would be many advantages in the adoption of such a plan. In the first place, it is reasonable to suppose that considerably less political influence would be exercised in the appointment of this staff than is now the case in the district attorney's office. Tradition in the police department would insist to a much greater degree upon noninterference by political influences with their activities. The staff would be subject to the direction not of a political district attorney who, if history is to provide guidance, will be a rather feeble public official, but of a police commissioner. They would be part of a working organization and subjected at all times to the demands of police officers who are anxious to present their cases in the best possible way.

Moreover, the establishment of such a group of legal advisers in the police department would centralize responsibility for presenting cases in the magistrates' courts from the standpoint of the State. It would eliminate the present tendency on the part of the police and the district attorney's office to push the responsibility of prosecution on to each other. As matters now stand, the district attorney's office blames the police for making arrests on insufficient evidence. The police, on the other hand, claim that the tendency on the part of the district attorney to avoid further prosecution of cases is an influence in the direction of minimizing the case which the police officers make. To quote a private opinion of an official of the police department: "Those district attorneys do not help us policemen; they abuse us." If the work of prosecution were centralized, such a state of friction could not exist.

Finally, placing the responsibility for prosecution in the police department would be a realistic recognition of the fact that if we cannot have prosecution of the enlightened type looked for by the Page Commission, we can, at least, expect competent and carefully prepared presentation of the People's case.

CHAPTER XI

THE THIRD DEGREE[1]

IN 1664, a London magistrate named Aleyn received a complaint that a house had been burglarized. He began a most vigorous and, as it proved, a most unscrupulous investigation. He interrogated servants and followed up clues. Finally he fastened his suspicions upon a man named Turner, questioned him, and because Turner denied the charge, "but not as a person of his spirit," he decided to investigate further. With another magistrate, Aleyn shadowed Turner and captured him at last in the possession of certain money which, the magistrates suspected, had been stolen. But conclusive proof was still lacking. Undaunted, the wily Aleyn then arranged that the prosecuting witness should testify falsely not to prosecute. The defendant was finally tricked into a full confession of his guilt.

Such were the duties of the magistrates after England had emerged from the Middle Ages. They included not only the function of passing upon the case itself, but that of conducting practically the entire preliminaries. They were arresting officers, detectives, prosecutors, judges, and magistrates all rolled into one. They continued to perform these duties far into the eighteenth century.

London grew and, with it, the problem of crime. Magistrates were unable to cope with the mounting tide. Moreover, they were corrupt and inefficient. Finally, after a

[1] This chapter is taken from an article of mine published in the *New York Times,* August 28, 1932.

number of preliminaries, such as the creation of the Bow Street Police in the eighteenth century, the Government of England provided for the great metropolis an organized police department equipped with means for the investigation of crime, the detection of criminals, and the making of arrests. It is significant that only a few years after, the function of the magistrates was severely whittled down. They became judicial officers, no longer expected or permitted, for that matter, to participate in the detection of criminals.

As the English magistrates, then, were transformed from active police and prosecuting officers and became judicial in their function, the police, on the other hand, built up the equipment necessary to do the prosecuting themselves, in an overwhelming number of cases. This is the status of criminal-justice administration in England now. The police are adequately equipped to conduct prosecutions. The magistrates serve as a means for the regulation and control of police activities in individual cases.

In the United States, where the development of judicial institutions closely followed English styles, something was lost in the transformation. The magistrates, except in the case of a few overactive justices of the peace in rural districts, became purely judicial officers, like the English magistrates. American cities created police departments in what they believed was the latest London pattern. But the work of prosecution became, in large part, a function of neither magistrates nor police. It was transferred to a distinctly separate officer—the district attorney. In this somewhat bewildering shuffle, the legal right to interrogate suspected persons was lost.

It is axiomatic that criminal justice cannot be administered unless someone is vested with the responsibility of questioning suspects, for when the prisoner is still frightened by his arrest, he is likely either to confess the truth or, if he attempts evasion, to bungle his story so hopelessly that the truth appears despite him.

On the Continent, the so-called accusatory system is used. The *juge d'instruction* conducts the interrogation of the accused. Those who have enjoyed the moving dramas of Brieux have caught glimpses of this system in action, oftentimes not completely complimentary to the magistrate. The *juge d'instruction* in *La Robe rouge* resorts to browbeating and trickery in his interrogation of a simple peasant. But in the United States there is no legal provision of any sort for interrogation. Neither magistrate, police, nor district attorney is directly authorized to perform this duty. So, inevitably, the police in our large cities have taken it upon themselves to fill the gap in the administration of criminal justice. The police question arrested persons unofficially.

This accident in the development of our institutions has placed the American police in a difficult position. The average policeman or detective is constantly under great pressure to achieve results—to get convictions. He confronts, every day, representatives of an underworld composed in part of shrewd, intelligent, experienced, and ruthless individuals. It is needless to say that the average policeman or detective is neither overly skilled in the art of cross-examination nor trained in the laws of evidence. He often faces skilful and unprincipled evasion which he himself is not clever enough to break down. He is given no help in questioning his prisoner except, perhaps, by fellow policemen who may be as poor a match for the prisoner as he. When he brings his prisoner before the magistrate, he has had no help in preparing his case from the deputy assistant district attorney, whose duty it really is to aid in the presentation of cases. He has prepared his own case. A harried magistrate conducts the examination amid great confusion, while the deputy assistant district attorney either maintains a lofty indifference or interjects a few questions which usually indicate his scant knowledge of the law and his total ignorance of the facts.

The policeman is a human being. Baffled by a prisoner shrewder than he, knowing that he will receive no help from the deputy assistant district attorney, and realizing at the same time that he must get convictions, he sometimes loses his perspective and, what is more regrettable, his temper. In order to obtain a confession, he uses his night stick, or a blackjack, or a rubber hose; deprives his prisoner of food; or takes away his clothes and leaves him in a freezing room for hours on end. These and other equally brutal practices have come to be known as the third degree.

There is so much evidence of the existence of these methods in the past that any general denial would be absurd. But the extent to which they are used today is conjectural. The Wickersham *Report on Lawlessness in Law Enforcement* pictures the police station as a veritable chamber of horrors. It has been pointed out, however, that the *Report* "uses the widespread public knowledge of the evil as evidence of its existence. . . . Beyond this repetition of already accepted beliefs, the Report really offers nothing. . . . Its conclusions are based only upon hearsay and opinion no more carefully analyzed and evaluated than by previous publications of one sort or another."[2]

In my opinion, third-degree methods are not often used in these days. For the most part, police departments throughout the country are doing a fairly good job. There is little reason to believe that third-degree methods are countenanced in New York City.

Those who have argued the case against the third degree wholly on the ground of brutality have been vastly unfair to the police. They have put the emphasis in the wrong place. The essential problem of the third degree is not so much whether this method of securing evidence is actually used as whether the public believes it is being used.

This very point was recently made by Judge Irving Lehman in the opinion of the Court of Appeals in the Mummiani case.[3] Mummiani was arrested two years ago for murdering a man in a restaurant in East Harlem. He was taken to a police station and kept there for thirty-six hours, in defiance of a statute, before he was arraigned in court. While he was detained there, he was questioned by five police officers. Finally he confessed his guilt; but in the course of his trial, he alleged that his confession had been extorted by third-degree methods. The police denied the charge.

Mummiani was convicted of murder in the first degree. His attorneys appealed the case, and the Court of Appeals reversed the judgment of the lower court and ordered a

---

[2] John Barker Waite, "Report on Lawlessness in Law Enforcement—Comment," *Michigan Law Review*, XXX, No. 1, 54–60.

[3] *People* v. *Mummiani*, 258 N.Y. 394.

new trial. At the second trial, however, he pleaded guilty to murder in the second degree and, after the trial, admitted that his defense in the first trial had been a fabrication. He had not been the victim of police brutality.

This decision of the Court of Appeals has been repeatedly cited in recent discussions of the third degree. It has been interpreted by some as an attack upon the police. Others have said that Mummiani's subsequent admission that he had not been subjected to the third degree makes the case without pertinence. Both of these positions are incorrect.

The Court of Appeals reversed the judgment of the lower court, not because they were convinced that the third degree had been used, nor because they were convinced that Mummiani was innocent, but because his defense had raised a strong suspicion which the prosecution did not adequately dispel.

We do not . . . say [reads the opinion] that upon this record, if we were triers of the fact, we should hold that the police officers were guilty of the wrong which they deny. We do say that this accused is entitled to a trial at which the jury will not be put in the dilemma of either accepting the bare denial of violence by the police officers or of branding them as false witnesses and allowing a possibly guilty murderer to escape the penalty of his crime. There can be a fair trial of a criminal charge only where there is no evasion of the issue.

This is an unemotional and unbiased statement of the essential problem with which any common-sense discussion of the third degree must deal. It is a penetrating warning that if widespread suspicion of the use of third-degree methods grows, unchecked, juries will simply not convict people brought in by the police.

This is precisely what has happened. Sharp criminal lawyers, in New York and elsewhere, have been quick to see the possibilities of the situation. They have discovered that juries, representing the sentiments of the community at large, believe that the third degree is frequently used. Occasional evidence that this is true feeds the suspicion. In the face of an otherwise hopeless defense, the cry of "Third degree!" is an effective way of securing an acquittal. An increasing number of guilty people are escaping the consequences of their crimes because of lack of confidence in the police.

In the interest, therefore, of convicting the guilty, wherever the evidence justifies it, the need is twofold. First, all suspicion of the use of the third degree must be dissipated. At the same time, provision for an adequate interrogation must be made. A substitute for the interrogation must be found, so that even in cases where the police might now be inclined to use force in obtaining a confession the use of such methods would be unnecessary.

A proposal to eliminate the third degree, containing a sound idea, but in many ways inadequate, was made by Judge Seabury in his report to the Appellate Division. It reads:

Legislation should be enacted providing that all persons, on arrest, regardless of the offense charged, should be taken directly before a magistrate, the charge read to them, the statement of the arresting officer taken upon record and an opportunity given to the prisoners, after first advising them of their rights, to make a statement of their own. . . .[4]

This proposal recognized that the fundamental need is to

[4] *Seabury Report*, pp. 207, 208.

remove suspicion from the police by having the prisoner taken not to a station house, an outpost of the police, but directly before a magistrate for examination.

A number of objections to this plan—some major and some minor—have been raised. It has been pointed out, for example, that such direct arraignment would take away from the police their present powers of fingerprinting arrested persons and of placing them in the police line-up before they are arraigned. These objections could easily be met—first, by permitting the police to place fingerprint experts of their own in the magistrates' courts, and second, by making attendance at the line-up one of the conditions of bail.

When these objections have been disposed of, however, there remain a number of a more serious nature. Professor John B. Waite of the Michigan Law School has pointed out that the Seabury recommendation contemplates direct arraignment before a magistrate in the fullest sense of the term. It means that a preliminary hearing of the case will be had almost immediately after the arrest. But as our laws now stand, a preliminary hearing before a magistrate is not an interrogation of the accused; it is an examination of the state's evidence to determine whether it is sufficient to justify holding the accused for further prosecution. It is held in order to find out what evidence the state has, and not to get evidence for the state.

Further, the Seabury recommendation would require that the person arraigned before the magistrate be informed of his constitutional rights. These include his right to counsel. If the importance of an interrogation of the arrested person is conceded, it follows that he must be examined before he has had the opportunity to consult with a lawyer, get "moral" support, concoct denials and alibis. He must be questioned alone.

In short, the Seabury recommendation is admirable in so far as it seeks to take arrested persons out of the hands of the police immediately after arrest. This would eliminate the possibility and the suspicion of the use of third-degree methods by them. The proposal is inadequate because it fails to provide a substitute for unofficial interrogation by the police.

Who can best do this questioning?

Professor Waite has suggested that the magistrate himself interrogate the prisoner before the preliminary examination. He proposes that this might be done either by statute or by informal agreement between the police commissioner and the chief magistrate. The statute he suggests would read somewhat as follows:

An officer who has arrested a person without a warrant shall, without unnecessary delay, take the person arrested before the nearest sitting magistrate in the county in which the arrest occurs and shall make before the magistrate a complaint which shall set forth the facts showing the offense for which the person is arrested.

When the accused is thus brought before a magistrate, the magistrate shall immediately inform him of the charge against him and shall further inform him that anything he says may be used against him and that he need not answer any questions but that his failure to answer questions may be used in evidence against him in case of trial.

The magistrate shall then proceed to question the accused as to his guilt or innocence of the offense charged and as to any other matters that may seem pertinent in respect to such guilt or innocence.

All questions put by the magistrate and all answers, if any, given by the accused shall be reduced to writing. The accused shall not be put on oath,[5] and if he refuses to answer, the questioning shall not continue. Under no circumstance shall the questioning persist beyond reasonable length nor shall any pressure either mental or physical be used to compel the giving of answers. If the accused declines to answer questions or any particular question, such facts shall be noted upon the written record of the interrogation.

Copies of questions and answers or failures to answer shall be made available to the accused or his counsel and to the district attorney. All such questions and answers shall be admissible as evidence in any subsequent trial of the accused so far as they may be relevant and otherwise admissible in respect to the question at issue. The fact that the defendant has declined to answer may also be given in evidence wherever it is relevant and material.

Professor Waite recognizes that some persons might assert that such a procedure would amount to compulsion which would make it unconstitutional. But he believes that the provision that the accused shall be explicitly told that he need not answer, that he shall not in any way be compelled to answer, and the fact that he is not put under oath remove any compulsion from the proceeding. His knowledge that refusal to answer may be used against him is no more compulsion, Professor Waite asserts, than the questioning which is now done by police officers.[6]

[5] Courts have held that putting an accused under oath before questioning him is compelling him to tell the truth and therefore compelling him to incriminate himself.

[6] A radical change in our law which would permit comment to be made upon the prisoner's refusal to answer questions at the interrogation would unquestionably be a long step toward the more effective administration of criminal justice. The constitutionality of any such change is, at the present time, however, a question of considerable disagreement. For a fuller discussion of this question, see Paul G. Kauper, "A Judicial Examination of the Accused—A Remedy for the Third Degree," *Michigan Law Review*, XXX, No. 8, 1224.

In my opinion, however, the proposal of police lawyers made in chapter x, suggests an infinitely simpler solution. Why should not these police lawyers be charged with the work of interrogating arrested persons? This should be done before the magistrate. The interrogation should be in no sense a judicial proceeding requiring a determination as to the sufficiency of the evidence. It should be made solely for the purpose of securing evidence. The magistrate would sit merely informally. Nothing would be required of him except his presence.

This plan would require no statutory enactment. It could be brought about simply by arrangement between the police commissioner and the chief magistrate. It should be noted, moreover, that no extra expense is involved anywhere in the plan. The presence of the magistrate at the interrogation could be required by simple act of the chief magistrate.

Getting a prisoner immediately before a magistrate would largely free the police of any suspicion of using the third degree, because, perforce, they would have almost no opportunity to use it. The mere presence of the magistrate would be a guaranty that it was not used. Providing the police with able, trained legal advisers would vastly reduce any necessity for physical force.

This is, I believe, a more practicable way of achieving the desired end than Professor Waite's proposal that the magistrate himself should interrogate the prisoner. Police lawyers would assist in the elimination of the third degree and any suspicion of it; but this would be merely part of the larger function of these police lawyers, who would vastly increase the effectiveness of the entire work of prosecution in the magistrates' courts.

CHAPTER XII

THE RELATION OF THE MAGISTRATES' COURTS TO OTHER COURTS

THE scene is the Night Court in Manhattan. The bridgeman calls the case and the complaining witness is sworn in. He is a detective employed in an automat. He charges that the defendant put slugs into one of the machines in the restaurant.

"Now, just a minute," says the magistrate. "Did you actually see him put the slugs in the machine?"

The detective shakes his head. "I saw a hand inserting something in the machine and watched the thing fall through the glass slot. When it got to the bottom, I saw it was a slug. I looked up at the defendant's face. He took his piece of pie and started to walk to a table. Then I called my partner, the other detective in the place. He looked at the slug and looked at the man walking to the table. We let the man finish his pie and then went over and nabbed him. We found more slugs in his pocket. Here they are."

"Let me see them," says the magistrate. He examines them. And then he says, after a minute: "How much time elapsed between the moment the slug dropped to the bottom of the machine and the moment you looked up into the man's face?"

"A second or two."

"There was nobody else near the machine? No chance of a mistake?"

"No."

"How soon after did your 'partner' come over?"

"The defendant was still walking to a table."

"There was no one else walking around—no other customers?"

"No. It was nine o'clock. We don't do much business then."

"Is your 'partner' in the courtroom?"

"Yes. He's right over there." The detective points.

The "partner" is questioned in much the same fashion by the magistrate. Their stories agree in every detail. Finally the defendant, a bold young man, is called forward. The usual preliminaries are gone through. Then the magistrate says:

"You've heard the testimony of these two witnesses. What have you got to say?"

"I didn't do it, Governor," says the defendant.

"You didn't put slugs in the machine?"

"I don't know nothing about it."

"What about the slugs in your pocket? Do you deny that you had them?"

"I had them all right. But I didn't put none in the machine."

"You had the slugs but you didn't put any in the machine. Is that correct?"

"Yea. I don't know nothing about it."

"Very well, then," says the magistrate. "I'll have to hold you for Special Sessions."

Ten minutes have been spent questioning the witnesses and the defendant. All the facts are before the magistrate. He has conducted what almost amounts to a trial. Nothing is left but for him to decide whether or not the defendant is guilty.

But as our laws now stand, putting slugs into a machine is a misdemeanor, triable by the Court of Special Sessions. Regardless of how clear the evidence against the defendant may be in such a case, the magistrate cannot convict and sentence him. The case must be held for the Court of Special Sessions and tried all over again by three judges.

The question which common sense asks is why three judges are able to decide a case of this kind any more justly than one magistrate.

The tendency in the last twenty years has been toward a widening of the jurisdiction of the magistrates. In 1909, in order to relieve the calendar of Special Sessions, the Page Commission suggested that two magistrates be designated to sit as Special Sessions judges until the calendar of bailed cases was reduced to three hundred or until December 1, 1909.[1] This measure was a purely temporary one. When the act of 1910 was drawn it "did not contemplate the exercise of Special Sessions jurisdiction by a magistrate except perhaps in the isolated instances of taking pleas of guilty in cruelty to animals and motor vehicle cases and in cases of violation of the Sanitary Code of the City of New York."[2]

In 1915 the Inferior Criminal Courts Act was amended,[3] giving the magistrates power to sit as Special Sessions judges in certain specified misdemeanors.[4] It had

[1] *Final Report of the Commission to Inquire into Courts of Inferior Criminal Jurisdiction . . .*, p. 6.

[2] Cobb, *Inferior Criminal Courts Act* (annotated), pp. 61–62.

[3] Laws of 1915, chap. 531, art. IIIA: Courts of Special Sessions Held by City Magistrates. *Ibid.*, art. VA: The Municipal Term.

[4] Cobb, *op. cit.*, sec. 44, p. 70: "*Procedure.* Whenever a defendant is "arraigned before a city magistrate for an offense which may be tried by "a court of special sessions held by a city magistrate, such city magis-

become necessary to relieve the Court of Special Sessions of some of its work, and "as lesser misdemeanors had always to be held in bail, however small, to answer in Special Sessions, grave hardship was caused to the ignorant and poverty stricken who were often locked up several days on some trivial charge while awaiting trial."[5]

The committee on reorganization of the magistrates' courts, in their report, which appeared shortly before the *Seabury Report,* recommended that magistrates be allowed to dispose of misdemeanors where a plea of guilty is entered. Judge Seabury went many steps farther and proposed that the illogical separation between the work of the two inferior courts in the trial of misdemeanors be wiped out. He recommended the abolition of the existing magistrates' courts, the Court of Special Sessions, and the Children's Court and their consolidation in a newly created Court of Special Sessions, with many divisions or "terms."[6]

From the standpoint of economy, this plan is admirable. It is obvious that consolidation of the three inferior

"trate after taking the information and depositions and the statement of "the defendant in relation thereto, or his waiver, may with the consent of "the defendant, after informing him of his right to be tried by three jus- "tices at the court of special sessions provided for in articles two and "three hereof, unless objection is made in behalf of the department in "charge of the prosecution for a violation of a code, rule or order of "such department, or in any other case by the district attorney, proceed "to hold a court of special sessions and try and determine such action "upon the information taken by the magistrate and the plea of the de- "fendant taken thereto by such court of special sessions and shall exer- "cise with regard thereto all the powers and jurisdiction of the court of "special sessions provided for in articles two and three hereof and may "from time to time adjourn such trial."

Misdemeanors triable by magistrates—see pp. 66–70, incl.

[5] Cobb, *op. cit.,* p. 62. For further explanation of how magistrates came to sit as Special Sessions justices, see pp. 62–66, incl.

[6] *Seabury Report,* pp. 182–183.

criminal courts into a single organization having separate
terms and headed by a conscientious and efficient chief
justice would result in a vast saving. The force could be
cut by a third and overlapping duties eliminated without
undue exertion by anyone.[7]

But even more important than the question of economy
is the basic common sense of the recommendation. Judge
Seabury asks

. . . whether there is any reason why the cases now held for
trial before three Justices at Special Sessions should not be tried

[7] *Seabury Report,* pp. 165–168. There are three separate inferior criminal court systems in New York City. By the end of 1932, $2,102,852 in
salaries will have been paid to the 671 employees of the magistrates'
courts; the 157 employees in the Children's Court will have received
$539,400; and there will have been a total pay roll of $554,200 in the
Court of Special Sessions, distributed among 119 employees. The total
cost to the taxpayers will have been $3,186,452 for salaries alone.

The magistrates are presided over by a chief, who receives $15,000 an-
nually and who has a secretary and a confidential clerk. The 49 magistrates are paid an aggregate amount of $588,000 a year. Then there are
a chief clerk and a deputy chief clerk, 37 clerks of court, 43 clerks, 89
assistant court clerks, 46 court stenographers, 40 interpreters, 182 court
attendants, 3 telephone operators, 3 messengers, a chief probation officer and 5 deputies, 107 probation officers, a clerical staff, a fingerprinting staff, etc.

The personnel of the Children's Court is headed by a chief justice,
who receives $17,500 a year and is provided with a secretary. There are
seven associate justices being paid $122,500 annually. There are propor-
tionately fewer clerks, etc., but the titles are just as varied with the addition of three psychologists, three medical examiners, and a laboratory
director.

In the Court of Special Sessions, in addition to the $18,000 chief jus-
tice, there are fifteen associate justices, with the usual clerks and stenographers, augmented by the addition of two prison matrons and an opinion clerk.

It appears that our courts are greatly overstaffed. There are three and
one-half times as many judges in the criminal courts of Manhattan as in
Detroit, and the population of the former is only one-fourth greater than
that of the latter city. Furthermore, conclusive proof of this overstaffing
is given by the fact that the judges and employees work only a few
hours each day and are not continuously occupied even then.

and disposed of by a single justice of the proposed new Court of Special Sessions, instead of the present procedure under which the magistrate, after sitting sometimes for days in a preliminary hearing, is required to send the case into Special Sessions to be tried all over again.[8]

The jurisdiction of the magistrates' courts has already been described. The jurisdiction of the Court of Special Sessions includes the trial of misdemeanors held for this court by the magistrates and the hearing of appeals from convictions in the lower court.

In 1931 the judges of the Court of Special Sessions acquitted or dismissed 3,393 defendants out of a total of 13,203 brought before them. Of the 9,810 convicted, 4,308 pleaded guilty. These latter, comprising approximately one-third of all the cases brought into Special Sessions, could have been sentenced as fairly and with much less waste of time and money by the magistrate who held the preliminary hearing. Under the present system

. . . in each of these 4,308 cases the time of the magistrate was taken up with arraignments, fixing of bail and, in many cases, holding preliminary hearings, and then there had to be informations filed in Special Sessions, new arraignments and bail in that Court, and then the three justices of the Court of Special Sessions had to sit in imposing sentence.[9]

There is nothing occult about the trial of misdemeanors which would place them beyond the comprehension of a competent magistrate who is able daily to dispose of offenses of an equally serious nature.

Objections to the plan that the magistrates try misdemeanors cannot be made on the ground that they would allow too many acquittals, because a magistrate now has

[8] *Seabury Report*, p. 172.   [9] *Ibid.*, pp. 172, 173.

the power to discharge prisoners after preliminary hearings if he feels that the prosecution has not made out a case against them.

Nor can it be argued that the responsibility for sentencing these defendants would be too great to rest in a single judge. One has only to read the reports[10] of the two courts to discover the answer to this argument.

The lesson to be derived . . . is that in practice the Court of Special Sessions imposes sentences no more severe than those which magistrates are authorized to impose in cases which they have the jurisdiction to try, showing that no argument against permitting a single judge to try and determine the cases which are now tried and determined in Special Sessions can be built upon the contention that the punishment which may be inflicted therefor is too severe to put within the power of a single magistrate. The magistrate at present has jurisdiction (Inferior

[10] "These show that out of 9,895 persons sentenced in the Courts of "Special Sessions throughout the City during that year, sentence was "suspended in 4,935 cases, 1,795 defendants were merely fined, 144 were "committed only because of their inability to pay the fine, and 1,770 "were sent to the Workhouse, the City Prison or the County Jail. Of "these 1,770 imprisonment sentences, 764 were for a month or less, 250 "were for two months, 303 for three months, 226 for four months, 10 for "five months, and 217 for six months; 932 were sent to the Penitentiary, "which means that the length of their imprisonment would be deter- "mined by the Parole Board, and 298 were sent to Reformatories. Of the "1,795 defendants on whom fines were imposed by all the Courts of "Special Sessions in the City of New York, 874 were paid in New York "County. Of these 874—the figure for New York County being used be- "cause we have no information as to the classification of the fines in the "other counties—797, or upwards of 90%, were in the amount of $25 or "less. One was $50, 9 were $100 each, 1 was $200, 3 were $250 each, and "4 were $500 each. The fines imposed in the magistrates' courts are fre- "quently greater than the vast majority of those imposed in Special Ses- "sions and the fines in the Municipal Term of the magistrates' court "reach as high as any imposed in the Court of Special Sessions and on "the average are probably greater than those imposed in the Court of "Special Sessions." *Seabury Report,* p. 173.

Criminal Courts Act, Sections 88, 88-a and 89) to sentence females in certain cases to correctional institutions for as long as
three years, in other cases to sentence males or females to the
Workhouse or the jail in Richmond County for six months. In
certain cases he may, in addition, impose a fine as high as $50
with alternative provisions for one day's imprisonment for each
dollar of the fine. Under Section 93 of the Inferior Criminal
Courts Act the magistrate may, in certain cases, send defendants convicted before him to the New York City Reformatory
for an indeterminate term which may last as long as three
years, subject to the action of the Parole Board.

Thus it is clear that we now invest magistrates, at least in
certain cases, with power to impose sentences greater than those
usually imposed by the Court of Special Sessions in the cases
which the magistrates must now send to [it] for trial. [So] far
as fines are concerned, the situation is the same.

It is, therefore, difficult to see any logical reason for the
classification under which magistrates are now permitted to
hear and determine some cases which come before them, while
in other cases, although they have authority to dismiss after
hearing the prosecution's case, they are required, if they do not
dismiss, to send the case into Special Sessions, there to be tried
all over again.[11]

It is, however, possible that a few cases might require a
hearing before three judges. Judge Seabury suggests as a
provision for such an exigency that "any case coming before a single justice could, upon the certificate of the presiding justice, issued after a showing of reasonable necessity therefor, be transferred for trial, in the first instance,
to the term presided over by three justices."[12]

As for the appellate work now done by the Court of
Special Sessions, Judge Seabury points out that it is not

[11] *Ibid.*, pp. 173–175.   [12] *Ibid.*, p. 171.

heavy.[13] He would provide a term of the new Court of Special Sessions

. . . presided over by three justices, which would hear the appeals from other terms of the court presided over by one justice. Whenever this Appellate part would be without sufficient business to keep it occupied, the President Justice would designate each of these justices to hold a term of the court over which he alone would preside.[14]

In short,

. . . there is no basis in logic or common sense for continuing the present practice, under which defendants are arraigned before magistrates, bail is fixed by the magistrates, and preliminary hearings are held before the magistrates, only to be followed, in the cases where the magistrates do not discharge the defendants, by the filing of informations, new arraignments, new fixing of bail, new pleadings and new trials of the same defendants before another court.[15]

So far as Judge Seabury has tried to eliminate waste by combining Special Sessions and the magistrates' courts, he has had the approval of social agencies and bar associations. There is another step in his recommendation which did not meet with such universal approbation—namely, the inclusion of the Children's Court in the plan of consolidation.

There are two questions to be considered at this point. First, shall the Children's Court and the Family Court be combined? Second, shall this combination take place

[13] "In 1931, the appellate part in the First Judicial Department dis-"posed of 156 appeals throughout the entire year, and the appellate part "in the Second Judicial Department disposed of 89 appeals in the entire "year, making a total of 245 for the entire year throughout the whole of "the City of New York." *Seabury Report*, p. 171.

[14] *Ibid.*, p. 171.   [15] *Ibid.*, pp. 176, 177.

within the proposed Court of Special Sessions or shall a separate court be constituted?

Regarding the first question, there is relatively little controversy. At the present time we have a Family Court judge at $12,000 a year dealing with the parents; a Children's Court judge at $17,500 a year dealing with children and through them with the parents; and a Supreme Court judge at $25,000 a year dealing with legal separations, divorces, and writs of habeas corpus for the custody of the children. Such a situation is obviously ridiculous. Besides the economic waste involved, social readjustment requires that the family be considered as a whole.[16] Judge Hoffman of the Court of Domestic Relations in Cincinnati says:

Owing to the divided jurisdiction characteristic of many of the so-called courts of domestic relations, their work shows lit-

---

[16] The Family Court, as it is now constituted, is largely a collection agency. Originally, the cases now heard there were mingled with the heterogeneous complaints in the district courts. Largely through the interest of social agencies, a specialized court was formed under art. v, sec. 74, of the Inferior Criminal Courts Act to handle these domestic problems. The jurisdiction of this court is limited to nonsupport cases and its chief concern is that "the taxpayer shall not be burdened with abandoned "families, destitute old people, and invalids who have immediate families "capable of supporting them" (*Seabury Report*, p. 210). It cannot grant divorces. This is a function of the Supreme Court. But it can offer to poor families a means of adjusting their immediate financial problems and so may keep them from becoming public charges.

Strictly speaking, the charge of cruelty may not be taken as grounds for action in the Family Court. However, art. v, sec. 74, of the Inferior Criminal Courts Act includes in its definition of a disorderly person one "who, by reason of his conduct, or his neglect or refusal to provide his "wife or children with the necessaries of life, renders it unsafe, improper "or impossible for them to live with him, by reason of which they are "without adequate support or in danger of becoming a burden upon the "public." This gives the court leeway in cases which are not based wholly on nonsupport, and cruelty may not be taken into account in allowing separate maintenance.

tle improvement upon the procedure of the ordinary court.
. . . It is a common complaint that the court of domestic relations and the juvenile court work at cross purposes. . . . No
court having jurisdiction in but one or two phases of family
trouble can function effectively, even though called a court of
domestic relations.[17]

The major argument occurs when the question of
whether the Children's Court and the Family Court
should be placed within the proposed Court of Special Sessions is considered. The Children's Court was at one time
a part of the Court of Special Sessions. As a result of the
efforts of social agencies, it became a separate court in
1924.[18] The agencies then desired to go a step farther and
take domestic relation cases out of the criminal-courts
system. A bill for this purpose was presented to the Legislature during the legislative session of 1932. It failed to
pass. While this bill presented certain admirable social
features, from the standpoint of efficient administration it
had weaknesses inherent in a compromise measure. Moreover, as Judge Seabury pointed out, this bill offered nothing unusual with respect to either organization or control.
It would simply have laid open a rich source of patronage
and influence to be tapped by the ruling political party.

Judge Seabury saw no reason for the establishment of a
separate Family Court. He recommended that instead the
Family Court should be made a special term of the newly
created Court of Special Sessions.

While the social agencies are, for the most part, willing
to see the jurisdiction of the Children's Court extended to
include family cases, they are violently opposed to putting

[17] *Trends of Probation*, p. 3.
[18] Laws of 1924, chap. 254—Amend. to art. vi, sec. 18, of the Consti-
tution.

children's cases back into the criminal-courts system. They argue that the problems of children and their parents are purely "social" and that they should be concentrated in a separate noncriminal tribunal. To handle them in a consolidated criminal court would, they urge, result in a retrogression to the standards of a decade ago.

This would hardly seem a logical conclusion. The mere physical incorporation of the Children's Court in the newly constituted Court of Special Sessions need not imply retrogression. The children's cases could be heard in their present building by specially assigned magistrates. Social agencies would be just as free to concentrate their efforts upon this special term of the court as they now are on the separate court.[19] Our knowledge of the handling of present social problems has progressed rapidly in recent years. We now know far more about the problems involved in juvenile delinquency than was formerly known. It is absurd to argue that such a consolidation as that proposed here would *ipso facto* cause any diminution of that knowledge or make more difficult the work of social agencies in applying it. Finally, the argument that the Family Court and Children's Court should be combined into a separate court, on the ground that these courts, as distinguished from the magistrates' courts, deal with "social problems," is untenable. Do not practically all of the cases which come before the magistrates involve social problems? Must each problem group be segregated into a separate and distinct court with all the expense and ineffi-

---

[19] It has also been argued that a stigma attaches to trial in a criminal court. In view of the fact that a child is *not* found guilty of a crime but is merely adjudged delinquent, it would hardly seem that any stigma of crime should be involved just because the children's term was administered by the same board which administered the inferior criminal courts.

ciency which such a plan would entail? If beggars, vagrants, peddlers, and the rest do not present social problems, what sort of problems do they present?

The expedient thing to do is to consolidate the three inferior criminal and quasi-criminal courts in the City of New York into a single court, saving the advantages which come from separate specialized courts by having such functions performed in separate terms of the court, while securing the benefits of unification and centralized control under a single, strong presiding head.[20]

However, the case for consolidation need not stand or fall on the inclusion of the Children's Court. Improvement in efficiency can be obtained without its incorporation in the criminal-courts system. If the time is not ripe for such a change to take place, then the jurisdiction of the Children's Court should be extended so that all family problems may be studied in a single court.

The consolidation of the three courts of inferior jurisdiction under one administrative head and the centralization of the widely scattered district courts of Manhattan into a centrally located building would create a gigantic organization within which, it must be repeated, it would be necessary to provide for specialization of interest by dividing the court into separate terms. One of the most important of these terms would be the special felony term proposed by Judge Seabury.[21]

In the magistrates' courts system at the present time, one of the special branches is known as the Homicide Court. In the boroughs of Manhattan and the Bronx, this court heard 1,124 cases. Approximately 72 per cent of the cases involved automobile accidents.

[20] *Seabury Report*, p. 180.   [21] *Ibid.*, p. 208.

The segregation of homicide cases in a special term is commendable. On the same principle, other felony cases should be heard in a separate court. At the present time, preliminary hearings in felony cases other than homicide are scattered throughout the district courts.

In the year 1930, 10,772 preliminary hearings in felony cases, exclusive of homicide cases, were heard in the courts of Manhattan and the Bronx, of which 9,056 were in Manhattan and 1,716 were in the Bronx.[22]

It is important to note that the magistrates dismissed 60 per cent of these cases.

As far as reliable comparative statistics are concerned, only one city has a larger proportion, Philadelphia, with 80%, while Chicago is below New York. Throughout the large cities of the country, the proportion of felony charges which are dismissed ranges from 20% to 50%. The proportion dismissed in New York is therefore large and deserves serious consideration. Either the police are charging a great number of persons with serious crimes without adequate evidence, or the magistrates are dismissing well-supported cases without justification. Both factors enter into the large proportion of cases thus handled.[23]

There can be no doubt that felony cases should be examined with great care away from the turmoil and hurry attendant on hearings in the district courts.

Judge Seabury's proposal that the inferior criminal courts of New York be consolidated is bold and sweeping. To achieve it will be difficult. Vast forces of conservatism oppose it. But the need of bringing together a scattered and, as a result, excessively costly machine will be more and more apparent as the need for economy grows. The whole growth of courts in New York City has been un-

[22] *Ibid.*, p. 208.   [23] *Ibid.*, p. 209.

planned and illogical. Politics retains the jobs thus provided with a tenacious hold. The bar looks on with conservative indifference, and social workers see only the interest so important to them. The voice of common sense and economy meanwhile is unheard.

CHAPTER XIII

THE MAGISTRATES THEMSELVES[1]

THE Seabury investigation disclosed all of the factors now so familiar in American inferior criminal courts —brazen frame-ups of innocent people, stealthy bribery, extortion, ignorance, and inefficiency. The stock *dramatis personae* crossed the stage—the careless clerk, the dubious lawyer, the greedy bondsman, the vermiculate fixer, and the rest.

But the most vivid light of the investigation fell upon a number of the magistrates themselves—their fitness for office, the way they were appointed, their conduct on and off the bench, their labyrinthine political connections and obligations. Quite worldly persons, it seemed, had been sitting in seats of magisterial authority. This is the chief issue that arises from the investigation—an issue which must concern all who are interested in the improvement of the administration of justice—for, in the last analysis, judges are responsible for the courts.

There were, and are, of course, magistrates of spirit, ability, and a deep sense of the proprieties. But, on the whole, the magistrates of New York City met their great responsibility with indifference. While there was legal provision for the leadership of a chief magistrate, there was neither the disposition nor the authority for a forceful central direction. The magistrates, so to speak, ran their courts in the plenitude of their own diversities. Those who

---

[1] Part of this chapter is taken from an article of mine published in the *Yale Review*, Vol. XXI, No. 3.

had the taste to do well found the going difficult. Those
with the taste to do badly found little restraint and vast
opportunity.

And who, it may be asked, is responsible for the judges?
Technically, it is the mayor of New York, to whom the
law gives the power of appointment. Two mayors were
nominally responsible for the entire bench as it existed
when the Seabury investigation began. A few survivors of
the days of Gaynor and of Mitchel had continued in office,
and a scattering of good men had been added. But for the
most part, the mayors had been guided by no high ideal of
magisterial fitness. In fact, they had distributed these offices in accordance with the demands of district and borough political leaders, and with certain rough principles of
apportionment, based upon the demands of active racial
or national groups, such as the Steuben Society. In general, this procedure yielded a choice variety of inadequacy. In many cases, the mayor practically indorsed the
district leader's choice, just as the president has come to
indorse senatorial choices in a higher sphere of politics.

The magistrates themselves made no bones of the reasons for their appointment. They had been active in politics, they said; were representatives of some racial or
national interest; had held a long line of subordinate political jobs; had the favor of powerful district leaders—
and the like. It did not occur to those who were examined
to mention intellectual or professional qualifications. A de-
cent modesty, perhaps, restrained this portion of the explanation.

Magistrate August Dreyer stated that when his law practice
dwindled, he explained his predicament to his district leader
and demanded "recognition" for his eighteen years of work for

the Party. His leader agreed, and in due time the appointment came. The Magistrate testified:

"I was a Democrat, and I belonged to the organization about eighteen years. This theatrical practice was going downhill fast, upon the ground that the National Vaudeville Artists started, which was taking care of all differences, which were settled by arbitration by the National Vaudeville Artists. The Equity was started with Mr. Paul Turner there, and they took care of all their differences, so that really what was left in the theatrical business was nothing but to take a divorce suit, and I felt that I did not want to take any divorce suits. I simply went around to my organization at the time, which was the 25th, and I spoke to George Donnellan, who was leader at the time, he is a General Sessions Court Judge. I said: 'Listen,—' he was not a judge at the time—I said: 'Listen, George, for eighteen years I never knew what a reference or receivership or guardianship was, never got a 5-cent piece, never held a political office. Here is my position, my practice absolutely gone, the National Vaudeville Artists settle their differences with the Actors' Equity who settle their differences through Paul Turner, what am I going to do? I think I am entitled to get a judgeship for all I have done for eighteen years, spent my time three times a week, never asked for anything, never bothered about references,' I said, 'I think I am entitled to some recognition.' Well, he says: 'I will be honest with you, you are entitled to some recognition. You never annoyed me or bothered me, other lawyers were after me to see what I could get for them.' I said: 'I think I am entitled to it.' "

When Magistrate Frothingham's place became vacant, the appointment went to a resident of his "district." Magistrate Dreyer began to lose hope; things looked "blue," but his leader encouraged him. "Don't give up hopes," he said, and finally Magistrate Dreyer went to see Mayor Hylan.

"* * * and I said: 'I am a Democrat, and here you have been a classmate of mine, and when the time came you asked me to do a favor and I did it for you. Many an afternoon I stayed in and told you just what happened. Now, there is an opportunity for you to help me.' Well, the result was I did not get any help. I waited and waited, and finally one day, I went down and I said: 'We will have it over with with the organization.' I wanted to know if my name was being sent down, and what was happening, if I was being fooled around with."

Subsequently, Mayor Hylan advised Mr. Dreyer that he was going to appoint him a magistrate, and he did.

Edward Weil, who, until his recent death, was a city magistrate, was quite frank in stating that he got his appointment as a reward for his long service to the Democratic Party, after threatening to get out of the party unless he got "recognition." His testimony reads:

"Q. How did you happen to be appointed magistrate? A. Well, I also spoke to Cosgrove—let me go back a minute. There was a vacancy for municipal court judge in our district which subsequently was filled by Judge Leary. There was a vacancy at the time. There was a municipal court judgeship to be filled in my district and I went to Commissioner Cosgrove and told him I would like to be the organization candidate for that position, for that judgeship. He said he would present my name.

Q. To whom? A. For consideration, to the executive committee of Tammany Hall. The night that the executive session was held I had quite an argument with my leader because I heard he had not presented my name but had presented the name of someone else and for two weeks I didn't go around to my organization and I didn't speak to Mr. Cosgrove. I met him on the street one day and we had it out and at that time I told him that I felt my political career was at an end, I was growing old in service and if I was not to receive any further recognition I would like to know it now because I could devote my time much more profitably in my profession, and if I was not going to get recognition I would like to get out of the organization. He told me to be patient and made excuses, and one thing and another, and later on, of course, when Judge Tobias died I was the logical candidate for this job.

Q. Why were you the logical candidate? A. Because I felt I should have had a job before Tobias had. I had been of much more service to the organization than Tobias. For twenty odd years I was a public speaker enunciating the principles of my organization in the streets, using my voice during campaigns, spending my evenings at the clubhouse trying to help those in the district after I became an attorney by being a free eleemosynary institution around there for years and rendering much more service than I felt I should have rendered for the organization. I will say this now, I have always felt and I frequently complained that I have not been adequately rewarded for my work for the organization. I feel that I should have been elevated to a much higher bench many years ago. I complained about that—

Q. To Commissioner Cosgrove? A. Yes, and when Tobias passed away and there was mentioned another man for my district, I said I should have it before he and I spoke to Commissioner Cosgrove and he spoke to Mayor Hylan and I have been advised Mayor Hylan inquired as to my work in the district attorney's office and evidently he was very well satisfied, and appointed me.

Q. Who took you down to Mayor Hylan? A. Mr. Cosgrove.

Q. Was that the first time that you called on the Mayor, with Mr. Cosgrove? A. That is the first time I have ever seen Mayor Hylan.

Q. You were then sworn in? A. No.

Q. What happened then? A. I was a member of the district attorney's staff at the time and Commissioner Cosgrove called me up and he greeted me as 'Judge.' I said, 'You have made a mistake,' and he said, 'No, meet me and go down to be sworn in tomorrow morning,' and I met him and went down and was sworn in the following morning."

In the case of former Magistrate McQuade, we have this testimony from the Magistrate himself:

"Q. Now, in your own words, Judge, will you state to the Court just how you came to be appointed magistrate? A. Well,

I was active around in politics, and so on, and I had the endorsement of Mr. Hyde, who was City Chamberlain at the time, and Senator Sullivan interested himself in me.

Q. Senator who? A. Sullivan.

Q. Tim Sullivan? A. Yes, sir."

*   *   *   *   *   *   *   *   *   *

"Q. Just how did you manage to get this new appointment? A. Why, I asked Mr. Murphy, who was the head of Tammany Hall, if he saw fit to give me the long term. Of course, I asked him to speak to the Mayor, if he would, at that time Hylan, and he did, and Hylan gave me the long term."

Magistrate Maurice Gottlieb described the circumstances leading up to his appointment as magistrate in these words:

"Q. Now, will you tell us a little more about the circumstances of your appointment to the bench, Judge? Was the appointment made upon the recommendation of Judge Mahoney or was it merely that he sponsored you through your district leader and through organization circles? A. Well, I can explain that. I have been a member of Tammany Hall over 40 years. I have lived in Yorkville for 30 odd years. My folks lived in Yorkville 50 years. I am a member of the Osceola Club for over 20 years. Judge Mahoney—I was very active with Judge Mahoney in helping to elect him leader, that must be 12 or 15 years ago, and I might say that when he became leader I was fairly well known as his right-hand bower. I took care of things politically. I helped get the house that our clubhouse is in. I have done things to help build up our organization in our district.

Q. Where is that clubhouse? A. 1019 Madison Ave. Then when Jerry was elected to the bench, well, we elected a new leader, Frank Briarly. He is a man who has been sick for five years with arthritis and never has been able to walk for five years. So that I stood back of him and helped him maintain his organization. Judge Rittenberg, my predecessor, was very sick. I had known Moe Rittenberg for probably 30 or 35 years. A call came for a man to fill his place, as temporary magistrate. I spoke to Briarly. There seemed to be no logical man for the position but myself. After all, I had spent money, time and help to build up the organization.

Q. Pardon me. Had Judge Rittenberg come from your district? A. Yes, from my district. The job, as we call it, really belonged to our district. That is a rule, sometimes broken, but I spoke to Briarly, and I spoke to Judge Mahoney."

Magistrate Earl A. Smith, after testifying that his district leader was Joseph McCormick, . . . continued:

"I had spoken to Mr. Whalen before, and Mr. McCormick told me that Mr. Whalen had spoken to him and recommended me for appointment, and the first thing I knew I was called down to Tammany Hall, I met Mr. Murphy, that was my last year in the Assembly, that was sometime before the appointment, the appointment was June 30th, I think there was to be one, and I was not eligible, being a member of the Assembly, my term did not expire until December 31st. He stated he might be able to do something for me later. The next year I did not run, and then Judge House was ill, in 1920, and so I was appointed rather unexpectedly."

Former Magistrate Henry M. R. Goodman gave the following testimony with reference to the circumstances of his appointment:

"Q. Now, can you tell us on whose recommendation or endorsement you obtained the appointment? A. Judge Friedlander. He was the president justice of the municipal court at the time. There was a sort of a steering committee or advisory committee.

Q. He was the chairman of this steering committee of the Democratic organization, do you mean? A. I don't know if you would call him the chairman. I assume that he was the man that represented the district.

Q. At any event, he presented your name? A. He did.
Q. To whom? A. To Mayor Hylan.

Q. Was it at your suggestion? A. It was. You see, I have to take you back, if you permit me.

Q. Certainly. A. It was some time prior to that when I suggested, or I had been asking for an appointment. If I could get a temporary appointment. I was in the district attorney's office and I did not desire a temporary appointment then—

Q. Suggested by whom? A. I suggested it and Sam Marks, I think, had spoken to Mr. Murphy. That was my information at that time. So when he died—

Q. Mr. Murphy of Manhattan? A. Charles F. Murphy. So that when he died, Sam Marks—when this vacancy occurred I spoke to Judge Friedlander about it and whether he spoke to Mr. Murphy or to Mayor Hylan I don't know, but I do know he spoke to Mr. Hylan because I had an interview with Mayor Hylan. I assume it took the usual routine.

Q. What is the usual routine? A. My impression was that the name was submitted to the county leader by the district organization and then submitted to the mayor.

*   *   *   *   *   *   *   *   *   *

Q. Coming down to your reappointment in 1929, who suggested that? A. I don't know what you mean by who suggested it.

Q. Did you apply for it yourself, did it come spontaneously from the Mayor, or did someone intercede in your behalf? A. I assumed it came spontaneously from the Mayor. I never even discussed it at the time. That was my assumption, but I found out my leader sponsored it.

*   *   *   *   *   *   *   *   *   *

Q. You said you had since learned that your leader had interested himself in your reappointment. You said nothing to him about it at the time? A. Of course I did.

Q. You did? A. Certainly. I spoke to him time and again, and he said 'Don't worry about it; it is all right.'

Q. Then you naturally assumed he was interesting himself in it? A. Well, I say I have since found out that he did. I assumed he did, too.

Q. I understood you had assumed it came spontaneously until you heard this. A. No. My impression was—the first I knew was a 'phone call from the mayor's office.

Q. About when was that? A. On the day I was appointed, to appear at the mayor's office at 4 o'clock, and when I arrived there I found my leader there. Up to that time I had assumed that it was just a call in the natural and regular way from the Mayor.

Q. Did he tell you at that time that you were to be reappointed or did he swear you in? A. Yes, that same day.

Q. Do you know what Mr. Solomon (the district leader) did in your behalf in that connection? A. Nothing, excepting to probably speak to Mr. Curry. I am only assuming this.

Q. You don't know that he did? A. I assume he did.

Q. Did he ever tell you he did? A. He might have. I didn't attach so much importance to it to go into it. I assumed it came in the regular course.

Q. What did he tell you about it? A. He kept telling me, 'Don't worry; you will be reappointed.'

* * * * * * * * * *

Q. Now, apart from your leader, did you ask anyone else to intercede for you for your reappointment? A. No, sir.

Q. You did not discuss it with anyone except Mr. Solomon? A. That is all."

Magistrate Silbermann testified that some years prior to his appointment, when a vacancy was created by the elevation of Magistrate Schulz to the Surrogate's Court

"I asked Mr. Murphy [Arthur H. Murphy, Democratic county leader of Bronx County] whether he would assist me in getting his unexpired term.

* * * * * * * * * *

Q. What did Mr. Murphy say to that? A. He said he couldn't.

Q. What? A. He said he could not.

Q. He could not assist you? A. Right.

Q. Did he give any reason for his inability to do so? A. No.

Q. Well, did you do anything else towards getting this unexpired term of Surrogate Schulz? A. I did not.

Q. You dropped it? A. I did.

Q. Did you drop it because you realized that without Mr. Murphy's support you could not get it? A. That is right."

Magistrate Silbermann was appointed in 1920:

"After my appointment * * * I learned that the Mayor decided to appoint a Hebrew from the Bronx and he communicated with Mr. Murphy and asked him to suggest a name of some Hebrew.

Q. That is, Arthur Murphy? A. Yes, Arthur H. Murphy.

Q. Yes, we are talking about Mr. Arthur H. Murphy. A. That he should suggest some Hebrew from the Bronx as a temporary magistrate in place of the late Magistrate Matthew B. Breen, who then was ill and who was a Bronx resident at that time. * * *

Q. Now, Judge Silbermann, what I am anxious to have you state, if you will, and if you know, is just why you, Jesse Silbermann, were selected to be magistrate up there rather than some other Hebrew up there in the Bronx who was a member of the bar in good standing. A. I have stated the reasons. I was active in the party; I was chairman of the Law Committee of the Democratic party up there prior to my appointment; I was active in politics."

Magistrate Silbermann held temporary appointments for about 2½ years. He looked forward to getting an appointment for a full ten year term.

"Q. Now, what did you do towards getting that? A. I saw my local leader, James W. Brown. I told him my term was expiring and I asked him to go up to see the county leader then, the present county leader, Edward J. Flynn, and ask him whether he was going to, or whether he would recommend me for the appointment for the full term of ten years.

Q. Is that the substance of your conversation with Mr. Brown? A. Yes, sir.

Q. What did Mr. Brown say? A. He said that he would go up to see Mr. Flynn.

Q. Well, did he come back and report to you as to the result of his conversation with Mr. Flynn? A. Yes.

Q. Tell us what he said to you? A. He said Flynn was taking it under advisement, he didn't see any objection to my appointment and that he would let me know.

Q. Well, did he subsequently let you know? A. He did.

Q. And what did he say? A. He said I was to be appointed.

Q. That is Mr. Brown telling you this? A. Yes.

Q. Is that all he said? A. Yes."

Magistrate Brodsky testified that a couple of months before his appointment he spoke to his district leader, James J. Hagan, about his desire to hold a public office.

"I spoke to Mr. Hagan and I mentioned the fact that I had rendered services to the organization and that I felt that I ought to get some recognition, that up to that time I had received none, that I had worked hard, and he said that if I waited a while, the first opportunity he would get, he felt I was entitled to it by reason of my experience at the bar and the work that I had done, that I had earned some recognition, and that is the substance of the conversation we had. * * *

Later on I understood there was to be a vacancy, a temporary vacancy, and Mr. Hagan said to me, 'Louis, there is to be a temporary vacancy; how would you like to take it?'

Q. Temporary vacancy where? A. For a magistrate. The judge then sitting on the bench was sick and there was to be this vacancy. I said I thought I would like to take it temporarily and he said that he would urge my appointment to the party. * * * I meant by that that he would urge it to the party, to the powers is what I really meant. * * * And then he did urge it and eventually I was appointed a temporary magistrate. * * *

Q. What do you know about his urging? A. Excepting that he told me so.

Q. What did he tell you? A. He told me he had presented my name.

Q. To whom? A. To the leaders of Tammany Hall; to the leader of Tammany Hall."

Magistrate Brodsky was then appointed for two successive thirty-day terms.

" * * *

Q. Now, then, you have told us about your original appointment. Coming now to your reappointment last year, what did you do in order to get that appointment? A. I continued—substantially nothing.

Q. Substantially nothing? A. Excepting to talk to Mr. Marsh Ingram.

Q. Who is he? A. He is the present leader who succeeded Mr. James J. Hagan.

Q. You mean in the district where you reside? A. In the district where I reside.

*   *   *   *   *   *   *   *   *   *

Q. Well, what did he do? A. I assume he presented my name to the leader of Tammany Hall.

Q. Did he tell you that he would? A. Yes, he said he would."

Magistrate Norris enjoyed something of an advantage over other aspirants to the magistracy. She was not obliged to intercede with any district leader; she was herself a co-leader of the Tenth Assembly District, the other leader being George W. Olvany.[2]

Now, the notions of district leaders as to magisterial fitness were quaintly direct. Secure in a sort of medieval proprietorship over the little principality of their districts, many leaders, it was shown, maintained an arrogant au-

[2] *Seabury Report*, pp. 31–44.

thority over those whom they had elevated to the magistracy.

Former Magistrate Goodman, after having testified that his District Leader was Alderman William Solomon, continued:

"Q. Has Alderman Solomon ever interceded with you with reference to any cases pending before you in the magistrates' courts? A. He has.

Q. How frequently? A. Whenever I would be sitting within the district which takes in his district.

*   *   *   *   *   *   *   *   *   *

Q. How frequently has he come to see you in reference to cases? A. I can't recall. Sometimes he may come in and sometimes he would call me at the house; sometimes he talked to me at the club.

Q. And sometimes at court in chambers? A. Well, he would come in chambers sometimes.

*   *   *   *   *   *   *   *   *   *

Q. Has Alderman Solomon ever spoken to you about cases when you were in other courts? A. He may have.

Q. Well, he may have or may not have? A. Well, I will say he did.

Q. On a number of occasions? A. Yes, I guess he has.

Q. In the same way, that is, either by telephoning you or speaking to you at the club or coming to see you at chambers? A. In the same manner.

Q. And I suppose other district leaders have also spoken to you about cases? A. They have.

Q. Any particular ones that you recall? A. I can simply answer that by saying I have seen a lot of people in chambers, district leaders and others.

Q. Yes, but I am asking about district leaders. A. I can't recall anyone in particular.

Q. Do you mean that you don't recall any leader that ever spoke to you? A. Oh, no. I say, I can't distinguish one from the other for any particular reason, but I might say that they all have spoken to me, or mostly all. I can cover it that way.

Q. Well, suppose you name some that have spoken to you? A. I have had McMahon, I don't know his first name.

Q. McMahon? A. I think that is his name. I am trying to start off from the lower end of the town. Congressman Sullivan, Ahearn, Dr. Goldenkranz, Commissioner Lazarus, Charlie Kohler, Clarence Neill, Warren Hubbard, Charlie Hussey, Mr. Teddy McKeever, Marsh Ingram, John McCormack—I daresay most of them.

* * * * * * * * * *

Q. Did the Bronx leaders see you also? A. The Bronx leaders did, too.

Q. That means some 30 or 40 leaders, then? A. I just don't know how many, but, as I say, most of them."[3]

One district leader calmly explained before Judge Seabury that in his office as tribune of the people he often spoke to judges in the interest of wayward "children." His answers, drawn out by a series of questions put in a delicately ironical manner, have a touch of droll realism.

Q. And you are stating here under oath, of course, that you don't think you have been to court to see Judge —— more than six times in all the ten years? A. Yes, Sir.

Q. You understand my question? A. I do.

Q. Well, now, were these social calls, these six times? A. No, no.

Q. What was it you went to see Judge —— about? A. Well, some of the neighbors' children get in trouble and I would simply go in and say a kind word for them.

Q. Say a kind word for them? A. Yes: ask the Judge to be as lenient as he possibly could in the matter.

Q. Yes. Now, is that all that you did with Judge —— in court, that if some of the children in the neighborhood got into

[3] *Seabury Report*, pp. 44–46.

trouble you would go in and ask him to be as lenient as he could? A. Yes.

Q. In other words, you interested yourself only in children? A. Oh no, I don't say that. I say when I say the neighbors' children I mean the neighborhood you know.

Q. I think I know what you mean. You mean that if a son or daughter of somebody living in the . . . A. Well, it could be the father just as well.

Q. Now, you see I took just what you told me. So you don't restrict your activities or your intercessions with Judge —— to sons or daughters? A. No, no.

Q. Now let us see. How shall we put it? That if anybody got into trouble you would go to Judge —— to ask him to be lenient; is that it? A. Absolutely.

Q. What would one have to do to gain your intercession with Judge ——? A. Well, some violation of a City ordinance or some minor offense. I never saw any magistrate, Judge —— or anybody else, on a felony or a stick-up or anything of that kind.

Q. Well, I am glad to get that answer, although that was not the answer I was looking for. But you say any other magistrate. Do you mean that you also see other magistrates? A. Absolutely. I have seen many magistrates.

Q. You go into the magistrates' courts, or you have been doing that, rather, and intercede with the magistrate to be lenient with defendants? A. Go in and say a kind word, testify to their good character to the Judge, and tell him you are acquainted— if it is a young fellow, you tell him you are acquainted with the family, and so forth, and you would like him to be as lenient as possible; if you could see your way to help him it would be all right; try to help him.

Q. Then you mean to tell us that you go to intercede for only such people as you know and can testify to their good character? A. Yes, that is right.

(At this point the counsel asked two men to stand, and the district leader said that he believed he had never seen them before.)

Q. Have you ever seen this man before? A. Not to my knowledge.

Q. Did you intercede with Judge —— for either of those two men at any time? A. I believe I did.

Q. Well, you didn't know them, did you? A. No, Sir.

Q. That was an exception to your rule, then? A. Yes.

Q. That you interceded for them although you didn't know them; is that right? A. That is correct.[4]

When one reflects that the "children" of the district leaders, added together, constitute the population of the world's largest city, it is clear how wide a field exists for the exercise of paternal solicitude.

It is not surprising that individuals thus selected should, in conduct both on and off the bench, leave much to be desired. The extent to which the private interests of a judge may have a bearing upon the quality of his service has long been recognized. Plato suggested that whenever magistrates "shall possess private lands and houses, and money, they will become stewards and farmers instead of guardians, and hateful masters instead of allies to other citizens."

The public hearings and the several intermediate and final reports of Judge Seabury to the Appellate Division provide a wealth of illustrations of most unjudgelike conduct on the part of a number of magistrates.

The Appellate Division ordered the removal of Magistrate Silbermann on the basis of several charges. It appeared that he had been influenced "by a person interceding who had been selected solely because of his supposed political influence with the respondent [Magistrate Silber-

---

[4] *Hearings before Samuel Seabury, Referee, In the Matter of the Investigation of the Magistrates' Courts, etc.,* I, 202 *et seq.*

mann] and who was unconnected with the case, uninformed of the facts, and had no knowledge of the character, career or surrounding circumstances of the offender." In another case, the hearings conducted by Magistrate Silbermann disclosed "an unfair attitude toward the complainant and his witnesses and unjudicial conduct on the respondent's part and indicated that he was actuated by improper motives." His conduct in still another case was characterized by the Appellate Division as "unfair and unjudicial."[5]

Magistrate Norris was also removed by the Appellate Division. One of the charges against her involved a change of, or an attempt to change, "official records, in material respects, to the prejudice of the defendant, in an endeavor to eliminate from the record on appeal remarks and rulings by her as a magistrate which presented evidence of unfair and unjudicial conduct at the trial and thus to prevent the substantiation in the appellate court as to what had in truth occurred. . . ." Another charge involved the violation of the constitutional rights of the defendant by placing "a twenty-year-old girl on trial summarily upon her arrest, without a warrant, and without counsel or the opportunity to obtain counsel and [convicting] her without advising her of her rights and on testimony which was obviously insufficient in law and almost exclusively hearsay. . . ."

Still another charge was concerned with the fact that Magistrate Norris owned some shares in a bonding company "with whose representative in the magistrates' court

---

[5] The quotations in the preceding paragraph are taken from the *Order of the Appellate Division Removing Jesse Silbermann from the Office of City Magistrate of the City of New York,* dated July 2, 1931.

she was in close contact and as to whose bonds she was frequently called to act and did act in her judicial capacity."

Finally, it appeared "that for money, Magistrate Norris underwent a course of treatment and sanctioned the exploiting of her judicial position in the advertising of a commercial product contrary to the essential dignity of judicial office." These charges, taken together, showed, in the opinion of the Appellate Division, "unfitness for judicial office and constitute[d] cause for removal."[6]

The charges against these two magistrates were concerned, of course, largely with judicial misconduct on the bench. But in the course of the investigation, it became clear that the issue in New York was most frequently the questionable activities of magistrates off the bench. In four instances, magistrates were so involved.

Magistrate Brodsky, whom a divided court kept in office, had engaged in vast real-estate and stock-market transactions.

Magistrate Vitale was removed, not long before the beginning of the Seabury investigation, because of the acceptance of a large loan from Arnold Rothstein.

The investigation brought to light a number of extraordinary facts with regard to the conduct of Magistrate McQuade. They were as follows:

That during and subsequent to the year 1919, he had been active in sponsoring the stock of a company known as Ajax-Texas Oil Corporation, a speculative venture of questionable merit. Witnesses were examined who had purchased the stock

---

[6] The quotations in the preceding section are taken from the *Order of the Appellate Division Removing Jean H. Norris from the Office of City Magistrate of the City of New York,* dated June 25, 1931.

of that company on the recommendation of Magistrate Mc-
Quade, and in one instance the stock had been transferred
from the Magistrate's own account to the purchaser. The Ajax-
Texas Oil Corporation is no longer in existence, and apparently
those who invested in its securities have suffered a complete
loss;

That the Magistrate had a financial interest in the Havana
Casino, and in the gambling room operated by such Casino. In
the spring of 1920 the Magistrate and certain of his associates
met a representative of the then owner of the Havana Casino
at the Pennsylvania Hotel in New York City, and discussed the
terms of a purchase by the Magistrate and his associates of the
Havana venture. At this conference it was explained that the
gambling room of the Casino was the principal source of profit
in the enterprise. Subsequently representatives of the pur-
chasers were sent to Cuba, where the property of the Casino
was inspected, and when the representatives returned from
Cuba they reported to the Magistrate and his associates, giving
full details as to the venture, and discussing specifically the
profits that might be expected from the gambling room. Thereafter, and late in the year 1920, a company known as Third
Securities Corporation purchased a 70% interest in the Havana
Casino, and in the gambling room of that Casino. Magistrate
McQuade received a 5% participation in the 70% interest thus
purchased. After this purchase, the books relating to the Casino
and to the gambling room were kept in Cuba, but the books of
Third Securities Corporation for the season 1923 to 1924 show
that the corporation advanced $150,000 to the gambling room,
and received back from the gambling room $312,960, or a profit
on its investment of $162,960. Of this sum, $8,148, or 5%,
was paid to Magistrate McQuade. The check for such payment
was drawn by Third Securities Corporation to L. M. Wilson,
and was endorsed by her in favor of Francis X. McQuade. On
August 1, 1924, this check for $8,148 was deposited by the
Magistrate in his account with Irving Bank Columbia Trust
Company;

That Magistrate McQuade, through a dummy, Jack Flanagan, was the owner of stock in a company known as Polo Grounds Athletic Club, Inc., and was active in the management of that company. The club was formed to sponsor prize fights in New York City. On August 5, 1924, a distribution was declared by the Polo Grounds Athletic Club, Inc. A check in the amount of $2,000 was drawn payable to Jack Flanagan, and such check was endorsed by Flanagan in favor of William Hoffman. Thereafter, and on August 8, 1924, the $2,000 check payable to Flanagan and endorsed in favor of Hoffman was deposited to the credit of Magistrate McQuade's account with the Irving Bank Columbia Trust Company. Other payments from the same source likewise found their way into the McQuade account. In some instances such checks were drawn to the order of persons who reduced the checks to cash, and who delivered the cash to Magistrate McQuade.

The evidence before the Referee tended to show that Magistrate McQuade, in addition to being active in the management of Polo Grounds Athletic Club, Inc., was also active in the management of the affairs of National Exhibition Company, owners of the New York Giants Baseball Club.

There was much evidence submitted in reference to Magistrate McQuade tending to show serious defects of temperament manifested in the discharge of his judicial duties. Notwithstanding what has been said about him, it is only fair unequivocally to state that no evidence was received by the Referee showing any act of corruption by Magistrate McQuade in reference to his judicial duties.

It was planned to present at public hearing the facts summarized above and additional facts. Magistrate McQuade was so advised. Thereupon he submitted his resignation to Mayor Walker on the morning of the day set for his public examination, and such resignation was accepted.[7]

Two other magistrates likewise resigned precipitately, just before they were to be examined by Judge Seabury.

[7] *Seabury Report,* pp. 50–52.

Magistrate George W. Simpson sat for many years as presiding magistrate in the commercial frauds division of the magistrates' court.

As the inquiry progressed, complaints were received by the Referee in regard to several cases in which this Magistrate had presided in the commercial frauds court. The persons lodging such complaints had been parties to litigation in that court, and they asserted that there had been irregularities in the disposition of the cases in which they had been involved.

In one case, which concerned the sale of obscene literature, the examination of witnesses by the Referee disclosed the existence of irregularities which, if known to the Magistrate presiding, would have necessitated the filing of charges against him.

Another one of the cases presented resulted in evidence being taken by the Referee which reflected in a very serious way upon the judicial conduct of Magistrate Simpson. Much other evidence was submitted in regard to the conduct of this Magistrate, and he was notified to appear for examination. Shortly thereafter he applied to the Chief Magistrate for a leave of absence for sixty days. The Chief Magistrate consented only to a leave of absence for thirty days. Magistrate Simpson availed himself of the denial of his request for a sixty day leave of absence as the excuse for tendering his resignation to the Mayor, which was accepted.[8]

A considerable amount of evidence was taken as to the conduct of Magistrate Henry M. R. Goodman, much of which suggested the need of further inquiry into his conduct. Much of this evidence related to practices that he had pursued in the magistrates' court. He was examined, and while his examination was pending he presented his resignation, which was duly accepted by the Mayor. The inquiry which would have been made in reference to matters complained of was not pursued after the Magistrate's resignation was accepted. Under these

[8] *Ibid.*, p. 52.

circumstances, I think it is fair not to comment in detail upon matters as to which no investigation was really completed.[9]

If one may draw general conclusions from the testimony which was taken concerning the conduct of magistrates, one is forced to the conclusion that many of these magistrates were so utterly ignorant of the standards of conduct becoming to a person wearing the judicial robe that most of their activities and associations were wholly innocent—that is, they actually did not realize that they were acting improperly. In the words of the *Report:*

That persons of the type of those above mentioned were permitted to hold judicial office is a sad commentary upon the political power that determined their selection, upon the mayors who vested them with the authority of office, and upon the public that suffered so long in complacent silence.[10]

[9] *Seabury Report*, p. 54.   [10] *Ibid.*, p. 55.

CHAPTER XIV

THE SEARCH FOR BETTER MAGISTRATES[1]

THE judiciary of the state of New York viewed in perspective has offered a picture of striking contrasts. In the immediate past in New York City, largely because of Judge Seabury's purposeful efforts and partly because of the press, the bar, and some of the judges themselves, dark shades have emerged. Ministers of justice have been caught in most unlovely poses.

In striking contrast is the distinction of the higher courts of New York State. An inquiry recently sent from a western university to the law-teaching profession of the country yielded the answer that the Court of Appeals in New York was regarded as incontrovertibly isolated in its preëminence. At its head, until his recent well-deserved appointment to succeed Justice Holmes, was Judge Cardozo, a jurist philosopher of the first order; and scattered throughout the courts below are many extraordinary judges. Moreover, the very investigation which has so scourged the unfaithful was conducted by a former judge at the direction of the high court.

This contrast is the justification of Judge Seabury's faith that the way to improve lower courts is to place them under the control and direction of higher courts and the way to get better minor judges is to have them selected by their judicial superiors. This singularly challenging proposal, offered as his remedy for the conditions

[1] This chapter is taken from an article of mine published in the *Yale Review,* Vol. XXI, No. 3.

he has exposed, is pertinent not only to the situation in
New York. It reaches beyond New York to every state
that ponders the question of how to get better judges and
more satisfactory justice.

While, no doubt, from the standpoint of the country as
a whole, such cases as those in New York are unusual,
they are, none the less, so related to the question of political control over the courts in other cities that they press
with more insistency than ever the problem of a judiciary
in politics. The question is a deeper one than merely the
avoidance of occasional misconduct. It reaches down to
the general development of a political bent of mind, in-
duced by the conditions through which judges pass in
achieving the positions that they occupy. If promotion
and progress are dependent, as apparently they are, upon
observance of certain political conditions, inevitable in securing public office, the minds of the judges must be
deeply influenced. This is not to say that a political bent
of mind is necessarily unsatisfactory in trying cases,
criminal or civil. However, the use made of this faculty
will largely determine the conditions under which such
judicial work is performed. It is not to be expected that
men whose formative years have been given to public
service in essentially political positions will be transformed when they reach the bench. They remain political.

The political mind has been admirably described by
Bernard Hart in his great work on human psychology and
behavior:

When a party politician is called upon to consider a new
measure, his verdict is largely determined by certain constant
systems of ideas and trends of thought, constituting what is
generally known as "party bias." We should describe these sys-

tems in our newly acquired terminology as a "political complex." The complex causes him to take up an attitude toward the proposed measure which is quite independent of any absolute merits which the latter may possess. If we argue with our politician, we shall find that the complex will reinforce in his mind those arguments which support the view of his party, while it will infallibly prevent him from realizing the force of the arguments propounded by the opposite side. Now, it should be observed that the individual himself is probably quite unaware of this mechanism in his mind. He fondly imagines that his opinion is formed solely by the logical pros and cons of the measure before him. We see, in fact, that not only is his thinking determined by a complex of whose action he is unconscious, but that he believes his thoughts to be the result of other causes which are in reality insufficient and illusory. This latter process of self-deception, in which the individual conceals the real foundation of his thought by a series of adventitious props, is termed "rationalization."[2]

It would seem that there are two marks of a political mind as shown in a judge's practice. The first is determined either by his ambition for further office or by his desire for continued and uninterrupted enjoyment of the one which he holds. The other is a certain striving on his part for what is "practical"; that is, a consideration in the making of every decision not only of the merits in the specific problem before him but of the effect that his decision will have when viewed by his public. That such a consideration is not entirely an independent one can be shown by certain examples of decisions upon problems involving numbers of people, where a decision must be made which will result in what is commonly called "social justice" in spite of temporary injustice in an individual case.[3]

[2] *Psychology of Insanity* (London, 1921), p. 65.
[3] This passage and the remarks on the political mind which follow are,

It is quite common for classical exponents of jurisprudence, both ancient and modern, to declare that such a consideration should be foreign to the mind of a judge and that the law should be enforced without regard to its effect in individual cases. This, of course, is based upon a fallacious conception of the definiteness of law. Another consideration in point, which the classical argument does not include, is the modern explanation of the process of rationalization. A judge who is a consistent exponent of the ruling order will produce not only good arguments for a given course of action but very often good law, in spite of his failure to realize that he is engaged in a process of justifying a prejudice.

There are notably favorable sides to the possession of the political mind by an American judge, resulting in qualities that often give him an advantage over some judges of a more independent mold. For example, the practitioner of politics becomes highly sensitive to currents in opinion which frequently may be evidence of new and highly important developments in social attitudes. The politically minded judge will become aware of the stirring of public opinion destined to determine the course of subsequent law, and through this awareness he will be able to anticipate legal changes and thus to accomplish something by way of bridging the gap which always separates public opinion and law. In the very process of seeking methods by which he can win public approval for himself, the judge with a political background will often become the constructive agent for important judicial in-

in substance, taken from my book, *Our Criminal Courts* (New York, 1930), pp. 247–250.

novations and reforms. He is able, particularly in criminal cases, to get the "feel" of the social situation from which a criminal act has emerged and to administer wise counsel and prescribe effective treatment. In all matters affecting changes in economic life, which so often become seriously involved in an outworn legalism, the judge with this background is able to make skilful and often wise adjustments. It is quite probable that the political mind is less likely than other types of mind to identify its own ideas and beliefs with eternal truth. The give-and-take of political life has taught the politician the fallibility of human ideas and human purposes. These characteristics are likely to be lacking in a judiciary entirely independent of the currents of popular thought. "My duty as a judge," said Judge Cardozo, "may be to objectify in law, not my own aspirations and convictions and philosophies, but the aspirations and convictions and philosophies of my time. Hardly shall I do this well if my own sympathies are with the time that is past."

But when all these points have been conceded, the stark fact remains that for a judge's decision, general social problems are secondary to a wise determination of what to do in an individual case, and the skill necessary to make this determination is only partly implanted by education in politics. It may be necessary for a magistrate to do unpopular things, and it certainly should be necessary for him to deny the claims of political influences, which are seldom based upon a clear, rational decision as to the needs of an individual defendant. Thus the political mind, in the administration of criminal law, has a tendency often to make temporary decisions which will seem to satisfy all concerned, when, in fact, such decisions are merely a means of deferring an ultimate grapple with pretty fundamental problems. The political mind in a judge permits considerations of expediency to assume determining proportions when what is needed is courageous and final action. It unfortunately lends itself to types of leniency or types of severity which accord not with honest examination of facts but with what an unenlightened public opinion demands. It is in these realms that the political mind fails as a factor in the effective enforcement of criminal law. A judge reaches the point where he must select a course of action in a world in which the plausible often poses as the truth, in which strident, emphatic people can easily be mistaken for the majority, in which the voice of propaganda may easily disguise itself as the voice of democracy, and in which the way of the majority may be the way of conservatism, devotion to the past, and, what is still more serious, devotion to prejudice.

Judge Seabury, in his final report on the magistrates' courts, made a bold and most significant suggestion, intended to reduce the influence of politics in the selection of magistrates. He suggested that the appointment of magistrates be taken from the mayor entirely and vested in the Appellate Divisions of the Supreme Court.[4] This proposal is based upon the argument that little improvement can be expected until there is a change in the whole complicated system of obligations upon which judicial tenure in these courts has rested. The Appellate Divisions are courts of appellate jurisdiction, in each of the four great departments into which the judiciary of New York is divided. They have a considerable, though unexplored,

---

[4] *Seabury Report*, pp. 184–187.

power of supervision and investigation over the lesser courts of the departments. Each consists, in New York, of elected judges of the trial court who are designated by the governor.[5] While they are elected, their terms are long, and tradition practically assures them of indefinite tenure. They are, in the main, composed of strong men, quite independent in their political relations, feared by the bar and respected by the public.

Thus New York offers certain rather exceptional advantages for such an experiment. The proposal has interesting possibilities as a solution for the general problem of judicial selection and control throughout the nation. It offers a combination of an elective with an appointive bench, the former to dominate the latter.

The appointive system has, of course, been almost completely superseded in this country by popular election. This, according to the conservative bar, has made the office political. More recent attempts to keep out party politics by a nonpartisan ballot have roused the dogs of another kind of politics. Appeal to the people by a judge of anything except a very high court means appeal to race, religion, and other political irrelevancies. It means cheap stunts for gaining publicity and slavery to the news-gathering exigencies of the city desk. This may be called the politics of nonpartisanship. With every judge his own political leader, his ear must be to the ground constantly, instead of, as under the old system, at those fortunately infrequent moments when the oracular voice of the boss rumbled a veiled request or an outspoken order.

On the other hand, a return to a method of appoint-

[5] There are seven justices in the First and Second Departments and five justices in each of the other departments.

ment raises the question of where the power of selection
of magistrates shall be vested. Executives are political,
and judgeships are precious cuts of patronage. Again the
voice of the boss is heard—sometimes, as in the case of
New York City, with thundering authenticity.

The conservative bar is likely to be deeply skeptical of
the proposal that lesser judges be selected by higher
judges who remain elective. The logic of it is all wrong,
they will say. Why subject judges of state supreme courts
to the winds of popular caprice and protect the small fry
of police courts? The answer is that so long as state courts
of final appeal hold vast authority in constitutional questions, they are, and should continue to be, political bodies.
Professional fitness is, of course, desirable; but that the
public should have the right to pass upon their social and
economic bias is necessary to a republican order of society. If, on this point, the conservative points to the
Supreme Court of the United States, the rank and file of
intelligent students of American law will point to the New
York Court of Appeals and say that not only in the matter
of technical competence but in the rare ability of adjusting an orderly process of change to a complex society, the
latter compares favorably with the former. Whoever
doubts this may ask the first ten nationally minded lawyers of distinction for an opinion on the subject.

The weight properly attached to a point of view on social and economic questions in appointments to courts of
final jurisdiction is well illustrated in a comment made by
Theodore Roosevelt in a letter written in 1902, when he
was considering the appointment of Holmes. His labor decisions, said Roosevelt, were "a strong point in Judge
Holmes' favor." Later Roosevelt noted with satisfaction

that another candidate was "right on the Negro question, right on the power of the Federal Government, right on the insular business, right about corporations, right about labor." Thus, for a high court, the premium should be on large questions of policy; but for a judge of a lower court, the premium is upon common sense, adequate professional standing, and, if you will, upon that indefinable but significant quality called personality. This imposes suitable limitations upon the sphere of politics in judicial selection; it makes clear the legitimacy of an elective system for courts of final appeal and equally clear that no legitimate right of democracy is denied by an appointive lesser judiciary.

To impose duties of judicial appointment upon a high court or upon the chief of such a court would, it may be claimed, take from the time and energy now given to writing decisions and to thinking of the legal questions involved. The answer is short: It would. This might make it necessary to enlarge the court by a member or two. The power might well be imposed upon the chief to make the necessary preliminary steps in appointment, to formulate information, and the like.

As to whether power of appointment should rest with the entire court or with the chief, there is little choice. Advantages and disadvantages are so evenly weighted that it is unnecessary to enumerate them.

Yes, it would involve the court in politics. The court is already in politics, to a limited degree. It is making decisions every day that, translated into the currency of politics, mean vastly more than the comparatively small value of minor judgeships. Every state has seen how large corporations and individuals seek and pay dearly for the aid

of political leaders in cases before the courts. If there is
to be a fear on this score, then we might as well withhold
all determinate power from our courts and leave them in
the pure state of vacuous unimportance. Where there is
power, the magic of influence will be brought to bear. It
is inevitable.

But political influence differs in amount and quality as
the method and direction of its application change. Let us
illustrate in the case of the proposed changes in New York
City. Most of the magistrates now holding office were
named almost directly by district leaders. They know it;
the district leaders know it; the mayor knows it; and so
do the lawyers who practice before them, the policemen
who bring cases to them, the bondsmen, the clerks, and the
newspaper men. The proprietorship is almost direct.

Judges of the Appellate Division usually rise from the
same ultimate source. Far away, deep down, the springs of
their power are in the districts. But the power of the district, flowing from such a source to the far-away Appellate
Division, is vastly diluted by the time it reaches its desti-
nation. Its course has been long, devious, indirect. Other
influences have trickled into the stream—the esteem of
the bar, the personal preference of the leader of leaders,
the individual bent of governors, the press, the church,
capital, labor, and more subtle currents. For this precise
reason, choice by the Appellate Division will far more
likely be influenced by the genuinely individual preferences of the appointing judges than by the preferences of
district leaders. In the face of many and diverse stresses
and strains, the decision will be on grounds more likely
than at present to be worthy of broad and general terms of
justification.

It is true that with many possible objections from many sources the choice may result in colorless and insignificant magistrates; but it is more probable that affirmative qualities easy to justify may be sought. And the person thus chosen, while he may be the loyal friend of his district leader, will be immeasurably conscious that between him and that leader is a tremendously complicated series of creating influences. Not knowing his political parentage accurately, he may find it best to follow what his instincts tell him is a course that is not only decently justifiable, but that will win the approbation of his superiors in the Appellate Division.

The proposal offers another advantage in the fact that judges ought to be, and probably are, better qualified than others to estimate judicial timber. They may find among the lawyers practicing in their courts many potential judges. They see how they behave in difficult and trying circumstances. Moreover, they know the conditions of the position, its hazards and requirements, because, like as not, they themselves have served as inferior-court judges. They have seen the effect of judicial office on many men, and they must know better than an executive official what sort of men develop and what others deteriorate in that office.

An inquiry among those conversant with the appointment of Federal, district, and circuit judges over a period of time reveals the belief that President Taft probably exercised more care and attained better results in these appointments than any other recent president. He was as president, in fact, always psychologically a judge, imbued with the best traditions of the bench.

Another consideration that commends the proposal is

the fact that under such a system it is likely that the higher court making the appointment will retain more of a guiding interest in the affairs of the judges and magistrates who are appointed. To take the New York magistrates again as an illustration, the mayor now makes the appointments and is little concerned with what happens later. Removal proceedings are vested in another authority, likewise the powers of investigation and inspection. Some cohesion among the courts from top to bottom is a wholly desirable and wholesome thing. The power of appointment is the most potent means of securing this sort of hierarchic control. Moreover, the courts, in the last analysis, should, and in the case of the New York magistrates do, have the power of control and removal over inferior-court judges. With this disciplinary power should be vested the power of selection.

Nor is there much substance in the theoretical argument that the making of appointments is not a judicial function. The drawing of a distinction between judicial and executive functions has no heavenly sanction, although practical lawyers invest the question with mystical importance. Judges do what the law tells them, just as executives do. What they can do best is a matter of fact and not of theory. It is a matter which should be weighed by considerations more articulate than the hollow mumblings of what history and tradition have found it expedient to place within the daily routine of a judge.

Any study of the increasing diversity of issues brought to the courts throws into sharp perspective the need for extraordinary judges. The work of the courts is in the current of epochal change. There has come to be a grotesque disharmony between what is forbidden by the criminal law and the means provided for its enforcement. In the New York magistrates' courts, three-quarters of the cases heard every year deal with traffic. What have these to do with the traditional pattern of a criminal trial, with solemn accusations, the requirement that "intent" be proved, and the like? These laws attempt to penalize people for doing what the law says should not be done. For what purpose? To move traffic with more expedition and safety. Fines are collected in the hope that compliance with the law, care, consideration for others, may be made less expensive to drivers. Fines assessed by some other means would serve as well. Obviously, the forms of law, of judicial proof, are vastly out of place here. So with innumerable violations of city ordinances—by peddlers, vagrants. What, for example, has vagrancy to do with "intent"? Or being a wayward minor or, indeed, a pervert or a prostitute? These are all questions of status, not of acts. They require another sort of treatment. None of them is much affected by punishment. Science may help more. And so the calendar of crime runs. Much of it is new; it pertains to modern problems. Society wants certain things prevented. To meet this demand we do not need new criminal definitions so much as new ways of applying restrictive legislation. Every type of offense must ultimately find its own means for enforcement. General patterns will not suffice.

A similar observation might be made with respect to the courts of civil jurisdiction. The mass of litigation there is equally at variance with the past. Again the automobile looms large. Many trial courts are confronting litigation three-quarters of which arises from automobile accidents. Modern society has wholly changed the character of the work that all courts must do. The forms developed over centuries do not work. Invention, experimentation, adaptation, to the end that there may be a wide differentiation in applying the law, are necessary. This is the central question of judicial reform.

New ideas may spring from a variety of sources—the bar, the press, the lay public—but it is clear that more may be expected when the working personnel of the bench is receptive to new ideas, ingenious in finding new ways to do things, and clear-headed in perceiving the many implications in the stream of litigation passing before them. The drive may come from outside, but the spirit of adaptation must come from the judges themselves.

A few reformers, recognizing that the many issues brought before both civil and criminal courts are involved in the disciplines of science rather than of law, would scrap the scheme of things entirely and substitute scientists for judges. The most concise form of this demand is for juries or tribunals of technicians. The answer is twofold. First, science, particularly in human relations, is less exact than it seems. It is, in fact, an art trying to become a science. The other side of the answer is that most judicial determinations, even when they deal with the most modern materials, are dependent upon a variety, a combination, of many techniques. Somewhere still there needs to be a wisdom of application, of integration, and the court and the judge must provide this. Common sense must, it would seem, lie at the heart of things.

This common sense must be chiefly embodied in a judge, aware of, although not expert in, a rich variety of knowledge—such a diversity as is enforced by the conditions of a highly specialized scientific age—a judge of knowledge and of scientific expertness as well as a judge of law, possessed, withal, of such initiative, taste, sensitiveness, and sympathy as may in the application of law to fact give meaning and reality to knowledge. This must be what Plato meant when he concluded that virtue and wisdom make justice.

CHAPTER XV

WHAT HAS BEEN DONE

ON June 15, 1931, while the Seabury investigation was in progress, a committee of magistrates was formed at the request of Mayor Walker for the purpose of making recommendations concerning the reorganization of the magistrates' courts.

The chairman of the committee on reorganization, Magistrate Jonah Goldstein, is a man of exceptional insight and enthusiasm. The report of his committee was made public in the latter part of December, 1931. Some of the recommendations which were made in this report have already been mentioned. Largely through the efforts of the committee, a number of changes have been made in the past year.

Five bills have been introduced and passed by the Legislature during the past season. These bills effect the consolidation of the bail bonds required in a case as it passes from the station house to arraignment, to examination, and finally to answer in a higher court; the removal of truancy cases to the Children's Court; a change in the wording of summonses, eliminating the threat of a twenty-five-dollar penalty for failure to answer—a threat which the law made no provision for carrying out; provision to enable a magistrate to issue a warrant where in good faith he has reason to believe a crime or offense has been committed, without being liable therefor unless it is shown that such action was malicious; and, finally, the amending of section 315 of the City Charter, changing the violation of traffic regulations from a misdemeanor to an offense.

The last bill deserves more than passing attention for it is closely associated with the problem of fines.[1]

In all magistrates' courts in New York City in 1930 a total of $1,498,026.32 was collected in fines. Of this amount $1,216,-249.32 came from two classes of cases—Vehicle and Traffic Law violations and Traffic Regulations. Thus over $81\frac{1}{2}\%$ of all fines were for some form of traffic violation. In addition it should be noted that the Sanitary Law provides for punishment for "smoking motor vehicles" and it may be that a part of the $57,031 collected in fines for violations of the Sanitary Law might be added. All in all, therefore, the problem of fines is largely related to traffic violations. Because a vast proportion of these cases are not contested, the proposal has gained favor that some means be provided by which a schedule of fines for certain offenses can be provided and that persons charged by the police with these offenses be permitted to plead guilty and pay fines without appearing in court at all. This argument gains weight because of the fact that of the 519,029 arraignments, 278,658 were for traffic violations. The fines were small. For example, in 104,928 cases during 1930, the fines were less than $5.00; in 102,664, the fines were $5.00. Thus in only approximately 20% of these cases were the fines more than $5.00.[2]

---

[1] "Sec. 110 of the Inferior Criminal Courts Act provides that:

" 'All fines or other moneys received by the clerk of any court shall,
" 'from the time of their receipt, be held in trust by the said clerk, who,
" 'on or before the fifth day of each month shall make report of the
" 'same to the comptroller and pay over such funds to the chamberlain.
" 'Such moneys shall be deposited in such depositories as the chamberlain
" 'of the City of New York may designate, and in the event of failure of
" 'such depository to pay by reason of insolvency, the clerk shall not be
" 'held responsible therefor.'

"No one person is responsible for the collection of fines. They are col-
"lected by the clerk of each court. Squads of men sent out by the com-
"missioner of accounts check up on the accounts of the clerks. A daily
"account is sent to the office of the chief clerk."

[2] *Seabury Report*, p. 198.

On January 30, 1931, Mayor Walker presented a bill to the Board of Estimate and Apportionment known as the Walker Minor Offense bill. The purpose of this bill was to reduce the "collection of fines to a routine business transaction." The bill proposes to establish a system of administering fines for the commission of certain minor offenses. It reads as follows:

Ch. 1574a. In the case of minor offenses constituting violations of the code of ordinance, including the sanitary code and park ordinances, and not involving serious danger to health, morals, safety or public welfare, the head of any administrative department the administration of which is concerned with any such violations is hereby authorized and empowered to prepare and promulgate a schedule of such offenses with fixed fines or penalties applicable thereto not to exceed five dollars for each such offense to be paid by offenders who admit violation of the same and who do not desire a judicial hearing. Said department heads are further authorized and empowered to make uniform rules regulating the giving of notice of such violations by department representatives. Any notice of violation hereunder shall be returnable at the office of the bureau of city collections, which shall make proper provision for the receiving of payment of such fines in the several boroughs and the giving of proper receipts therefor. Each department, on the service of any such notice, shall immediately notify the city collector thereof, and in case any violator shall fail to appear and pay such fine within the time specified therefor the city collector shall inform the department issuing such notice, which shall thereupon cause a summons to be served on said violator. Nothing in this section contained shall prevent the police or representative of any department from serving a summons in a proper case or making an arrest as provided by law.

Section 2. This local law shall take effect immediately.

Judge Seabury, in indorsing this bill, pointed out that

it would eliminate the loss of time and the inconvenience which are now involved in answering summonses for minor offenses.[3] In spite of Judge Seabury's indorsement, the year 1931 passed without any action on the bill having been taken, and hence it died. Meanwhile, the Legislature amended section 315 of the City Charter, changing the violation of traffic regulations from misdemeanors to offenses. Finally a bill was passed by the Legislature authorizing municipalities to arrange for scheduled fines in minor traffic violations to be paid without personal appearance at court. This bill became effective on September 1, 1932. The next move must come, then, from the local authorities.

Other changes have been made without recourse to legislation. A full-time Family Court for the Bronx has been provided; a stagger system in traffic summonses will even the load carried by the court by making summonses returnable at different hours. In the Family Court in Manhattan, play space indoors and out, a restroom, a Board of Health nurse, and milk and crackers for the children whose parents' cases are being heard have been provided, largely through the efforts of Magistrate Goldstein. Provision has also been made for feeding prisoners arrested after midnight, who, because of lack of funds and lack of provision, were without food until after arraignment in the court the following morning. The Criminal Medical Clinic which was established in the Criminal Courts building has been made available to magistrates who wish to have defendants examined, under section 931 of the Code of Criminal Procedure.

[3] *Seabury Report*, pp. 199–200.

Finally, Chief Magistrate McDonald has sanctioned a plan for an adolescent court. This project was recommended by the committee on the reorganization of the magistrates' courts and sponsored by a number of social agencies. While much has been done for the children in our system of justice, relatively little attention has been paid to delinquents between the ages of sixteen and twenty-one. They have been left to mingle with the heterogeneous stream in the district courts, where their cases have been passed upon without undue attention to their special problems. The Wayward Minors Act attempted to meet this situation by affording a means by which young people might be brought before the court by parents or agencies for the purpose of discipline. But the Act has not been very extensively evoked. The *Magistrates' Court Report* for 1930 shows only 233 "wayward minor and miscellaneous" cases,[4] yet 41,147 defendants were between the ages of sixteen and twenty-one.[5]

The problem is indeed one of major importance. The new adolescent court is in the nature of a laboratory experiment which has as its chief objective the determination of how best to handle the adolescent offender. As there will not be sufficient facility for handling all the cases, some selection will be necessary at first.

There still remain many major problems to be solved. The method of appointing magistrates remains unchanged. The bail system has only been tinkered with. Immediate arraignment is only a subject of dinner-table conversation. The clerical staff has not been reorganized. The

[4] *Magistrates' Court Report*, 1930, p. 28, Table XVI.
[5] *Ibid.*, p. 26, Table XIII.

problems of prosecution and defense have not even been touched. The recommendations as to a centralized probation bureau have not been carried out. Separate hearings in felony cases, centralization and consolidation of the inferior courts, are only hazy dreams.

CHAPTER XVI

REFLECTIONS

THE outcome of the Page Commission Report is a perfect illustration of the limitations of purely formal reform. To a great extent those who wanted reform were able to write their own prescription. The elaborate Inferior Criminal Courts Act was the result. But underlying conditions remained the same; the evils recurred in a new and particularly vicious form.

Relatively, there has never been much trouble in getting new governmental machinery created by the New York legislative authority, especially when the cost is to be saddled upon the huge budget of Greater New York and there is an active group of proponents drawn from the welfare and civic agencies of the city. There are two reasons for this. First, the political machine is willing to throw its power behind any measure that creates more jobs or increases rewards for those which already exist. Second, the burden of carrying new expenditures is thrown upon the richest taxing district in the world.

But the trouble is, as sad experience has shown, far deeper than these changes in form can eradicate. It goes to the qualities of personnel and the atmosphere in which the work of the court is done.

A laconic statement can set forth the difficulty. The machine in the selection of magistrates through the years has followed the policy of giving as poor a quality of appointments as public opinion will permit. When driven by the sting of a public shocked by raw scandal as in the past two years, there is improvement. Also, when a Murphy grows to supreme power over the district leaders and is enlightened by a more rounded view of civic morality, there is an improvement. But these are temporary, partial, incidental improvements. Underneath, the muddy current of machine practice and policy runs undisturbed.

This current is discolored by two influences. First, there are the enormous demands made upon the public service, which means in monetary terms the public treasury, for political service. One could endure the political domination of New York City with much more equanimity if it were less expensive. As this book abundantly shows, roughly half of what goes to support the magistrates' courts in New York City yields no return in the actual administration of justice. It goes either to political work or to utter waste and inefficiency.

The other influence that stains the current is a tendency to temper the course of justice everywhere in order to do private favors. Perhaps there is a deep socio psychological explanation. It is not necessary here to examine it in detail. But it is easy to see that more often than not the politician is so much for the "under dog" that he often turns aside the course of justice most unwisely. In the warm, intimate atmosphere of the district the law is too often not a fool but an alien. The offender is near, human, and, what is most important, grateful. He gets the breaks.

Perhaps he should. Certainly the treatment of him by hard authority shows no brilliant results. The devices of men for the correction of criminals cannot claim much credit. Failure seems more evident than success.

But the background upon which success is to be measured is not a world in which justice is badly administered but a world in which it is not administered at all. Upon the basis of such a comparison, even the pessimist must see a value in law enforcement. And we cannot help but see that if the law itself, intelligently and without improper influence, had a chance, the gain might be much more apparent.

Before this can happen the authority that rules politics in New York City must bend itself low before the altar of self-renunciation. The candid observer, however, cannot yet discern even the portents of such a miracle.

APPENDIX TO CHAPTER VIII
WAYWARD MINORS

THE Women's Court has jurisdiction over prostitutes—
these have constituted the bulk of the cases—wayward
minors, and conducts preliminary hearings in petty larceny
cases (shoplifting). A word should be said with regard to the
second group before leaving the subject of the Women's Court.
The wayward minor presents one of the most important problems in the magistrates' courts today, not because of the number of cases which occur—this is relatively small—but because
of the youth of the offenders. For the moment we are concerned
only with the illegal commitments of wayward minors in the
Women's Court. On January 8, 1931, there were in "Bedford
Reformatory"[1] fifty-one inmates who were "held by virtue of
defective commitments."

"Their commitments were either irregular upon their face, as
tested by the appropriate statutory provisions, or irregular because, although proper enough in form, they were improper by
reason of the absence of a hearing on competent evidence, as
required by the statute. There were fourteen girls on parole who
were liable to revocation of their parole and to be returned to
custody under similarly defective warrants of commitment,
while six parole violators were at large but being sought by the
Reformatory by virtue of identical commitments. There were,
further, three others who had served out their sentence, who
had been held under commitments faulty for the above reasons,
and a scattering of three more who had originally gone to Bedford under illegal warrants. The total of the cases, then, affected by this situation, as disclosed by the Investigation, was
seventy-seven.

---

[1] New York State Reformatory for Women at Bedford Hills.

"Section 913-b of the Code of Criminal Procedure provides that a wayward minor may be so adjudged by a magistrate,

'where the charge is established upon competent evidence upon a hearing.'

In the case of *People ex rel. Deordio* v. *Palmer*, decided in the Appellate Division of the Second Department, October 10, 1930 (230 App. Div. 397), the warrant of commitment stated that the relator is

'duly charged with being a wayward minor, who has been wilfully disobedient to the reasonable and lawful commands of her parents and in danger of becoming morally depraved therefrom in violation of Section 913-a of the Code of Criminal Procedure, was duly arraigned on said charge and was duly informed of her rights under the law; and whereas said charge having been duly established by the confession of the defendant on her plea of guilty.'

There was no hearing in this case. The Court found that according to Section 913-b, Code of Criminal Procedure, the charge must be established not by a plea of guilty but 'upon competent evidence,' and that therefore a commitment on a plea of guilty was without question illegal under the law.

"Mayor Walker, in conference with the Corporation Counsel, the Chief City Magistrate, the Police Commissioner, and Mr. Worthington of the Committee of Fourteen, criticized the presentation of the question of illegal commitments in wayward minor cases. It was pointed out that commitment had been made according to a printed form, HS 121—Reformatory Commitment (Section 913-c, Code of Criminal Procedure), amended by Chapter 389 of the Laws of 1925. There were two alternatives contained in this form, (1) 'upon competent evidence upon a hearing' and (2), 'by the confession of the defendant by h... plea of guilty.'

"The Mayor said that in the *Pogoda* case, decided by the Appellate Division, Second Department, in 1926 (217 App. Div. 763), this form of commitment 'by the confession of the defendant on her plea of guilty' was sustained. The *Pogoda* case, however, was different; in that case the minor was charged with and found guilty of a specific offense and the Appellate Division held that the plea of 'guilty' to that specific offense was proper—and for that reason the Appellate Division was obliged to dismiss the writ even though there may also have been a charge that the relator was a wayward minor, which latter charge could not have been sustained by a plea of guilty.

"Every person committed as a wayward minor since 1923, without a hearing at which competent evidence was presented, was illegally incarcerated. In the seventy-seven cases offered in evidence, the papers show that there was no trial and that a commitment was issued only upon the confession of the minor. In all but a few of these the words of the statute, namely, 'upon competent evidence presented at a hearing,' compliance with which alone would render the commitment valid, had been stricken out. Each of these seventy-seven commitments was, therefore, plainly invalid upon its face.

"As a result of the disclosures in this Investigation with respect to the wayward minors who had been committed without competent evidence presented at a hearing, a writ of habeas corpus was procured, to bring up the question of the legality of the detention of one of the girls then being held at Bedford Reformatory. In that proceeding the writ was sustained and the alleged wayward minor discharged. (*People ex rel. Peltz* v. *Brewster*, 139 Misc. 161; 232 App. Div. 1; 256 N. Y. 558.) Upon the authority of that determination, the other alleged wayward minors, held under similar defective commitments, were also released."[2]

[2] *Seabury Report*, pp. 132–135.

INDEX

Acuna, Chile Mapocha, 44, 119–121

Adolescent court, 260

American Bar Association, 184

American Federation for Sex Hygiene, 115

American Social Hygiene Association, 115

American Vigilance Association, 115

Appellate Division, 39, 42, 166, 177, 181–182, 246, 247, 250–252

Assistant clerks, method of appointment, 55, 73; salary, 73; functions, 73, 74; testimony of, before Judge Seabury, 74; evidence of corruption, 75–77; recommendations of Judge Seabury as to, 82, 84

Association of Grand Jurors of New York County, 91

Attorneys, 30, 46, 160–163; Judge Seabury's findings as to, 171, 172, 173–175; Judge Seabury's recommendations as to, 176–177, 181–182

Bail, recommendations of Page Commission as to, 32; original theory of, 87; springing up of professional bondsmen, 87; growth of corporate sureties, 88; John Doe hearing in 1921 to investigate abuses, 89–90; legislation in 1922 concerning, 90; legislation in 1926 concerning, 93; action of Superintendent of Insurance in 1927 and 1929, 93, 94; central bail-bond bureau proposal, 94–95; establishment of bail-bond bureau, 95; findings

of Judge Seabury regarding, 97–107; recommendations of Judge Seabury regarding, 108–109; action of committee on reorganization, 110

Bar Association of the City of New York, 181

Board of magistrates, recommendations of Page Commission as to, 27; functions, 55

Brodsky, Louis B., 48, 229–230, 236

Burlingham, Charles C., 50 f.

Cantor, N. F., quoted, 167

Centralized court proposal, 60–62; recommended by Judge Seabury, 61

Charity Organization Society, 21

Chicago Crime Commission, 175

Chief magistrate, recommendations of Page Commission as to, 27; designation, salary, 55

Children's Court, 163, 164, 207, 208 f., 212–216

Clerical staff, organization, 63–64; cost, 1931, 80; cost, 1932, 85; recommendations of Judge Seabury as to, 81–84

Clerks, method of appointment, 55, 64; functions, 64; salary, 64; testimony of, before Judge Seabury, 64; report of observer as to activities, 69–73; recommendations of Judge Seabury, 81–82

Cobb, Bruce, quoted, 53, 116, 206 f., 207 f.

Commission to Inquire into Courts of Inferior Criminal Jurisdiction

INDEX